MEDIUM AEVUM MONOGRAPHS

EDITORIAL COMMITTEE
K. P. CLARKE, A. J. LAPPIN, S. MOSSMAN,
P. RUSSELL, C. SAUNDERS

EDITOR FOR THIS VOLUME
A. J. LAPPIN

MEDIUM ÆVUM MONOGRAPHS XLI

DIALECT VARIATION IN NORTHERN MIDDLE ENGLISH

Scribal Language and Dialect
in Northern Manuscripts of
The Pricke of Conscience

J. GILBERT

The Society for the Study of Medieval Languages and
Literature

OXFORD 2022

THE SOCIETY FOR THE STUDY OF

MEDIEVAL LANGUAGES AND LITERATURE

OXFORD, 2022

http://aevum.space/monographs

© J. GILBERT, 2022

ISBN-13:
978-1-911694-04-5 (pb)
978-1-911694-05-2 (hb)
978-1-9911694-06-9 (e-book)

British Library Cataloguing in Publication Data

A catalogue record for this book is available from the British Library

For Athena — thanks for all the wisdom

CONTENTS

ABBREVIATIONS xi

INTRODUCTION xiii

Medieval Dialectology 1
   1.1.   Scribes and their methodologies in ME texts 2
   1.2.   The translating scribe: code-switching and the relationship between orthography and phonology in ME texts 6
   1.3.   Scribal error 12
   1.4.   *A Linguistic Atlas of Late Mediaeval English* and *A Linguistic Atlas of Early Middle English* 14
   1.5.   *LALME*: its uses and limitations 20
   1.6.   Scholarship on Northern Middle English 24
   1.7.   Northern Middle English and its relationship to Scots studies 32

Methodological Approaches 39
   2.1.   Selection of base text for study 40
   2.2.   The questionnaire for data analysis: compilation 49
   2.3.   Approaching and using manuscripts to accrue data 51
   2.4.   The base manuscripts and their scribes 53
   2.5.   Limitations observed in the questionnaire method, and subsequent additional methodologies 58
   2.6.   Applications of selected methodology 60
   2.7.   Language dictionaries as aids to study 61
   2.8.   A further note on *LALME* 64

Consistent Differences in Orthography 69

The Textual Tradition of the *Pricke of Conscience* 95

Codicological Evidence and Sociolinguistic Contexts 117

    5.1.   Codicological review of manuscripts 118

    5.2.   Scribal training and education: linguistic and orthographical features and what they indicate 128

    5.3.   Collating textual and manuscript evidence 134

    5.4.   Conclusions 142

Setting Data in Context 145

    6.1.   The *Northern Homily Cycle* 146

    6.2.   The lyrics of Richard Rolle 151

    6.3.   The epistles of Richard Rolle 152

    6.4.   Durham Literary Manuscripts 154

    6.5.   Compiled data and its indications about varieties of NME 156

    6.6.   Identified varieties and their characteristic features 168

    6.7.   Re-assessing *Sir Tristrem* in the context of these varieties 168

    6.8.   Conclusions 172

Conclusion 175

    7.1.   Improvements to traditional dialect models 176

    7.2.   The NME region as home to many different language varieties 177

    7.3.   Conclusions about scribes and manuscripts based on codicological evidence 181

APPENDIX 1: Manuscript Transcriptions 187

1.1. A – Rawlinson C.891 187
1.2. B – MS. Rawlinson Poetry 175 191
1.3. B2 – MS. Harley 4196 201
1.4. C – MS. Cotton Galba E.ix 205
1.5. D – MS Wellesley 8 214

APPENDIX 2: Questionnaire 221

BIBLIOGRAPHY 227

ABBREVIATIONS

DSL	*A Dictionary of the Scots Language* at https://dsl.ac.uk/
EME	Early Middle English
LAEME	*A Linguistic Atlas of Early Medieval English*, compiled by Margaret Laing [http://www.lel.ed.ac.uk/ihd/laeme2/laeme2.html]. Edinburgh: Version 3.2, 2013
LALME	*A Linguistic Atlas of Late Medieval English*, accessed for this work in the form of *eLALME*. M. Benskin, M. Laing, V. Karaiskos and K. Williamson. *An Electronic Version of A Linguistic Atlas of Late Mediaeval English* <www.lel.ed.ac.uk/ihd/eLALME/eLALME.html> (Edinburgh: The University of Edinburgh, 2013)
LME	Late Middle English
MED	*Middle English Dictionary*, ed. Hans Kurath, Sherman M. Kuhn *et al.*, in the *Middle English Compendium* (Ann Arbor, MI), at http://ets.umdl.umich.edu/m/med/
NME	Northern Middle English

INTRODUCTION

Northern Middle English (NME) is a general term used to describe the Middle English written and spoken from around the time of the Norman Conquest to about the year 1500 in the northern counties of England: Northumberland, Durham, Cumberland, Westmorland, and Yorkshire, 'excluding the southwestern part of the county' (Lewis and McIntosh, 1982, p.20).[1] This study uses NME as an umbrella term for the dialects of the Northern region – describing, indeed, an 'umbrella dialect' that can encompass a number of more specific regional dialects, which may distinctly differ from one another but which all share a number of common features, in the same way that 'London English' is a term that encompasses a number of different London dialects.[2] Within Northern scholarship, however, insufficient work has been done to differentiate the umbrella dialect, originally described by Victorian scholars such as Richard Morris and Walter Skeat, from the language varieties it encompasses. Furthermore, NME in the late medieval period is generally discussed – where it is discussed at all – as if it were a homogeneous dialect, within which there has been little attempt to establish any more specific varieties.[3] This is not an especially useful way to look at the region, and, as this study will indicate, this idea of the NME area is fully within our scope to challenge, where study is approached from new avenues.[4]

---

[1] For a more detailed description of Middle English, see Horobin (2009, pp. 15–28).
[2] For a discussion of "London English" and its types, as defined by M.L. Samuels, see Samuels (1963, pp. 81-94).
[3] For a definition of a 'fully Northern' dialect form, see Lewis and McIntosh (1982, p. 20). In *A Linguistic Atlas of Late Mediaeval English* (Benskin, Laing, Karaiskos, Williamson et. al., 1986; 2013; henceforth cited *LALME*), texts adhering to this description are described as 'NME' – Northern Middle English. Language descriptions from Morris (1863)and Skeat (1912) will be discussed in more detail later.
[4] See Lewis and McIntosh (1982, pp. 20–21), for a discussion of apparent homogeneity in this region and its probable relation to 'scanty' compiled evidence available for study.

Dialectology, or dialect geography, is a field of study that properly began in 1876 with Georg Wenker's study of grammatical and phonological variation across the dialects spoken in Northern Germany at that time (Chambers and Trudgill, 1998, p.15). Many people continue to think of dialectology as a study of spoken dialect, and this is in fact the focus of most dialectologists – the overriding reason being that dialect is usually the preserve of spoken language, no longer reflected in the standardised written record. For scholars of historical languages, however, this situation changes, and dialectological studies can equally be conducted from written witnesses, where these reflect dialect variation.

Among ME studies, dialectology is a particularly illuminating scholarly avenue, and for good reason.[5] The ME period was defined by dialectal variation and the lack of a written standard; it came to a close with the rise of the printing press on the eve of the sixteenth century (Strang, 1970, p.224). – Although the idea of a neat switch towards a London-based 'Chancery Standard' has been thoroughly debunked by Michael Benskin (2004, pp. 1 – 40) and others, English did certainly, at this time, begin converging towards more standard forms which represented the antecedent of the language we speak and write today.

Because English was not, during the ME period, the official language of either the Church or the state, it lacked even the loose standardisation it had begun to develop in the late Old English period, and devolved instead into a complex system of different written dialects, varying from region to region according to sociolinguistic factors (Benskin, 2004). Consequently, a considerable amount of scholarship has been conducted on dialectal variation in England and Scotland across this period, particularly between 1300 and 1500.*A Linguistic Atlas of Late Mediaeval English (LALME)*, completed in 1986 (Benskin, McIntosh, Laing, Samuels, Williamson; henceforth cited Benskin et al., 1986; or 2013 for specific reference to the electronic revision), used data from a wide range of literary manuscripts and 'anchor texts' – texts firmly localised to particular areas – to present an accurate dialectal picture

---

[5] For an excellent concise discussion of its many potential applications and how studying a text's dialect in context can aid in the solution of many scholarly problems, see Horobin (2012, pp. 59-78)

of the area. One region that remains comparatively little illuminated by this study, however, is the NME area, with which region this book is concerned.

There is no lack of source material from the NME area at this time. On the contrary, the great draw of studying NME is that there are a very large number of known manuscripts still available to us in NME dialects, ready to be mined for data. The greatest difficulty of studying NME, however, is that much of this data still remains locked within the manuscripts, simply because the manuscripts have never been studied or edited. Close study of those manuscripts that have previously been little examined is the key to this project. This study utilises the vast and rather underused resource of the popular Northern poem, the *Pricke of Conscience*, extant in multiple Northern manuscripts, as a basis for dialect study. Despite the fact that this poem exists in more witnesses than any other from the period – 115 in all – it has been fully edited only once by Richard Morris in 1863, and then revisited within the past decade by Ralph Hanna and Sarah Wood in their amplified version of Morris's edition (Hannah and Wood, 2013). While Morris's edition was, in its day, ground-breaking, it works from only two manuscripts, and as such does not represent the wide variety of orthographic and lexical differences found in the NME region within manuscripts of the *Pricke of Conscience* alone. Hanna and Wood's edition considers nine manuscripts in order to improve upon Morris's initial collated text, and will undoubtedly prove hugely useful to scholarship, but its aims are to produce a reading edition of the poem which more closely resembles the authorial original than Morris's copy did. As such, it is not intended as a resource for the study of dialectal variation between the texts of the poem, nor does it seek to thoroughly analyse or compare the language of the manuscripts. This study makes use of the vast resources lying unremarked by scholarship in the form of northern manuscripts of the *Pricke of Conscience* which have previously never been independently edited or closely examined from a dialectologist's standpoint, although three of them have been consulted by Hanna and Wood.[6] The traditional scholarly picture of the Northern dialect area is a narrow and shallow one, where texts must either fit an accepted list of

---

[6] Hanna and Wood's text is discussed more thoroughly in Chapter One.

features, or be considered anomalous. Further manuscript study in the NME region will not only increase scholarly understanding of the range of language features seen in this region, but can also help to illuminate how Northern scribes handled texts, and in what contexts they were written.

In large part, the reason a properly detailed picture of the NME area has not yet been achieved is that sufficient work (transcription, and subsequent sociolinguistic investigation, of manuscripts) has not yet been undertaken to make it possible. In their 1982 study, *A Descriptive Guide to the Manuscripts of the Pricke of Conscience*, Angus McIntosh and Robert Lewis identified thirteen 'fully Northern' texts of this work, characterised broadly by their 'retention (at the appropriate date) of some form of unrounded vowel (normally spelt a) in words descending from OE and Old Norse <ā> – for example, texts that give STANE, BATH instead of STONE, BOTH' (Lewish and McIntosh, 1982). They did not, however, make any attempt to assign specific positions to these texts, stating that they had not the means to go about this within the scope of their study, although 'this is not to say that it will remain impossible to do so.' Furthermore, they did not attempt to divide the languages of the texts into narrower language varieties with specific features, although differences can certainly be identified between the languages of texts broadly classified as NME. The *Pricke of Conscience* is an invaluable resource for the dialectologist, and because there are so many Northern manuscripts, it is ideal as a base text for this study. Comparison of different versions of the same text enables direct line-by-line comparison, as well as application of the questionnaire method which will be presented more fully below. This study analyses, in detail, four manuscripts of the *Pricke of Conscience* classified as 'fully Northern', and assesses the similarities and differences between them, setting them in proper context in order to demonstrate that they are not all written in an identical dialect, and to discuss why this may be the case.

Within the past twenty years, some small-scale studies have been conducted in the field of NME. Keith Williamson's 2002 study works from the data collected by *LALME* and from the Edinburgh Corpus of Old Scots to note variation in third person plural pronouns and in infinitive markers across the north of England and the southernmost part of Scotland, dismissing the 'geopolitical' line usually drawn between NME and Older Scots (Williams,on, 2002, pp. 253-86). He concludes that variation within the late fourteenth and fifteenth centuries was greater in this area than has previously been believed. However, while his study, alongside a very few others,[7] has made some advances and paid some long-warranted academic attention to this neglected area of scholarship, it remains constrained by the limitations of its source material. It does not seek to propose any improvements upon the NME model popularly accepted, nor does it distinguish any varieties within NME. Victorian scholarship presented NME as a largely homogeneous dialect area, within which all texts demonstrated an identical set of linguistic features. These features, usually based upon those presented by Morris in the introduction to his 1863 edition of the *Pricke of Conscience*, once represented a true reflection of what Morris had learned from his studied texts; but they have become somewhat cemented in scholarship as if they represented a far more definitive idea, which little has been done to question. In order to interrogate this model in an informed fashion, a scholar would need to evaluate data from those many Northern manuscripts which have never been edited or studied. Generally, however, there has been little drive in scholarship towards this goal (Lewis and McIntosh, 1982).[8]

The lack of attention paid to the NME region is not inexplicable. A lack of anchor texts may be largely to blame. 'Anchor texts' are those which can be localised to a particular vicinity, such as wills and parish records. They are the means by which studies such as *LALME* have traditionally begun to create dialect nets within which other, non-anchored, texts can be fitted and localised. Any text can be an anchor text, provided that it is in English and its origins are known. The problem with NME, and perhaps the reason it has been so little explored despite the large number of Northern texts, is that there are very few anchor texts from this region at this time. Latin prevailed in the North for even parochial uses for far

---

[7] Williamson's study is discussed more fully as part of the literature review, alongside the other studies alluded to here. See Chapter One.

[8] for a discussion of the obstacles presented to Middle English dialect study by the lack of sufficient drive towards transcription, see McIntosh (1989a, pp. 92–93); see also Benskin (2002) and, with specific reference to lack of study in the NME area, McIntosh (1989b).

longer than elsewhere in England, and consequently it has been almost impossible to conduct dialect study of this region by the usual method. However, this need not, and should not, mean that we cannot approach this area via other avenues. This study approaches dialect study of the NME region from the angle of textual and codicological evidence from manuscript witnesses, demonstrating how much can be learned from a comparison of new data.

Localisation has long been one of the primary aims of many dialectological studies. Localising a dialect – pinpointing its place, or probable place, of origin – can be achieved through a number of means. The features of the dialect itself can be compared to those of other anchor texts. One can also use the extralinguistic features of the manuscript to make a localisation judgement. The manuscript may contain the name of a person or place, or betray production methods that are only found in certain regions. However, in some cases it is not possible to make a localisation with any degree of certainty. It has long been thought that this is the case in much of the North, due to the lack of anchor texts.[9] It is difficult to know what dialect features relate to any particular place if there are no anchor texts to work from; and because localisation has become so paramount an aim in dialect scholarship, the idea that it is not always possible in the North has dissuaded many scholars from approaching this region. However, it is possible to glean a great deal of useful information without prizing localisation as the only or ultimate goal. Moreover, once one has acknowledged that the acquisition of more Northern data is useful in its own right, we may find that some degree of localisation does become possible.

As well as presenting a good deal of new data and suggesting new dialect models of its own, this work is also a study of the dialects of four NME manuscripts, set in their sociolinguistic contexts. Hopefully it may serve as a model for further studies of Northern dialects in the late ME period, demonstrating how we can advance our limited knowledge of NME through close reference to the many manuscripts whose word stocks have not yet been added to the

---

[9] For a discussion of the problems perceived by *A Linguistic Atlas of Late Mediaeval English* in categorising Northern dialects, see *LALME* 1, Preface, p. viii.

collective 'word hoard'.[10] The ability to distinguish more forms of Northern English will be useful to scholars in its own right: the more we know about what certain language features connote, the better we are able to draw connections between texts and scribes. For many Northern manuscripts, precise localisation may never become possible. However, over the course of this study it has been possible to identify a number of new linguistic truths about variation within the region, often connected to sociolinguistic variation, simply through the acquisition of more data, and to distinguish language varieties within the NME model, even where these cannot, at this juncture, be tethered to a place. It is evident that there are far more varieties of NME than previous models suggested. It is evident, too, that many dialects in the NME region do not necessarily conform to the language description set out by Morris in 1863. Indeed, we might question the usefulness of any attempt to define stratified dialects at all – we will later discuss how the imposition of boundaries between 'Scots' and 'NME' has sometimes proved problematic. It might be more useful to approach each region as containing geographically varying features that may all have different boundaries. At any rate, it is helpful to approach the NME region as something more complicated than what the older models imply.

For example, one of the issues discussed in this study is that of *Mischsprachen*, or apparent mixtures of two or more dialects found in a single text – something especially difficult to assess when so little is known to begin with about the dialects of a region. As will be explained, the lack of understanding of the NME region has led scholars to classify the language of the ME text *Sir Tristrem* as, potentially, a *Mischsprache*, due to the anomalous 'non Northern' forms it exhibits (McIntosh, 1989b). There are a number of texts like *Sir Tristrem* whose provenance is hotly debated and whose language has been viewed as problematic. This study demonstrates that once we have rejected the idea of NME as a homogeneous language with a single set of language features to which all texts

---

[10] See McIntosh (1989a,p. 94) for a discussion of uncatalogued manuscripts and their potential data; Lewis and McIntosh (1982) describe 113 manuscripts of *The Pricke of Conscience*, 111 of which have never been edited or transcribed for publication.

adhere, we are better able to assess such texts properly and in context. Previously, any text showing language features that deviate from those described as NME has appeared 'anomalous'. This study demonstrates how varied language features in this region truly are, showing that some so-called linguistic anomalies are actually quite commonly attested in this region, once we have more texts to take into account. The more information we have about the variation in dialects across this region, the better we are able to determine whether a text could accurately reflect the consistent usage of one scribe, rather than a combination of various separate dialects inconsistently mixed.[11] When features previously thought anomalous are found represented consistently in other Northern texts, as here, they cease to be anomalies and become simply a part of the linguistic mixture noted in the NME region.

Effectively, then, the overarching aim of this book is to demonstrate that the current idea of the NME region as an area with little dialectal variation needs to be reconsidered, and that, moreover, it is possible to replace this outdated model with one that shows the area as dialectally heterogeneous, simply by paying more scholarly attention to the texts available. We are not in possession of a large number of anchor texts, but we do have a number of other vital witnesses at our disposal, and once localisation is disregarded as a starting point, it is possible to see that much information can be gleaned from unexplored manuscripts on their own. Where manuscripts are studied in their full context, such that language is viewed as a product of a human scribe and his origins and training, it is possible to observe patterns in the data that anchor to considerations other than place. To this end, my study places considerable emphasis upon the value of sociolinguistic considerations.

Sociolinguistics is, in essence, the study of two things: firstly, the effect that any and all aspects of society, such as cultural norms, expectations, education and context, have upon a person's language,

---

[11] For a full discussion of *Sir Tristrem*, how previous scholarship has approached it, and how acquisition of new data can aid us in determining more accurately what is *Mischsprache*, see Chapter 6, p. 201.

and secondly, the effect that language use itself has on society.[12] Any study of written dialect must keep in mind that languages and the societies that use them are inextricably entangled. The contexts in which the texts were produced inform how the scribes have treated the texts, and we can identify evidence of this by comparing the texts to each other. Basic linguistic considerations enable us to state that two dialects are different, but application of sociolinguistics is what enables us to explore why this difference might exist. We can then consider what this can tell us about where the texts may have originated, and what factors may have been at work on language change and variation in the region at this time.

There is very little data about NME texts because so few of them have been studied or processed, which means there is very little data available for comparative analysis.[13] Furthermore, because of the lack of anchor texts, it is not always possible to consult *LALME* and see where a text may have originated according to the linguistic maps *LALME* has drawn up, as many NME texts are not entered on these maps. Therefore, because our avenues are already limited, it seems pertinent to use all possible information to differentiate the dialects of our chosen texts.

In this case, that means acknowledging that all our languages are the products of scribes, who are human beings. If we can identify any changes to the text made by the scribe which seem to indicate what their social circumstances might have been, we can then perhaps deduce that a particular feature, such as longer forms of words, for example, might have been the result of exposure to a certain sort of education. Chapter Five explores this issue more fully.

As noted, my study takes as its base text the *Pricke of Conscience*. This devotional text, which is discussed more fully later, is fundamentally useful to us because it exists in so many

---

[12] For a general overview of the history of sociolinguistics and its various definitions and usages within modern scholarship, see Van Herk (2012), especially pp. 2–7.

[13] See Hanna (2002) for a discussion of some of the many texts produced in Yorkshire in the fourteenth century which have gone largely unexamined by scholarship, specifically p. 109. In this essay, Hanna discusses textual transmission out of the Yorkshire region, and also briefly discusses some of the Northern *Pricke of Conscience* hands examined in this study, so it will be returned to later.

manuscripts, and is Northern in origin. Many of the Northern manuscripts of the poem have never been studied independently, so the data they contain is not readily available to scholars. My study explores in detail four Northern manuscripts, comparing tranches of them against each other line-by-line.

The linguistic information they yield can be compared using the traditional dialectologist's method of the questionnaire, as is discussed in Chapter Two. However, as noted, this study also focuses upon what can be learned of, and from, scribes' sociolinguistic backgrounds – the sorts of houses in which they may have worked and their intentions with regard to the text. Line-by-line comparison is useful here in that it enables us to see, as a questionnaire does not, when a scribe seems to have changed a line for sense, perhaps revealing a religious difference of opinion, or when he has edited for rhythm or flow. As will be discussed in more depth later, this sort of consideration enables us to see where variation is purely dialectal, and where there may be other scribal reasons behind it. It can also help us to guess at where the scribe may have worked or been trained, which can ultimately be a means of explaining why one dialect may differ from another, where, for example, one dialect is that of a clergyman, one of a university-educated man, and one of a noblewoman. Another important witness in this regard is the physical manuscript itself; this book therefore includes a codicological study, examining what the books' construction can tell the scholar about where and by whom they may have been produced, enabling us to make deductions in consequence.

In order to make the fullest use of the four core manuscripts I have considered, this study approaches them from a number of different angles, and attempts to set them as fully as possible in their context. The first chapter of the book reviews the current state of scholarship in this area, paying particular attention to the methodological approaches available to the dialectologist, and which have been developed in recent years. This chapter discusses the different processes of translation a text can go through in a ME scribal context. It discusses the relationship between orthography and phonology in ME texts, scribal methodology and scribal error. It then discusses the two most major scholarly developments in ME dialectology, *LALME* and *A Linguistic Atlas of Early Middle English*, and determines what these projects can, and cannot, offer the

Introduction   xxiii

dialectologist. The chapter then details specifically what attention has been paid to NME, how this scholarship is related to Scots Studies, and what gaps remain.

Chapter Two deals with this study's base text, the *Pricke of Conscience*, and the reasons behind its selection. Following on from the broader methodological review in the first chapter, it explains which methodologies are used in this study and why. It reviews the methodological development of the project, identifying why I determined the comparison of multiple manuscripts of the same text, rather than of different texts, to be most appropriate in this instance. It discusses the compilation of a questionnaire, and subsequent additional methodologies applied. This chapter then also presents and describes the core manuscripts used in this study, and their hands. It goes on to exemplify, through the use of initial data, why the selected methodologies are appropriate, and discusses why *LALME*, while a vital resource, should not be over-relied upon by scholars of NME.

Chapter Three is largely a data analysis. It presents and analyses data taken from the questionnaire, as well as other observed data, and explores it, forming a substantial response to the question of whether or not these dialects are all homogeneous, and demonstrating the extent of their differences.

Chapter Four discusses textual transmission and the textual tradition of the *Pricke of Conscience*. It is an analysis of large-scale textual variation and how this is related to scribal practice and textual scholarship, using evidence taken from the transcriptions of texts A, B, C and D. It identifies differences between these texts and discusses the importance of considering scribal influence in differentiating dialects.

Chapter Five is a codicological review. It presents the manuscripts and scribes in their sociolinguistic context, utilising codicological evidence from the physical manuscripts to expand upon and illuminate deductions made from linguistic data. It posits possible origins and occupations for a number of previously undiscussed scribes.

Chapter Six sets the above data in the context of other, edited manuscripts from this time. It demonstrates how the accrued data and conclusions work in the already established context, taking data from other Northern manuscripts to demonstrate how patterns begin to emerge across the Northern area, and how the new data challenges older scholarly ideas. Conclusions are also drawn as to what sociolinguistic factors seem to correlate with the emerging pattern. The chapter concludes by grouping the manuscripts according to their language features. It then proposes, and describes, a number of specific dialect groups that can be identified from the data, and discusses what sociolinguistic factors, if any, we can connect to these dialects.

In summary, this book seeks to utilise previously unmined data – processed by means of transcriptions, a dialect questionnaire, line-by-line comparison, sociolinguistic investigation and codicological assessment – in order to build upon and reconfigure ideas about the Northern dialect area in the fourteenth century. The data mined for this study offers additional information for our scholarly understanding of NME, identifying a wider range of linguistic variation than that traditionally attributed to this region. Working from textual and codicological evidence, the study also posits possible sociolinguistic circumstances within which the four major scribes may have developed and worked. Consequently, it invites a more complex view of dialect variation in this region, demonstrating observable patterns within the evidence, indicating how certain instances of linguistic variation may be connected to scribal behaviour and influences, and offering thereby a new perspective from which to view NME.

CHAPTER 1

Medieval Dialectology

The core focus of this book is upon Northern dialects of English during the medieval period. Specifically, the question is how far such dialects do exist – rather than constituting the homogeneous 'Northern English' form which has become scholarly shorthand – and whether we can hope to differentiate them from each other, either into unlocalised groups or, ultimately, into more specific regional, or training-based, varieties. Developments will necessitate new, closer consideration of manuscripts rather than reliance upon what has already been transcribed, because this is, as Lewis and McIntosh (1982) attest, insufficient for the purpose of narrowing the dialectal net. This sort of study, within the ME period, is usually largely dependent on manuscripts that have been copied – texts that are not 'originals', but have been recopied by a scribe.[1] In some cases, the texts may have been copied unchanged, but a large number of the available manuscripts will have been translated: both those of Northern origin which have been apparently translated from one local dialect into another, and those which began life in Southern dialects. There is available a certain amount of material untouched by a copyist's hand – parish records, for example, or occasional legal documents in English – but the majority of the dialectologist's source material comprises texts which exist in multiple copies, and upon which one scribe, or many, will have exercised some influence.

To the dialectologist, the anonymous scribes who transmitted works from one end of the country to another represent a vital resource. We cannot examine texts as if each is a mechanical reflection of the language of its area of origin. The languages of texts are dependent upon their scribes, and upon important factors such as personal preference, personal motivation and ideology, and, significantly, scribal training. As such, before one can begin to

---

[1] For an overview of dialect study in this period and the manuscripts it relies upon, see Horobin (2012, pp. 59–78).

debate the dialectal implications of changes made in copying, it is vital to understand scribal methodology. Many scribes were peripatetic; especially in the later ME period, with the centralisation of government and the emergence of a professional book trade, a large number of scribes appear to have migrated from the provinces to centres of production in the south, such as London and the university towns (Horobin, 2012, p.61). As such, the language of a manuscript is a reflection of the scribe's area of origin or training, rather than, necessarily, its place of production. In Chapter Five, we will consider evidence for scribal training in the select manuscripts used as the basis for this study, but let us first examine how scribal methodology is generally understood to differ in ME texts.

1.1. Scribes and their methodologies in ME texts

Prior to the commencement of *LALME*, begun in 1959 and published ultimately in 1986, translated texts were often held as suspect by ME linguists. The earliest ME dialect surveys, such as those conducted by Samuel Moore, Sanford Meech and Harold Whitehall (1935), relied largely upon authorial holographs, such as Thomas Hoccleve's fifteenth-century manuscript of his own works, and localised parish records in the vernacular. This evidence, while valuable, is unfortunately scanty. Most ME texts are anonymous, with authorial holographs very small in number; there are none at all from the North or West. Local records are dated and firmly localised, but are usually short and restrictive in the lexis they use.

By these early studies, the vast body of anonymous, unlocalised ME writing was dismissed as potential evidence, because it did not represent the language of a text's 'original' author' – although ideas of authorship in this period were, in themselves, very different from the modern conception.[2] The *LALME* project represented a leap forward for medieval dialectology in that it recognized and acknowledged the language of the scribe as being as valid as that of the author, and to the dialectologist, often vastly more useful. This project utilised securely localised texts, or anchor texts, such as those used by Moore, Meech and Whitehall (1935, pp. 1 – 60), as a

---

[2] For an interesting discussion of, for example, 'communal authorship' in the Ancrene Wisse, see Savage(2003, pp. 45–55).

means of localising other texts by comparison of the language used. As far as possible, every manuscript containing ME was studied, by means of a questionnaire, and mapped onto a matrix according to its relationship to these anchor texts, and to the other unlocalised texts that had been fitted already. This method, known as the 'fit technique', dramatically increased the amount of data available to ME scholars, because, for the first time on a large scale, the language of scribes was accepted as valuable evidence (Horobin, 2012, p.62).

Angus McIntosh (1989c, p.39) argues that 'if a competent scribe took on the task of turning a text from one dialect to another then he usually made a very thorough job of it' meaning that the resultant text serves as good evidence for the dialectal features of the scribe, quite independent of those of his exemplar.[3] Simon Horobin (2009, p.24), in a discussion of how palaeography has enabled the identification of certain scribes, concurs that this evidence has demonstrated the consistency with which translating scribes translate into their own dialects:

> [...]for instance, palaeographical analysis of Trinity College Cambridge MS R.3.8 and Bodleian Library MS Rawlinson A.389 showed that both were copied by the same scribe, while linguistic analysis of the two revealed striking similarities even down to the minute details of spelling. Such evidence supports the view that LME scribes [who translated] consistently translated the language of their exemplars into their own dialects.

Not all scribes, however, took on such a task of translation. McIntosh (1989a, p.92) identifies three scribal *modi operandi* encountered during the compilation of *LALME*:

A. He may leave the language more or less unchanged, like a modern scholar transcribing such a manuscript. This appears to happen only somewhat rarely.

B. He may convert it into his own kind of language, making innumerable modifications to the orthography, the morphology, and the vocabulary. This happens commonly.

---

[3] For a full discussion of *LALME*, its achievements and limitations, see later in this chapter.

C. He may do something somewhere between A and B. This also happens commonly.

As McIntosh indicates, both Type A and Type B texts are valuable sources of primary source material for dialectal and word-geographical studies. Where a Type A text will usually yield little information, textually speaking, about the copying scribe, but only about the dialect of the exemplar's copyist, Type B texts are excellent resources for students of the scribal dialect, where we can be sure that they are translated texts. However, as Simon Horobin (1998, p.14) notes,

> the detection of types A and B is particularly tentative, as certainty can only truly be achieved through comparison of a scribal copy with its immediate exemplar: a very rare privilege given the erratic survival of ME manuscripts. The distinction between these two types and C is therefore one of degree rather than kind, and depends greatly on the amount of text analysed.

Type C texts are those written in *Mischsprache*, or mixed speech' – that is, where the scribe has combined two or more dialects, to a greater or lesser degree. Although these are less readily useful than Type A or Type B texts, dialectologically speaking, McIntosh (1989a, p.93) indicates that they 'can usually be recognised' and frequently discounted as evidence.

Michael Benskin and Margaret Laing (1981, p.55) identified three possible explanations for the retention of 'exotic' forms in the work of a scribe. The first is that the word may be a relict, a single example of an orthographical form not found elsewhere in the scribe's work, a result of direct transcription by a scribe whose practice is otherwise to translate. These may be retained accidentally, or perhaps because the scribe did not understand the word. The second scenario refers to unusual word forms found clustered in certain tranches of the text, particularly near the beginning of a copied segment. These, Benskin and Laing posit, represent sections of text that were transcribed directly before the scribe moved distinctly into translating his exemplar instead. The third type of retained words are those kept consciously by the scribe by 'constrained selection'. Here, the scribe attempts to accommodate the usage of the exemplar within his own work, in some attempt to replicate the 'flavour' or 'sense' of his original through the retention of signature forms of the exemplary scribe. A scribe making use of constrained selection is likely to distribute these retained forms throughout the entirety of his text (Ibid, pp.55-57).

If there is a shortage of material, C texts may be examined more closely, in hopes of identifying and separating the dialectal strands. Where a text's *Mischsprache* is a mixture of two quite distinct dialects, this is often not too challenging, and allows the scholar then to utilise the text as evidence for two or more dialects simultaneously. Where, however, the dialects combined are similar to each other, it is not only difficult to disentangle the two, but it may also be that the *Mischsprache* nature of the text passes unnoticed. As such, although we might derive evidence from a C text combining one Northern dialect with a London one, it is unlikely that a C text mixing two Northern dialects could be effectively split into dialect layers (Ibid., p. 60).

Ideally, in order to consider most fully the ways in which a scribe has altered a text, it would be necessary to consider two texts – firstly, the exemplar from which he was working; and secondly, his or her final product. When working with a widely distributed text which exists in a large number of manuscripts, this is usually a very difficult, often impossible undertaking, as it necessitates the existence of a reliable proposed *stemma*, identifying the probable exemplar for the output text, something often not easy to discover. Where we are able to identify a number of manuscripts as the work of a single scribe, the question of this scribe's methodology might be pursued through identification of potential 'exotic' forms; where these are found distributed throughout the scribal canon, they are, evidently, more likely to indicate personal or dialectal usage than examples of constrained selection or simple relicts (Ibid. p.61). But this is not always possible either. It is more important to recognise that the dialect of a text is still a worthy witness, whether it is ultimately the dialect of a translating scribe or of the scribe of an exemplar.

6   *Dialect Variation in Northern Middle English*

1.2. The translating scribe: code-switching and the relationship between orthography and phonology in ME texts

The sort of thorough translation McIntosh describes – the capacity for a sort of multilingualism, which allows the receptor (here the scribe) to understand, and automatically translate, syntactical, phonological and morphological forms from a different language or dialect without any conscious thought – has been described by Charles F. Hockett (1955, pp.10-25) as 'code-switching'. Hockett's descriptions do pertain largely to the process as detected in speech, but even in modern English, it can be applied to the written language – it is, for example, immediately apparent to a British English speaker that *color* signifies the same concept as *colour* – and in ME, which had arguably at least as many possible written as spoken forms, the idea can be applied almost as thoroughly to the reading/writing process as to that of speaking/listening.

According to Hockett's model, units of content – morphemes – are 'coded' by each individual in an idiosyncratic way, the many facets of which reflect dialectal differences, idiolectal tics, and so forth. These morphemes are then 'decoded' by the receptor – the listener, or, in this case, the translating scribe. Hockett bases his descriptions of these processes around the idea that every human brain contains a General Headquarters, or 'GHQ', where all language processes are carried out. Hockett (Ibid.,p.11) states that

> when the morphemes leave Jill, the effect of her speech [or writing] is to lead Jack's GHQ into a series of states and state-transitions paralleling more or less closely those through which her own GHQ passes as she speaks. Jack "understands" Jill – that is, communication is effected – if this parallelism is close enough.

This he describes as the fundamental basis of all communication: if there is sufficient crossover between the 'codes' of any two people, the decoding of another person's morphemes, and subsequent recoding of them into one's own, will happen unconsciously. For example, if as part of an email exchange I am asked by an American friend, 'What color are your bedroom walls?' I might reply, 'White – what colour are yours?' The decoding and recoding of *color* to *colour* has here happened without any need for conscious thought at all. This is interesting for our purposes, because the difference between *color* and *colour* is, after all, so minimal that translation is, in fact, unnecessary, but this does not prevent the automatic recoding from happening in the great majority of instances.

When confronted with a familiar word spelled in an unfamiliar way, Hockett's model suggests that it is more likely than not for a scribe to recode unconsciously according to his own, more familiar orthography, in the same way that we do not replicate the pronunciation of other people in conversation. Tiny variations in the spellings of words, particularly where these do not appear to affect the pronunciation, might then be seen to reflect this unconscious tendency to translate, even where unnecessary, into one's own recognised form. The theory of code-switching might lead us to infer that certain variant spellings of words reflect forms favoured in certain areas, for it would otherwise be most logical to leave a word unchanged, if intelligible, and if no other form was more favoured. Consequently, it may be possible to localise manuscripts more specifically according to apparently unremarkable differences in orthography – albeit only where we have access to a sufficient number of localised manuscripts for correlation.

Although code-switching has only very recently begun to be applied to written language by modern linguists, scholars of medieval English have applied the theory of code-switching to the written landscape of trilingual medieval England for some time; Päivi Pahta (2012), for example, notes that while there are challenges deriving from the lack of body-language and inflection, scholars of written "codes" also have advantages, too, such as "the use of ambiguous graphic symbols, attention catchers, headings, subheadings, or other graphic devices". Arja Nurmi and Pahta applied the theory of code-switching to great effect to the Helsinki Corpus of English Texts, conducting a corpus-linguistic analysis which ascertained that the "endemic multilingualism and pervasive language contact" of the Middle English period led to various patterns of code-switching, the explanations for which did not "lie exclusively with demographic variables" (Ibid).

The fact that a scribe's translation into his own dialect may be more or less unconscious does not necessarily preclude him from being presented with difficulties where lexis or orthography are widely variant. However, in many cases, we find that scribes translate accurately despite these greater differences. According to Hockett (1955, p.19):

> divergence between the codes of two people who communicate with each other via speech can be regarded as...code noise. The signal which leaves one person contains, in terms of his own total code, a great deal more evidence as to what message he is transmitting than the minimum which he himself would have to receive to understand the message. Some of this evidence is irrelevant for a particular hearer, but if a sufficient percentage of it falls within the identical portions of the two codes, the hearer will still understand.

In other words, the scribe is not translating the word as an unattached entity, but in context, where it is often fairly easy to intuit the meaning of a word one has never encountered before. Furthermore, when dealing with dialects, transmission of the appropriate message will be aided by the 'crossover' between the two dialect forms. Hockett identifies two factors as enabling effective communication despite divergence. In the first instance, 'the set of idiolects involved share certain features: the whole set of shared features we shall call the *common core* of the set of idiolects. Barring channel noise, speech in any one of the idiolects is understandable to speakers of all the others so long as it remains within the common core, while any momentary resort to the features peculiar to the speaker's idiolect and not shared by the others constitutes code noise.' This, again, we may extrapolate into the arena of the medieval written language. Even if a scribe had never before encountered text in the dialect from which he is translating, the degree to which the most fundamental parts of language cross over between dialects permits the scribe to decode and recode fairly easily. The context provided by word forms which diverge only slightly from his own dialect enables him to make educated guesses at those he does not understand. Of course, sometimes these guesses are fallacious, and result in translations based upon similarity of form, but whose product words carry an entirely different meaning from that intended by the original signifier. More often than not, though, contextual inference enables scribes to translate unconsciously much that would otherwise have proved inexplicable.

Secondly, Hockett (Ibid., p.20) notes that 'a given speaker [or writer] may constrain his own speech [or writing], largely or wholly, to the bounds of his own code, and yet be trained to understand speech which falls well outside ... [One could describe] an inner circle marking the bounds of his own (productive) idiolect, while the outer circle marks the bounds of what he is trained to understand. Speech from A may thus fall outside the productive idiolect of B without automatically constituting code noise: it constitutes code noise only if it falls outside the larger circle for B.' This is particularly pertinent when considering general scribal translation, as it accurately reflects the level of understanding a practised scribe would have gleaned over his years of experience in translation: exposure to other dialects is likely to have increased the number of words and variant forms which would not constitute code noise to a translating scribe, even though his own productive idiolect has not been increased through this exposure. This facet of scribal practice can be dialectally enlightening – where a scribe has translated, accurately, a piece of lexis that bears little relation, beyond semantic similarity, to his choice of word in his own dialect, one must question whether this was due to scribal knowledge, due to general local exposure to the source dialect, or something else. On the other hand, this depth of scribal understanding beyond his own dialect can also problematise our analysis of translated texts, as it may sometimes have been the case that the scribe left words unchanged because he understood them – and perhaps because he felt that his readers would have understood them – although they would not have fallen within the productive idiolect of anyone in his dialectal area. It is in these cases that analysis of the apparent purpose of a translation can be useful, as the translating scribe of a text for the use of 'lewed men' is more likely to have translated such words into their appropriate dialectal equivalents, as the readers of the text would by no means have had a similar level of exposure to other dialects. Thus, if the text appears to be for the use of the less well-educated and does retain words whose currency within the dialect we would question, we might deduce that these words would have been generally understood, even if not commonly used, in that area.

Hockett's model functions well when reapplied to the realm of medieval scribal behaviour, but, as stated, it was not originally intended as an explanation of such behaviour. Margaret Laing (2008, p.6), however, in her consideration of the relationship between listening, hearing and reading specifically in the context of medieval scribal production, has drawn a number of similar conclusions. She emphasises that 'written Middle English is not phonetic transcript', but rather, a 'nexus of sound and symbol', within which there may easily have existed, by the late ME period, that tendency to re-code words into extant 'preferred forms' as described above. As she notes, 'since Luick's day it has been shown that regional spelling variation in some of its features may be independent of phonetic variation – in other words, written ME is not simply a mapping of all and only the features of the spoken language' (Ibid., p.7). While languages being written down for the first time might, as Laing argues, be expected to show high levels of conformity between their written forms and their spoken expression, it is undoubtedly true that, when once any form of written systematisation has begun, the correlation between the two will often lessen with the passing of time, especially once a standard has become established and entrenched. Spoken language and pronunciation cannot be systematised in the way that schools and scriptoria might attempt to systematise their local written dialects and orthographies, and will always develop more swiftly. Laing quotes Henry Sweet (1888, quoted in Laing, 2008, p.7):

> When there is no traditional spelling handed down, as when such a language as Old English was first written down in Latin letters, spelling can hardly help being phonetic; where, on the other hand, there is a large literature, and, perhaps, a class of professional scribes, the influence of the traditional orthography becomes stronger and stronger, till at last, the invention of printing and the growth of the newspaper press make changes of spelling as inconvenient as they were formerly easy.

By way of clarifying her discussion, Laing refers to the spelling reform movement of the late nineteenth and early twentieth centuries, which held that English orthography ought to be reformed in order to bring it back into line with the phonetics of the language. She refers to Henry Bradley's counter-assertion that 'to an accomplished reader it does not...matter a jot whether his native language is phonetically spelt or not; what is important to him is that the group of letters before him shall be that which habit has led him to associate with a certain word' (Bradley, 1919, cited in Laing, 2006, p.7). This is entirely in line with the above application of Hockett's theory to the written language, where *color*, for example, will be read and understood unthinkingly by a British English speaker, but automatically re-coded to *colour* when replicated in the receptor's own hand, as this is the group of letters s/he habitually associates with the word.

That ME scribes in certain areas did have pre-existing associations between signifying letters and signified words is evident in the extent to which OE spelling conventions continued to be utilised and adapted throughout the period. The work of the monk, Orm, is an obvious example of the utilisation of OE spelling conventions in ME – for example, the consistent employment of a doubled consonant to indicate shortness in the vowel preceding (White, 1852). His spelling system is almost uniquely self-conscious and conviction-based, but there are many examples of less systematic application of these conventions. For example, 'a number of Middle English scribes regularly double the final 'd' of GOD to differentiate it from GOOD', while 'linguistic historians (like the Worcester Tremulous Scribe) adapted those OE models to be more suitable to their contemporary written English' by conflating them with other models with which they were familiar – specifically Latin and Anglo-French (Laing, 2008, p.11).

Accordingly, it is likely that, to a scribe trained in the copying of material in a number of different dialects, several combinations of letters might be familiar as signifying the same thing, even where only one such combination would be his own preferred. Laing (Ibid., p.14) notes that, as it is unlikely that a scribe would copy in single-word units, a translating scribe would in a real sense be writing to his own dictation – 'reading it, as it were, aloud'. She suggests that the stage at which active translation occurred would 'depend on the extent to which the exemplar's writing system was familiar and/or transparent to him and on the extent to which he used eyes as well as ear in the process' – that is, how far the exemplar's signifying orthography translated automatically to the appropriate signified concepts in the translator's own mind:

> Imagine, for instance, a copyist whose own pronunciations were [brixt] in variation with [bri:t] for BRIGHT, and [ni:t] for NIGHT. This scribe, on meeting <bricht>, would presumably recognise it by eye as a realisation of something like his own version of [brixt] and could easily arrive at his own spelling of, say, <bri3t>. But a further audio-visual substitution would be needed before he could arrive (unconstrained by the exemplar) at his other variant, spelled, say, <brit>.

This scenario, however, does necessitate the variant spellings in the exemplar being familiar, to some extent, to the scribe. Laing (Ibid., p.15) describes two main scenarios which may occur when a translating scribe is copying an exemplar whose dialect is unfamiliar to him:

> 1. In spite of being in an unfamiliar dialect, his exemplar's writing system is nevertheless fully transparent to him. He reads by eye and takes in a word or phrase. He then dictates to himself using his own spoken language system. He produces his own spellings for the tranche of text that he self-dictates.
>
> 2. His exemplar's writing system is not fully transparent to him. He is obliged to read "as it were, aloud". He decides what a segment of text means, including what word or words in his lexicon any particular string of letters might represent in context. For each word he then selects (one of) his own preferred spelling(s).

A single scribe may employ a mixture of the two responses throughout his production of manuscripts, dependent upon the situation. Taking as an example the scribe of Digby 86, Laing notes calculable differences in his behaviour dependent upon his familiarity with the language of his exemplar. This scribe is known to have copied 22 texts, of which Laing estimates 18 appear to have been in dialects similar to his own. These 18 texts show differences in the relative frequencies of spellings of some words, which Laing reads as an indication that his selection of variants was, to a certain extent, constrained by the usage of his exemplars. In the remaining four texts, for which Laing believes he had exemplars in more foreign dialects, 'his language shows signs of linguistic mixture, it being apparent that his exemplars for these texts ... contain[ed] features alien to his own usage. So the Digby scribe may be characterised as both a constrained translator and a mixer depending on circumstances' (Ibid., p.15).

1.3. Scribal error

As is the case with the majority of medieval scribes, it is evident that, on some occasions, discrepancies between dialects caused serious difficulty and errors in transmission. In the Digby scribe's copy of *Le Regret de Maximian*, some lines are completely garbled, where 'the Digby scribe appears to have got into a muddle with his personal pronouns in the transfer from the exemplar text to his own' (Ibid., p.16). Laing suggests that when the Digby scribe realised that he was 'in deep syntactic trouble', having attempted to translate pronouns not easily mappable onto his own preferred ones, he 'resorted to literatim copying' (Ibid., p.17), hence complicating matters further. In this way, one scribal error can lead easily on to another, as well as causing the scribe to alter his method of translation – factors the dialectologist must consider.

Janet Cowen and George Kane (1995, pp.79 - 80) emphasise that it is sometimes difficult to ascertain how far any alteration to the text between manuscripts represents authoritative intervention on the part of the scribe, and how far unconscious translation or simple error. They identify the following as attributable to unconscious behaviour: repetition of copy, omission of letters, transposition of letters, misreading of letters, confusion of letters, misreading of contractions and suspensions, miscounting or misreading of minims, misreading of the general shape of a word, misreading of homographs, misdivision, homoeoarchy, homoetoteleuton, inducement of preceding copy, inducement of both preceding and following copy, grammatical attraction, inducement of a common collocation, transposition of words, approximations, and small omissions.

The above textual issues largely represent posited explanations for unimportant or obviously erroneous differences, such as misspelling or repetition of lines. Cowen and Kane (Ibid., p.81) note, however, that 'there is a large group of variants where it is impossible to distinguish between variation attributable to imperfect attention to copy and that arising from scribal preference or habitual substitution. These are variants of dialect and construction and vocabulary equivalents which appear to be habitual and which do not materially affect the sense in any determinable way. Many of these produce unmetrical lines.' Thus, just as a scribe may substitute a combination of letters unthinkingly for another, he may also substitute preferred synonyms for other words with barely more thought. In the same way as a British English speaker might translate the word *faucet* to *tap* without hesitation, we may hypothesise that certain scribal word substitutions were of this sort.

As Cowen and Kane (Ibid., p.84) indicate, however, it is sometimes difficult to tell whether or not the scribe has intended something by his alteration. As classes of variation which definitively do 'invite analysis in terms of the copyists' response to and participation in the meaning of the text', they give the following: more explicit readings, more emphatic readings, easier readings, modernisation, sophistication, variants affected by other errors, inducement by another error, compensation for error, further variation from hypothetical exemplar error, compensation for hypothetical exemplar error, metrical smoothing consequent on error, compensation for final *-e* (scribal uncertainty about the metrical value of it), compensation for endings in *-e, -en*, other sophistications of metre. Where these sorts of variation occur, the dialectologist is advised to consider what factors other than simple translation may have influenced the scribe, and to analyse their effect upon dialectal information gleaned from the text. For the purposes of this study, where we have little information about the precise origins of manuscripts, any variation that may shed light upon a scribe's possible sociolinguistic circumstances is important, and can aid us in assessing what factors, social or geographical, may have influenced his use of language.

1.4. *A Linguistic Atlas of Late Mediaeval English* and *A Linguistic Atlas of Early Middle English*

The two most important works on ME dialects have been, to date, *LALME* and its successor, *A Linguistic Atlas of Early Middle English (LAEME)*. The original project, *LALME*, drew upon anchor texts, localised by internal evidence, to localise others where such information did not exist. Texts were interrogated using the questionnaire method, and the results compared, such that non-anchor texts could be 'fitted' onto maps according to how closely their language was related to those of the short formulaic documents used as anchors. For each manuscript studied, a Linguistic Profile was drawn up to show its language forms, and most are also shown on a Dot Map, giving the proposed location of the manuscript's dialect relative to that of others. The process is 'inherently self-refining': the more texts are localised to a particular area, the more complete becomes the dialect matrix for that area, enabling more accurate localisation of further texts. Some areas, however, where anchor texts are lacking, have far less complete dialect matrices than others (Horobin, 2012, pp.62 – 64).

The *LALME* team worked on the basis of questionnaires derived from tranches and scans. For the *LAEME* project, effectively the entire available corpus of early ME texts was loaded and logged into an electronic system, with each word tagged as being a form of a single main signified term – that is, all forms of the item SHOULD, for example, would be tagged as such. The tags are lexico-grammatic, indicating the type of word each item is grammatically, and to which item of lexis it corresponds. Text dictionaries, or text profiles, were generated from the tagged texts. These text dictionaries are the equivalent of the linguistic profiles generated in *LALME* from questionnaires, but they record all words in the text and their frequencies. Here, in the difference of technique between *LALME* and *LAEME*, we may note the importance of varying one's methodology dependent upon extralinguistic factors and availability of material, which will be discussed more fully in the next chapter.

The *LALME* team had a vast number of documents at their disposal. The evidence for late ME, once one accepts that translated texts can be used, is plentiful. In order to cover as much ground as possible, therefore, *LALME* applied a questionnaire to the texts it examined, noting the form given in each text for a number of common items. The most immediate difficulty in applying the questionnaire method to early ME lies in its dependence upon plentiful linguistic evidence, and particularly upon anchor texts, those which can be more or less definitively associated with a particular place of origin, whose language is likely to reflect the local usage. For *LALME*, there existed numerous documentary texts which fitted this criterion: short, official, legal or administrative texts, largely uninteresting to non-linguists, but sufficient to construct a 'network of information for different words of items and their variant forms' (Laing, 1991, .p.28). The information garnered from these short texts was then plotted onto maps of the country, creating an initially simple dialectal network, into which other, unplaced texts could be fitted.[4] The plentiful available anchor texts (in most areas) means that the network can be more closely interwoven than would otherwise be possible; and, furthermore, the greater the number of 'fitted' literary texts, the more detailed the picture becomes, and the easier it is to fit further texts. The process

---

[4] For a full explanation of the fit technique, see *LALME 1*, §2.3.

is tedious, but effectively simple, and certainly ingenious, requiring nothing more as a starting point than a decent number of relatively well-dispersed anchor texts. But it is completely impractical as a method for *LAEME*, for the simple reason that no such number of anchor texts exists for Early Middle English, or EME.

EME, surviving as it did in the context of a post-Conquest, Norman-dominated England, existed in a context very different from that of later ME. Where writing in English did continue, it was often in the form of copies of old texts made in monasteries – although the *Peterborough Chronicle,* which includes twelfth-century continuations, newly composed, is an important exception.[5] New writings in EME – such as the *Ormulum,* the *Lambeth* and *Trinity Homilies* and the homilies in the Cotton Vespasian manuscript – overlap chronologically with new versions of OE texts, and the disparity in the languages used make it evident that, very often, the copyists of older texts indeed did not modify the language of their exemplars, although the English they themselves spoke was, presumably, far closer to that of the *Ormulum.*[6] Obviously, this problematises the use of copies of OE texts as evidence. However, the canon of documents from which we might glean any information at all about EME is so slight that they cannot be discarded. *LALME,* for instance, noted examples of *Mischsprachen,* as Laing and Lass (2006, 17.2.4) indicate, but did not use them. However:

> for *LAEME,* we have so little surviving source material that we cannot afford to discard linguistically composite texts without at least attempting to analyse them and to isolate their different linguistic elements. In some cases it has proved possible to extrapolate from different linguistic layers inventories of forms that may be taken to represent genuine regional usage.

Where we find *Mischsprachen,* the language of the manuscript is not internally consistent, but is, instead, a mixture of two forms of language: that of the scribe, and that of the exemplar. This can, of

---

[5] For a discussion of the evidence for Early Middle English, see Horobin (2009, pp. 15–20).

[6] There are a number of interesting articles on this subject in Swan and Treharne (2000). For an overview, see pp. 3–10.

Medieval Dialectology 15

The *LALME* team worked on the basis of questionnaires derived from tranches and scans. For the *LAEME* project, effectively the entire available corpus of early ME texts was loaded and logged into an electronic system, with each word tagged as being a form of a single main signified term – that is, all forms of the item SHOULD, for example, would be tagged as such. The tags are lexico-grammatic, indicating the type of word each item is grammatically, and to which item of lexis it corresponds. Text dictionaries, or text profiles, were generated from the tagged texts. These text dictionaries are the equivalent of the linguistic profiles generated in *LALME* from questionnaires, but they record all words in the text and their frequencies. Here, in the difference of technique between *LALME* and *LAEME*, we may note the importance of varying one's methodology dependent upon extralinguistic factors and availability of material, which will be discussed more fully in the next chapter.

The *LALME* team had a vast number of documents at their disposal. The evidence for late ME, once one accepts that translated texts can be used, is plentiful. In order to cover as much ground as possible, therefore, *LALME* applied a questionnaire to the texts it examined, noting the form given in each text for a number of common items. The most immediate difficulty in applying the questionnaire method to early ME lies in its dependence upon plentiful linguistic evidence, and particularly upon anchor texts, those which can be more or less definitively associated with a particular place of origin, whose language is likely to reflect the local usage. For *LALME,* there existed numerous documentary texts which fitted this criterion: short, official, legal or administrative texts, largely uninteresting to non-linguists, but sufficient to construct a 'network of information for different words of items and their variant forms' (Laing, 1991, .p.28). The information garnered from these short texts was then plotted onto maps of the country, creating an initially simple dialectal network, into which other, unplaced texts could be fitted.[4] The plentiful available anchor texts (in most areas) means that the network can be more closely interwoven than would otherwise be possible; and, furthermore, the greater the number of 'fitted' literary texts, the more detailed the picture becomes, and the easier it is to fit further texts. The process

---

[4] For a full explanation of the fit technique, see *LALME 1,* §2.3.

is tedious, but effectively simple, and certainly ingenious, requiring nothing more as a starting point than a decent number of relatively well-dispersed anchor texts. But it is completely impractical as a method for *LAEME*, for the simple reason that no such number of anchor texts exists for Early Middle English, or EME.

EME, surviving as it did in the context of a post-Conquest, Norman-dominated England, existed in a context very different from that of later ME. Where writing in English did continue, it was often in the form of copies of old texts made in monasteries – although the *Peterborough Chronicle*, which includes twelfth-century continuations, newly composed, is an important exception.[5] New writings in EME – such as the *Ormulum*, the *Lambeth* and *Trinity Homilies* and the homilies in the Cotton Vespasian manuscript – overlap chronologically with new versions of OE texts, and the disparity in the languages used make it evident that, very often, the copyists of older texts indeed did not modify the language of their exemplars, although the English they themselves spoke was, presumably, far closer to that of the *Ormulum*.[6] Obviously, this problematises the use of copies of OE texts as evidence. However, the canon of documents from which we might glean any information at all about EME is so slight that they cannot be discarded. *LALME*, for instance, noted examples of *Mischsprachen*, as Laing and Lass (2006, 17.2.4) indicate, but did not use them. However:

> for *LAEME*, we have so little surviving source material that we cannot afford to discard linguistically composite texts without at least attempting to analyse them and to isolate their different linguistic elements. In some cases it has proved possible to extrapolate from different linguistic layers inventories of forms that may be taken to represent genuine regional usage.

Where we find *Mischsprachen*, the language of the manuscript is not internally consistent, but is, instead, a mixture of two forms of language: that of the scribe, and that of the exemplar. This can, of

---

[5] For a discussion of the evidence for Early Middle English, see Horobin (2009, pp. 15–20).

[6] There are a number of interesting articles on this subject in Swan and Treharne (2000). For an overview, see pp. 3–10.

course, also apply to manuscripts where a scribe has copied *literatim* from an exemplar whose scribe has created a *Mischsprache*. Texts such as these, although difficult, can still yield dialectal evidence, where the two 'strands' of language, or the two varieties, can be differentiated from each other. Moreover, manuscripts that begin as *Mischsprache* can sometimes be identified as becoming more consistent later.

Documentary evidence for ME, then, requires a great deal of attention to detail for a small return. Many post-Conquest copies of pre-Conquest documents are, apart from other concerns, difficult to access and unedited: a historian will, of course, tend to print the earliest available version, rather than later copies in which the OE has been 'corrupted' by a ME scribe. A greater problem, though, is the fact that so many ME scribes were reluctant to make any changes at all to the language of the original. As Laing (1991, p.34) indicates, 'the language of the main scribe [of the *Peterborough Chronicle*], working as early as 1122, is quite different from the OE produced by contemporary or later copyists', most of whom, unlike the Peterborough scribe, continued to copy in what we can deduce to be a form of OE based on loose pre-Conquest conventions. These 'authentic' OE productions, then, are frustrating for the linguist. However, there is an increasing tendency towards the late thirteenth century for the scribe to copy OE in a modified form, showing evidences of his own dialect, as in the documents in the *Sacrist's Register* at Bury St Edmunds. Texts such as these – particularly those localised to Bury St Edmunds, Canterbury, Winchester, and so on – are valuable as anchor texts; nevertheless, they remain unfortunately few (Ibid., p.34).

There are few surviving parish records and legal documents from the EME period, and certainly very few records in English. Consequently, the majority of genuine EME texts are literary or historical works. This encompasses extended narrative and instructive works, such as the *Ancrene Wisse,* which afford large amounts of linguistic data, as well as shorter lyrics and tags in Latin texts. Here of course there are difficulties, such as the fact that verse form might affect language use, as might the language of the original and the fact that most manuscripts are copies. However, these problems were equally faced by the *LALME* team, and 'the entire feasibility of ME dialectology relies on the fact that it is nevertheless possible to isolate examples of genuine individual and local linguistic usage' (Laing and Lass, 2006). Literary and narrative texts, such as the *Peterborough Chronicle* or *Ayenbite of Inwit*, can be used as anchor texts where no others are available, as they can often be confidently associated with particular religious houses – although, as Angus McIntosh has indicated (1989a., p.93), 'a surviving early Middle English text may be the culmination of a process of transmission in which the local characteristics of the person who produced the final copy may only be sparsely represented.' Margaret Laing (1991., p.34) points out that 'it may not have seemed necessary, or even desirable, that the written forms of English should mirror the regional variations of spoken English'. Analysis must be made of the slips and accidents in such texts, detecting pieces of local information in order to attempt localisation with reference to other texts, for which *LALME* is an incredibly useful resource, although its language is later.

Obviously, where linguistic information is so hard to come by, all of it is precious. The idea of using a questionnaire for *LAEME*, as for *LALME*, was untenable (Laing and Lass, 2006):

> A theoretically "ideal" questionnaire for early Middle English would have to register so many variables that in practice it would be unmanageable...A questionnaire is itself a highly selective tool. The more tractable we make it, the more likely we are to miss valuable information: the simpler the questionnaire, the coarser the net.

Improvements in technology, as well as the reduced size of the corpus, have meant that the *LAEME* scholars could, instead, transcribe and electronically 'tag' their available texts. All the available linguistic data is thus stored to sort and examine, analyse and manipulate, allowing 'the inductive emergence of significant categories whose existence we might not otherwise have expected' (Laing, 1991, p.34). All spellings of the item THROUGH, for instance, have to be tagged so that the computer knows that they represent the same word. Text dictionaries can then be generated from these texts. These serve the same purpose as the linguistic profiles derived from the *LALME* questionnaires, but are all-inclusive, rather than selective, containing all the information provided by a witness or scribe. Information on items of interest can be taken from the text dictionaries to create form dictionaries of variant spellings, which would serve the same purpose, on an electronic level, as the County Dictionary in *LALME*. The vision of the *LAEME* editors is that, rather than referring to pre-drawn maps as with *LALME*, users of *LAEME* will be able to select items of interest for their own research, and generate the appropriate map electronically.

The maps in *LALME* represent 'a dialect atlas of Middle English', treating texts as 'examples of a system of written language operating in its own right' (Ibid., p.34). Laing and Lass (2006) indicate that the reason for this great emphasis on the value of written evidence was 'the post-Bloomfieldian view then (and to a large extent still) that writing is of no independent linguistic interest, but merely "parasitic on" speech', but are quick to clarify that this does not mean that *LALME* saw phonological interpretation as unnecessary. There is, rather, phonological commentary throughout: even the Dot Maps depend on our acknowledgement of the relationship between sound and symbol. *LAEME* is created on a very similar understanding: orthography, certainly, is taken very seriously as an independent resource, but phonology is equally a part of the study. As Laing and Lass (2006) describe it: '*LAEME* is not an atlas of early Middle English orthographic forms, but an atlas of both first-order data and the second-order but equally important information deducible or otherwise arguable from it. The history it portrays is that of orthography, phonology and their interactions.' Indeed, two orthographies of the same word could not logically be recognised as being forms of the same word unless a phonological system is assumed; each set of orthographies must also have a lexical identity, and therefore a 'meaning'. Primary data in *LAEME* is understood in the same way as it is in *LALME*, and will be displayed on the same sort of map, albeit electronically generated.

To a certain extent, however, we might challenge this assertion of the importance of phonology in a study based purely on written words. Laing and Lass's remark about the necessity of an assumed phonological system would not seem to be universally applicable, in actuality – some languages, such as sign languages, do not have phonological systems at all. In the same way, although ME as a spoken language would have had a phonological system, the written ME we are studying does not allow us to access this in the same way as we might if studying a spoken dialect, such that, in a way, it almost becomes irrelevant. McIntosh (1989d, p.24) complains of scholars' unwillingness 'to look at written texts without seeing them purely and simply as a sort of encoded form of some variety of spoken Middle English', suggesting that 'the proper way to treat written dialectal material for the purposes we are considering is to record the graphemic forms as such. Thus if there is a contrast <bane> : <bone> between the North and elsewhere, then for our purpose it is best treated as a contrast in graphemes irrespective of their phonemic 'value', or, to speak in more mediaeval terms, as a contrast in *figurae* irrespective of the *potestas* of each.' This is in accordance with Horobin's (2012, p.60) note that

> [...] any inferences about the nature of the spoken language must be reconstructed from the written language [...] Some spelling variants are of purely graphemic significance; that is, they are concerned only with spelling, such as the variation between *shall* and *sall*, where we can be pretty sure that the spelling difference does not reflect a difference in pronunciation. [...] Other written features can be assumed to have some relationship with spoken distinctions, such as differences in the spellings *ston* and *stan*, where one has an unrounded, and the other a rounded vowel. These features can be mapped geographically, but it is important to remember that we are primarily mapping the spellings of words, not their pronunciation (even though the two clearly have some kind of relationship). A map of the different forms of *stan* and *ston* in a group of Middle English texts would simply reveal the areas in which the scribes chose to use the *stan* spelling, and areas where scribes chose the *ston* form.

In other words, in studying a written language such as ME, although we can assume that there are, in some cases, phonological implications, this will be largely immaterial to the fact that the study will be primarily of orthographical differences.

1.5. *LALME*: its uses and limitations

A Linguistic Atlas of Late Medieval English is undoubtedly, as has already been acknowledged and discussed, an invaluable resource for the medieval dialectologist. However, when one's sphere of interest lies within the NME area, *LALME* is rather less helpful than it would be to a scholar of medieval London English. In the introduction, I discussed the lack of scholarly attention that has been paid to the Northern manuscripts of the *Pricke of Conscience*. A perusal of *LALME's* linguistic profiles indicates that the *LALME* team have not afforded the manuscripts, in some cases, as much attention as has been devoted to those of more southerly origin. In Lewis and McIntosh's *A Descriptive Guide to the Manuscripts Of the Pricke of Conscience,* we find, in the appendix, a map showing the distribution of texts of the Main Version. The notes to the map, though, explain that 'the line through Yorkshire separates the "fully Northern" area from the rest of the country' (1982, p.170). The sixteen texts believed to belong north of this line are inset in a single group: no attempt has been made to place them more narrowly than 'from somewhere within the fully Northern area'. Lewis and McIntosh were writing, here, in 1982. By the time of the publication of *LALME* in 1986, some few developments had occurred, but only a very few. An examination of *LALME's* descriptions of the manuscripts in question shows some increased specificity of localisation, but many of them remain barely considered, leaving the area wide open for scholarly intervention.

Where, in 1982, Lewis and McIntosh's Northern sources were all simply described as 'fully Northern' – or, in *LALME's* terms, as 'N(orthern) M(iddle) E(nglish)' (Benskin et. al, 1986, vol 2., p. 114) – *LALME* does identify some of them more specifically. Oxford, Rawlinson C 891 and Hand A of London, Sion College Arc 80 are located to Yorkshire's West Riding; Oxford, Rawlinson Poetry 175 to the North Riding; British Library, Harley 2394, to the East Riding. Cambridge, St John's 80 and British Library, Additional 3395 are located to North West Yorkshire. *LALME* vol. 3 (Benskin et. al, 1986, p. 201) describes Harley 6923 as belonging possibly to 'the North Riding of Yorkshire, or South West Durham', but it is ultimately recorded simply as NME. The uncertainty of this designation is reflective of the fact that these manuscripts seem to have been less thoroughly considered by the Atlas than many others. As we might expect under such circumstances, we see a consequent lack of representation of Northern manuscripts in the dot-maps and profiles. The remaining fully Northern manuscripts of the *Pricke of Conscience* – British Library, Cotton Galba E ix; Wellesley 8; BL Harley 4196; BL Additional 24203; Dublin, Trinity 157; Hand B of the Sion College manuscript and London, Lambeth Palace 260 – are all simply described as 'NME'.

Of the Lambeth Palace manuscript, *LALME* states that it is 'possibly N(orth) R(iding) Y(orkshire) or S(outh) Durham, but may be mixed with E(ast) R(iding) Y(orkshire) usage. Analysis ff. 101 – 107. Not entered on maps' (Benskin et. al, 1986, vol. 3. p. 300). This descriptor goes some way towards explaining both why there are many Northern manuscripts not afforded specific determinations by *LALME*, and also the reason why the current study is necessary, and why any linguistic discoveries it makes are essentially new, purely because it uncovers data not contained in *LALME* or any other published source. A great many of the manuscripts in question have been analysed by *LALME* based upon only very small tranches – sometimes only four or five pages. We also find that six of them are 'not entered on maps'. The entry for Cotton Galba E. ix – the basis of Morris's edition, and one of the most famous manuscripts of the *Pricke of Conscience* – provides no information beyond a statement that the manuscript is considered to be NME. There is no linguistic profile number, as is usually found for even those manuscripts said to be unmapped. *LALME* refers the reader, instead, to Lewis and McIntosh (1982, p.59), where we discover that the manuscript contains six separate Northern hands, but nothing else of especial consequence, and no explanation for *LALME's* omission. It might be assumed that there is no linguistic profile because interested parties might refer, instead, to Morris's edition, which is largely based upon this manuscript.

The very great majority of all other manuscripts considered by *LALME* are assigned a 'linguistic profile', or 'LP'. This constitutes, effectively, a basic list of the word forms found in the manuscripts for the items in the *LALME* questionnaire. The *LALME* questionnaire does not vary across any of its many hundreds of manuscripts, in order to incorporate more words specific to the sort of text under examination – indeed, it cannot do so, as the very point of the questionnaire is that it be suitable for making a general survey of every ME text. The result of this is that the words considered are necessarily those which would commonly occur, and therefore perhaps show most variation, across any manuscript, rather than concentrating specifically upon those words that might be most prominent in religious poetry such as the *Pricke of Conscience*. The *LALME* team were not concentrating especially upon either this text or upon the Northern dialects. They could not transcribe every manuscript, and, as such, often completed questionnaires based upon brief tranches, as described above, and sometimes scans of the text, where certain items could not be found within the tranche. The current study has an advantage in that focuses upon the Northern manuscripts of the *Pricke of Conscience* specifically; and, within this, upon a selection of manuscripts that can be studied in more depth and utilised to make an informative but manageable initial survey of differences and similarities. As such, this study is able to make a more thorough survey of the far smaller number of manuscripts it considers, for the purposes of presenting fuller accurate data on each.

LALME is intended to serve only as a guideline and resource for dialectologists, allowing them to make analyses themselves, rather than be provided with dialectal theses as such. However, the non-placement of so many Northern manuscripts means that the scholar of NME is unable to make use of *LALME* in the same way that a scholar of South West Midlands English might, where his or her relevant manuscripts are all specifically localised and well documented. The fact that *LALME's* tranches of so many Northern manuscripts are so small is a contributing factor to its inability, in some cases, to provide any information on the manuscripts at all – although the lack of anchor texts is the most critical factor behind the fact that so many are not entered on maps.

Many basic features of Northern dialects, of the sort that might be found in the questionnaire, are, indeed, very similar to each other. However, as will be demonstrated over the course of this study, many are also consistently different, in a way that strongly suggests dialectal variation within the NME area. Although the questionnaire is useful to us, especially because some of the manuscripts used were not interrogated fully by *LALME*, what would be necessary to move beyond the rough and unmapped linguistic profiles of *LALME* would be direct, line by line comparison of one manuscript with another, showing not only differences in orthography and phonology, but also, crucially, differences in lexis and in sense.[7]

---

[7] This will be discussed more fully in the subsequent chapter on Methodological Approaches.

1.6. Scholarship on Northern Middle English

This study investigates a number of those items of dialectal interest discussed above: among them, the question of how texts are changed in translation; how great an impact the motivations and ideology of the scribe have on this process; and what sorts of features the dialectologist needs to consider in the study of dialect, and in what volume. The study incorporates elements of word geography, of philological analysis, and of sociolinguistic exploration. However, its concern is with NME, and the single most important question this study responds to is, as set out in the introduction: Is it really useful to discuss 'Northern Middle English' in the late medieval period as if it were a homogeneous dialect? Does close manuscript study support or refute this idea, and can it enable us to present a more accurate and complex one?

Victorian scholarship established a set of features that generally characterise a text as 'fully Northern'. These are still used by many modern scholars, particularly in texts that address English and ME generally. These features place texts within a geographically massive Northern area, but allow no further localisation or narrowing of features into groupings. Traditionally, accounts of Northern dialect will generally comprise a list of language features, such as: that *thair* and *tha(s)* are observed as the possessive and demonstrative pronouns; *-s* inflexions are found on 3sg. present indicative and present indicative plurals; OE /a:/ is not raised and rounded (Fernandez-Custa and Rodriguez-Ledesma, 2008, pp.91, 94). This simplistic model can be seen in such histories of the language as Charles Barber's *The English Language: A Historical Introduction* (1993), John Burrow and Thorlac Turville-Petre's *A Book Of Middle English* (1992) and many others. The intention of this study is to demonstrate, through study of some of the many Northern manuscripts that have yet to be examined closely (or indeed at all) that this set of features is broad and simplistic, and a more nuanced reading can be presented. A far wider variety of features exists within the region than is usually indicated, and it is possible to present an improved model, potentially suggesting subdivisions of features.

This study is based upon Northern manuscripts of the *Pricke of Conscience,* for reasons which will be more fully outlined in Chapter Two's methodological discussion, but which revolve around the plentiful number of manuscripts, the poem's Northern origins, and the number of Northern dialect copies which exist. Until the publication of Ralph Hanna and Sarah Wood's revision in 2013, the only extant edition of this Northern poem was Richard Morris's 1863 production, which prefaces the poem with a discussion of the manuscripts and the poem's language. In discussing the dialects of the NME region, Morris does begin by making the valuable point that to describe Northern English based purely upon 'that portion of it spoken in the North of England' is inadequate, suggesting that one needs to consider texts from lowland Scotland as well (Morris, 1863, p.v). However, his explanation for this – that, apart from some very minor differences, 'in Grammar and Vocabulary the idioms North and South of the Tweed belong to one and the same dialect' – is problematic and, as this study demonstrates, misleading. There are certainly problems inherent in conducting scholarship around the traditional geopolitically-motivated dividing line between 'Northern Middle English' and 'Scots'. This does not represent an appropriate linguistic border, and it is limiting to scholars to keep their studies only on one side of it, if they wish to get a clear picture of how dialects interact and vary across the border region. If Morris's comment is intended to indicate solely that the border between Scots and NME should not be artificially drawn, then this is an idea with which the current study agrees. However, Morris takes this idea further, implying that consideration of this border is especially unhelpful because 'one and the same dialect', with very little linguistic variation, exists across the entirety of Northumbria and Southern Scotland. Although Morris does not state that there is no linguistic variation at all within this region, his consideration and classification of it as largely homogeneous is evidently also problematic. Other scholars, such as Walter Skeat (1912), continued to approach and describe the region in the same way until the early twentieth century.

Morris, of course, was writing in 1863, before scholarship had turned towards the influence and importance of the scribe and his context on textual and dialect study. He might be excused for his disregard for orthographical differences as constituting any form of dialect variation; there is no distinction made between written and spoken dialects in his discussion, and no acknowledgement that written dialects can be worthy of study in their own right. But Morris's account of the Northern dialect, his description of it as if it were homogeneous and his disregard of orthographical variation as important, has continued to be accepted as a valid general view of the NME region, as we see in the figure presented by Charles Barber (2000, p.137), showing 'fully Northern' as one of the major varieties of ME. Even modern linguistic scholars such as Lukas Pietsch (2005), in his intensive exploration of potential reasons behind the development of the Northern Subject Rule, discusses NME only as a 'major dialect' within which many similar developments took place across a wide area. Pietsch's discussion of language change is deep and thorough, but it catalogues changes across a very large Northern region, rather than addressing heterogeneity of language use within this dialect area.[8] The idea of NME as a homogeneous area has become so entrenched that, in many cases, even the most illuminating and investigative scholarship works from this concept as a base, rather than challenging or exploring it directly.

Morris (1863, p. xiii), laying out a set of features that is echoed by many other subsequent scholars, describes some of what he considers to be the major characteristics of 'the Northumbrian dialect':

1. In nouns, 'the genitive singular ends in -es, -s, occasionally in -is, -ys. Very frequently the sign of the case is omitted, as "Fader house"'.
2. 'All words ending in -yng, -ing, are substantives and not participles'.
3. For numerals, 'much of the Anglo-Saxon orthography is preserved', e.g. 'ane, twa, thrin' for one, two, three.
4. Þa serves as a demonstrative adjective before plural nouns; þas usually demarcates 'those'.
5. The comparative degree is formed by -er or -ere, occasionally by -ar or -are.
6. Pronoun forms found in Northumbrian are: 'sco, sho, thai, thair, tham, yhe or yhou, yhow, you'; with the relative pronouns 'wha, wham, whilk'.

---

[8] Pietsch's research is not constrained only to Northern Middle English, but addresses variable grammars in modern Northern dialects too. For his work on Middle English, see specifically section 3, p. 45–62. Not purely a Middle English scholar, Pietsch relies upon *LALME,* and is consequently constrained by its limitations, as discussed above.

7. 'The conjugation of the Northumbrian verb is extremely simple, one form in s being used for every person in the present tense.' Morris states that this is 'a test by which Northumbrian may be distinguished from other dialects' (p. xviii)
8. Morris also notes that 'the most striking peculiarity perhaps' of the Northern dialect is 'the preservation of the long a in words of Anglo-Saxon origin containing this vowel'.

As a broad set of features by which to broadly identify a text as 'Northern', these are sufficient, but only as a means of determining which texts are suitable for further interrogation in order to shed true light on the Northern dialect area. It is evident that more and better questions need to be asked of the chosen Northern texts in order for us to make better use of them in dialectological studies. If we are able to increase our knowledge of variation in language features in the North, then this could ultimately enable us to determine how far these features differ from text to text and why this might be. Ultimately, it might even be possible to narrow down potential areas of origin for each, or at least to establish which features cross over between manuscripts, and what these manuscripts might have in common.

In his 1994 paper on textual transmission in ME, Richard Beadle discusses the fourteenth century shift towards the North, 'perhaps mainly to Yorkshire', for the composition of devotional and instructional texts, such as the *Pricke of Conscience, Speculum Vitae*, the *Cursor Mundi*, and those texts traditionally attributed to Richard Rolle (Beadle, 1994, p.71). As he notes, these texts make up a significant proportion of the surviving corpus of ME manuscripts, their composition and mass production stimulated by the force of institutionalised religion. The fact that these Northern-composed texts were such a significant part of ME literary output makes the lack of scholarly attention to them still more surprising. As Beadle comments, the distribution of Northern texts such as the *Pricke of Conscience* is gratifyingly large, but the map he provides illuminates again the situation in Northern scholarship: a line divides the 'fully Northern' area from the rest of the country, below which every manuscript is dot-marked to a localisation. The dots above the line are contained in a box to the side of the map itself, their precise distribution impossible to map, due to lack of evidence and study –

even though Beadle feels that the *Pricke of Conscience* may have been originally composed within this precise area, north of Yorkshire (Ibid., p.79).

Beadle's list of localisations for every remaining copy of the *Speculum Vitae* shows that the 'centre' of distribution for this text probably lay in Yorkshire (Ibid., p.84). It also demonstrates again, however, both the value of *LALME* as a tool for scholars working on texts south of the 'fully Northern' line, and the need for further material for scholars working north of it. In truth, Beadle has only localised those manuscripts with origins in Yorkshire and the more southerly counties – that is, those within the part of the Northern area more thoroughly explored by *LALME*. The three remaining, 'fully Northern', non-Yorkshire manuscripts are assigned only to 'Northern area.'

What study has been conducted within this area is limited in its usefulness by its reliance upon place-names and surnames in documents where they are often the only English words, as in Gillis Kristensson's 1967 study of the Northern counties, based upon Lay Subsidy Rolls. Kristensson's survey is extensive, but it has a heavy phonological concentration, and seeks to disregard anything that might be judged a scribal eccentricity, the effect of migration, or anything else he views as 'anomalous' (Kristensson, 1967, p.5). As such, what conclusions he presents are without scribal context and do not necessarily reflect the behaviour of scribes writing full documents in English. Such information would seem insufficient to use alone as a basis for identifying or localising fully Northern English texts; certainly *LALME* did not judge Latin documents containing place-names as sufficiently reliable to use as anchor texts, and Kristensson's conclusions have not been used by Beadle or Lewis and McIntosh. Nevertheless, the variation noted by Kristensson within usage of <o> and <a>, <i> and <y>, and similar, contributes to the suggestion that there is far greater variation within this region than has been properly recorded to date, and a scholar might certainly compare his or her findings against the maps Kristensson presents – his suggestion, for example, that <o> spellings are commoner in the south of the fully-Northern region is certainly a useful one.

The Historical Linguistics Research Group at the University of Seville is currently (2008 – ongoing) engaged in a research project which ultimately 'aims at identifying those features of contemporary

Northern dialects which can be traced back either to Old Northumbrian or to innovations that appear in Middle English' (Fernández-Cuesta, 2013). The goal of the project is related to the history of standardisation: they hope 'to ascertain what features are most resistant to the process of standardisation and discover the possible causes of their resilience.' This project has utilised *LALME*, but has also taken into account twelve documents from the Late Middle English (LME) period, including Cotton Galba E.ix (Fernández-Cuesta and Rodriguez-Ledesma, 2008, p.109). No full account of this project has yet been published, but it appears that a questionnaire method of sorts was applied, with the forms of selected items for each manuscript collated in a database alongside those items from the available Linguistic Profiles in *LALME* (Ibid., p.92). Currently, two of these LME documents are available online as part of the team's SCONE corpus project, which aims to make available a searchable corpus of Northern texts. These are both legal documents: 'The award of William Chiry, mayor, et al., against William Asselby et al., for 'diuers and orrible tripas' against mayor, bailiffs and burgesses' and 'The will of John Smyth of Rolleston' (Fernández-Cuesta, 2013). The other texts used are as yet not available to the general public.

This project certainly shares some of the concerns of this study. Julia Fernández-Cuesta and Maria Nieves Rodriguez-Ledesma express a desire, through their presentation of data, to 'modify the somewhat simplistic and general views (of Northern English) found in most histories of the language' (2008., p.91). Again, the primary concern of these writers is with investigating which features are most resistant to standardisation. They are particularly concerned with legal texts, and with which non-standard features remain in these texts after the point at which 'standardisation' is supposed to have taken place (Ibid., p.92). Dialect differentiation, as such, is not the aim, and the study suggests no new localisations, within the scope of what has already been published, beyond those given in *LALME*. The study is not concerned with sociolinguistic or codicological features, nor the motivations of scribes. There are no two copies of the same text compared.

However, in their presentation of some examples of data accrued, and of data already available in *LALME,* the paper demonstrates that the number of varieties actually extant in NME is vastly greater than what the usual homogeneous presentation suggests. For example, they note that there is variation in the plurals of THAT, beyond what simplistic grammars of NME suggest (Ibid., p.105). As yet, the amount of data made available by this project is insufficient to much illuminate the current study; furthermore, its focus is different to mine, and it is primarily concerned with a different type of manuscript. The full results of this major study, when they become available, will doubtless be of great interest to Northern scholars. In the meantime, the current study, utilising different methodologies and with different concerns, finds similar evidence of a picture more complex than what is generally indicated.

Another group of scholars who have made significant recent contributions to Middle English dialect study is that led by Merja Stenroos and Kjetil V. Thengs at the University of Stavanger, where the *MELD* (Middle English Local Documents) project is based. Like the current study, this project maintains that there remains much underresearched linguistic evidence available to Middle English scholars: while local documents have often been disregarded as 'formulaic', Stenroos and Thengs (2020, pp.4 – 5) point out that, unlike literary texts, local documents are not difficult 'to place in a specific historical context.' Instead, local documents can 'be related directly to specific historical contexts: people, localisations, institutions and communities' and are often very precisely dated. For the Middle English scholar, one of the primary difficulties of any attempt to work with local documents is that there has been little attempt at digitization or extensive study, largely because interest among scholars has been so lacking. The focus of the corpus has not been on Northern Middle English in particular, and the Northern texts that have been studied have yet to be made available by the group. However, the principles of the study utilize fresh approaches to considering Middle English dialect which take into account all available aspects of texts within their context, including the known or assumed social context, the other texts in the corpus, and codicological elements, as well as the actual language of a text. These are principles I have adopted in my own study; when *MELD* is fully available to dialectologists, it will offer unique new avenues down which the dialectologist might usefully progress. However, at the current time, no *MELD* information is available in the NME area under discussion in this study.

Hanna and Wood's revision of Morris's *Pricke of Conscience* is a significant, relatively recent contribution to NME scholarship. Their intention is 'to render the poem approachable by modern scholars', and the primary focus of the edition is to produce a literary text that resembles, as closely as possible, an authorial original (Hanna and Wood, 2013). Palaeographic descriptions of the manuscripts considered are very thorough, but the descriptions of each text's language are cursory and drawn mostly from *LALME*. The appendices of the edition indicate clearly where variants occur between texts, but the presentation is not intended to form the basis of a dialectal or linguistic study. Rather, the most significant instance of dialect investigation in this edition is concerned with the rhyme scheme of the poem, which Hanna and Wood conclude indicate an authorial original emerged in north Yorkshire (**Ibid.**, pp. xxxix–xlv). Importantly, Hanna and Wood have conducted their enquiry as part of a search for evidence about the dialect of the poem's original author, in order to further illuminate the origins of the poem itself. They do not undertake dialect analyses of the manuscripts independently, but rather consider what the early Northern manuscripts indicate as a whole.

Hanna and Wood took, as their base text, an electronic copy of Morris's edition, itself based on British Library, Cotton Galba E. ix. and British Library, Harley 4196. They correct any instances of silent emendation by Morris. They then utilise Derek Britton's suggested stemma for the early copies of the *Pricke of Conscience* to determine which manuscripts should be used as preferential reasons, in order to achieve a final text as close as possible to the original (Ibid., **pp. lxiv–lxix**). Because of this concern with reproducing an original text, Hanna and Wood judge the significant authorial changes made by the scribe of Wellesley 8 – in this study, Scribe **D** – to be 'errors', citing as such, for example, 'his decision to suppress all the poem's Latin' (Ibid., p. lxix). The palaeographical and codicological suggestions made by Hanna and Wood have proved very useful to the current study, but the focus of this study is upon what variation can indicate, and upon sociolinguistic context, and as such, for our purposes, as will be seen, Scribe **D**'s manipulation of the text is not a concern, but a point of interest.

Hanna and Wood do not present a description of what constitutes NME.

1.7. Northern Middle English and its relationship to Scots studies

In his book *The English Language: A Historical Introduction,* Charles Barber (2000) presents a figure showing the major dialects of ME. As has been noted earlier, it is representative of many such figures in histories of the language, showing 'Northern Middle English' as the language of a block of land between the Humber and the Scots Border. Barber does state that this is a simplification. However, he then goes on to make a number of other comments which exemplify some of the problems encountered by scholarship on Northern English. For example, Barber states that 'Northern' is 'divisible into Scots and Northern English', and then goes on to state that 'the separation of the Northumbrian dialect of Old English into the Scottish and Northern English dialects of Middle English is in part due to the political separation of the two regions, which led to the emergence of a Scots literary language in the course of the Middle English period' (Ibid., p.138). In the introduction, I have suggested how this artificial idea of Older Scots as distinct from NME may have compromised scholarship within the Northern dialect area, working analogously backwards from the later, literary language of Middle Scots to encourage the idea that texts from north of the Border fall within a completely different field of study. Speaking of modern Scots, Jeremy Smith (2012, p.6) notes that 'the twenty-first century border between Scotland and England certainly corresponds with a frequent correspondence or 'bundling' [...]of isoglosses [...]where one linguistic feature gives way to another.' But Smith is speaking here of spoken dialects. Moreover, the correspondence between political and linguistic borders is one that has developed since the Middle Ages, when written English usage in England was affected by a process of standardisation that took far longer to spread north of the border; it seems that this modern political difference has sometimes been retroactively over-emphasised in the period that actually pre-dates it. Smith identifies the 'separateness' of Scots as beginning during the later fifteenth century, when Scots became 'elaborated', or available for use in high prestige situations. The LME period, and specifically the manuscripts used for this study, correspond with the Early Scots period (1375 – 1450) when 'it seems that the Anglian-derived variety spoken in Scotland was not viewed by contemporaries as distinct from English. The term

"Inglis", used to describe the non-Celtic language of the Lowlands of Scotland, was only joined (and not replaced) by Scottis in the late fifteenth century' (Ibid., p.8). As such, the assumption of a firm linguistic boundary at this time would seem anachronistic and unprofitable, creating sharp and unhelpful divisions reliant on political, rather than linguistic difference.

Some scholars have, of course, taken these difficulties into account. Walter Skeat (1912, pp.44 – 45) considered it obvious that '"Old Scots" is, of course, the same thing as Northumbrian or Northern English of the Middle English period, which may be roughly dated as extant from 1300 to 1400 or 1450' and indeed 'that the language of the Scottish Lowlands is in all important particulars the same as that of the Northern counties of England, as is evident to any unbiased reader who takes the trouble to compare the Scottish Dictionary with the glossaries of Brockett, Atkinson and Peacock.' Obviously this makes the case too simplistically in the opposite direction, but the point is that scholarship does not seem to have continued in this direction, but has rather chosen to cut off study in the middle of the region North of the Humber for political reasons. Studies in medieval Scots are wide-ranging and numerous; if we were able to discourage recognition of a 'border' between Scots and NME and apply some of that manpower to the many unstudied Northumbrian manuscripts, NME could soon become as well catalogued and understood as its Scottish cousin. Within my own study, I have noted much evidence of the fluidity of language in the 'NME region' even across only four manuscripts; it would be interesting to continue this study on a larger scale to include Scots manuscripts of the poem, the better to illuminate a wider dialect area, rather than cutting off study at the border. Further study, exploiting all the benefits of direct text comparison across manuscripts, would enable us to determine how far the 'Scots' manuscripts of this text differ from those we have already looked at, and in what ways.

There has been a small amount of relatively recent study in this direction. Wojciech Gardela (2009) published a paper on 'Spelling variants of the present participle in a selection of Northern English and Scots texts of the late 14th and the 15th centuries', seeking to emphasise both that it can be useful to consider Scots and Northern English together, from the point of view of the dialectologist, and also that such variants do exist. Gardela notes that *LALME* already presents us with some suggested dialectal variants of this participle, divided up by region – <aunt> (Durham, North Riding), <ende>, <eng> (Durham, Northumberland), <inde>, <ond>, Lancashire, but we already know the limitations of *LALME* with regard to the Northern dialects. Anchor texts for this area are thin; therefore the net for plotting by dialect is coarse. Further investigation and cataloguing of specific, largely untranscribed and unstudied manuscripts must be undertaken in order to refine the net, in the same way that *LAEME* made use of mass transcription and tagging in order to enable dialect plotting for the earlier period. Gardela, rather than narrowing by text, focuses upon a particular linguistic point. He considers it across the NME area and also in relation to Old Scots manuscripts, with reference to *The Helsinki Corpus of Older Scots*. He concludes that 'the present participle in NME and ESC shows some variation in the forms of spelling', suggesting that the change in the form of the present participle from AND to ING was moving at different rates across the broader dialect area – supporting the theory that these were several different, regionally specific, independently developing dialects, moving at their own rates, and that it is unhelpful to consider them only within the traditionally demarcated 'NME' area. As will be demonstrated later, these are all suggestions that my own findings support, but Gardela's study exemplifies how very much work the dialectologist must expend for a small return, and it is one among few such studies. The more we can turn away from recognising the old dialect boundaries as set, demarcating distinct homogeneous regions, the better.

Keith Williamson utilises this idea too, stating that the two language labels of Northern Middle English and Older Scots are 'used to distinguish geopolitically what is perceived to have been a common speech area, or *sprachgebiet*' and choosing to disregard that unhelpful geopolitical labelling in his own study (Williamson, 2002, p.251). He works from both *LALME*, which we have described in detail before, and the *Edinburgh Corpus of Older Scots (ECOS)*, which is an archive of fully transcribed documents more similar to *LAEME* (Ibid., p.252). Williamson's conclusions from these sources are that 'the fifteenth century was a[n unprecedented] period of linguistic divergence within the Northumbrian *sprachgebiet*, both between Lowland Scotland and Northern England and within these respective areas'. The data collected in my own study have evidenced this kind of divergence in evidence a century before, in the early fourteenth century. Again, Williamson is working only from what *LALME* and *ECOS* have recorded; in the case of *LALME*, 'only from the prima facie datable documentary material', which greatly restricted the usable area. This demonstrates further how manuscript study, and consideration of linguistic features in their sociolinguistic and codicological contexts, can actually present a different and more complex picture than can be gleaned from the limited amount of textual information from this region that has already been logged into *LALME*.

Williamson notes variation in third person plural pronouns and in infinitive markers. In discussing the infinitive markers, he is able to state that 'in N England, TIL occurs only sporadically in documents' (Ibid., p.270) but without direct reference to the manuscripts in question, this is not a starting point from which further study could easily be conducted. This, again, exemplifies why it is useful to investigate these markers in their context. Williamson also suggests that between 1380 and 1409, *gif* rather than *if* is 'only sporadic' in the North of England whereas it is 'dominant in Scotland', with the variant only increasing in the record after 1409 (Ibid., p. 273). As will be seen later, this is an interesting comment in light of what I have observed in the period before 1380. The language of manuscript **A,** as will be fully discussed in Chapter Three, uses *ȝif* consistently. Can one then infer, using Williamson's evidence, that this dialect is likely to have its origins in a more northerly part of the country than **B, C** and **D,** which all use *if*? I would posit instead that, without more manuscript study, we cannot trust this picture as fully accurate, due to its reliance on the limited amount of data in *LALME*. Further application of the *Pricke of Conscience*-based comparative method, transcribing and comparing copies of the same text, to a larger number of manuscripts – again, preferably to include some beyond the 'geopolitical' boundary – would be useful here. The more textual study that is embarked upon, the easier it will be for scholars of Northern English to write from a basis of logged and attested data, as Scots scholars are able to, rather than producing small, isolated studies out of a scholarly vacuum.

Like Williamson, Vibeke Jensen (2012) examines orthographical variation within the Northern region, but again, like Williamson, Jensen relies upon texts localised by *LALME,* such that her study of the consonantal element <th> in late NME is restricted to the West

Riding of Yorkshire and the City of York. Her study seeks to build upon the idea of a Northern 'system in which the voiced fricative is spelled <þ>or <y>and the voiceless fricative is spelled <th>', to determine any geographical variation within the area, using manual questionnaires and analysing tranches of the same texts, so it does utilise more data than that provided by *LALME*. However, Jensen finds 'no clear geographical pattern' to the variation she notes although she does determine that religious texts are more disinclined to use <th>, and that in documentary texts, <th> appears to be used more in the eastern part of the county (Ibid., fig 4). Jensen's survey demonstrates that there is language variation from one text to another, but its dependence upon *LALME* localisations restricts it to a fairly small part of the Northern area, within which we would not expect such wide geographical variation as we might find between, for example, texts from Yorkshire and texts from the northerly parts of the 'fully Northern' region. Her suggestion that variation may also be based upon more than geographical factors also supports the idea that sociolinguistic contexts should be investigated in order to illumine NME further – and that restriction of studies to localised or localisable texts does not much aid scholarship in illuminating the lesser explored region north of Yorkshire.[9]

The NME region is not a homogeneous language block, isolated dialectally from the others around it. Much of the time, scholars such as Barber note that it is considered as such only because it has been difficult, to this point, to do much else, for reasons largely related to the lack of scholarly attention paid to these Northern texts. This is certainly a valid assertion (although not a situation that cannot be altered). McIntosh (1989a) notes the complexities of 'differentiating the various subtypes of Northern Middle English' on several occasions and notes that 'some important texts...have not been published at all: this means that not even the word-hoards of the "best" Northern version of these poems [*Speculum Vitae, The*

---

[9] Within the Yorkshire region particularly, Matthew Townend has conducted considerable useful work on English as viewed *coexisting* with Old Norse – and the subsequent influence of Norse upon Northern forms of English. Townend's work offers an interesting sociolinguistic consideration of Middle English in its context, although his primary focus is on the earlier period of coexistence between Old English and Old Norse. See, for example, Townend (2002).

Scale of Perfection, Rolle's Commentary on the Psalter] figure in...any Middle English dictionary' (Ibid., p.99). Consequently, we are unable to take these words into account and use them to further study of the Northern dialects. Because of the broadness of *LALME's* focus, and the fact that it was begun in the 1950s, mass transcription and logging of texts could not be undertaken, leaving this work to specialised scholars. Subsequently, there has not been a mass emergence of many such specialised scholars willing to transcribe and edit these valuable hoards of information about NME. In order to move forward in this scholarly arena, it is necessary to stop working solely from editions and *LALME's* data, which are insufficient for in-depth studies of the NME region. Evidence must be mined from the manuscripts themselves, new data collected for future use, and sociolinguistic contexts must be considered in order to ensure that the greatest amount of useful information is gleaned from this raw material.

Scholarship on ME dialectology, as described above, has established an excellent basis from which to work, but a number of significant gaps remain. For the most part, these gaps are concentrated in the unexplored area above the 'fully Northern' line set out by Lewis and McIntosh and used by subsequent scholars such as Beadle. Lack of anchor texts in the NME region has meant that very little attempt at localisation, or differentiation of dialect, has been attempted north of Yorkshire, but the existence of so many unedited and unstudied Northern manuscripts affords the scholar many opportunities to approach the NME region in an evidence-based fashion, accruing new data and interpreting it in its scribal context. As I have discussed, consideration of scribal behaviour is vital to any in-depth manuscript study; moreover, where there are no anchor texts against which to contextualise newly collected data, evidence of the scribe's sociolinguistic circumstances and origins can serve as an alternative method of contextualising and interpreting what new evidence is collected. Understanding of the scribe as a human being becomes all the more important.

This study seeks to illuminate the NME region through the collection of additional data and the close examination of it in relation to the scribes whose languages we are studying. As its primary research questions, it seeks to examine the idea of NME as a homogeneous dialect area, and to interrogate the extent to which existing descriptions of 'fully Northern' English are accurate representations of the data that emerges. Working from manuscripts that have been little examined, it seeks to determine what can be discovered about these manuscripts and their possible origins based upon textual and extratextual evidence, without recourse to anchor texts to aid in localisation. It will then question whether the dialects of these manuscripts can be divided into different language varieties, and, if so, whether we can determine any connections between these varieties and what the evidence has indicated about their scribes. Fundamentally, it seeks to improve the current picture of NME through new acquisition of data and a method of comparison that takes into account the importance of scribes and the amount of information they imprint on their textual witnesses. This new data can then be added to what already exists, so that any patterns can be observed in context. We will, moreover, then be able to see whether the reconfigured picture can better explain and accommodate debated language varieties, such as that in *Sir Tristrem*. Much previous scholarship has been hamstrung by a lack of access to the information, of various kinds, bound up in Northern manuscripts: this study, in bringing some of this information to light, will put it to use in expanding what is known of NME, and will contribute to scholarship a fuller picture of the number of linguistic variables recorded in this region.

CHAPTER 2

Methodological Approaches

The methodology of the dialectologist is invariably, by necessity, comparative. It relies upon an analysis of a text's language as compared, factor by linguistic factor, against that of another. Meanwhile, the scholar must also consider what sociolinguistic and scribal factors may have influenced these differences, beyond straightforward dialect variation. The research questions of this study, and the limitations of the evidence for NME, require a methodology that not only appropriately collects language data about the manuscripts in question, but also enables that evidence to be fully analysed within its sociolinguistic context.

April and Robert McMahon, in their *Language Classification by Numbers* (2006, p.25), posit that historical dialectologists need 'quantitative methods', stating that 'waiting in the hope that better evidence will simply emerge is not an option'. In the latter statement, this study is fully in agreement: waiting for new evidence is insufficient. Dialectologists wishing to know more about unexplored areas must move beyond what previous scholars have been able to achieve from limited transcriptions, and explore the raw manuscript data themselves. However, the formalised, computer-based methods proposed by the McMahons, while perhaps applicable to their study of historical language groups, do not constitute the sort of methodology this study could usefully employ. In protest against the current *status quo*, the McMahons assert that 'the comparative method [...] is sometimes presented as a mystery into which one can only be initiated after years of philological training; moreover it is suggested that numbers are anathema to its practitioners' (McMahon and McMahon, 2006, p.28). However, it is clear from such studies as *LAEME* that numerical data has been utilised appropriately and extensively by modern historical dialectologists; it is simply that it must be combined with and facilitated by the 'subjective' analytical skill of a human linguist before conclusions can be firmly drawn. While a purely formalised, quantitative, 'provable' method may hold appeal for certain studies, this rejection of the human factor in both the input variable (the scribe) and the output variable (the scholar) is not useful to us in advancing understanding of an under-considered area like the NME region.

It is necessary that the student of historical dialects consider the input and influence of the scribe as part of his or her methodology, for the language under consideration is not a language of mechanical amanuenses, but of people. Although the scribes we are dealing with have only in very rare cases left us their names, they have on many occasions left us, to greater or lesser extents, some evidence of their identities as imprinted upon the texts. It is vital that we consider this when determining what their motivations may have been for the alterations they have made, how far these therefore represent simple dialectal differences, and how far other factors impinge upon the scribe him or herself. It is undeniable that the comparative method presents the scholar with difficulties; it is also true that no linguistic analysis can, at this historical distance, be conclusive. However, a study which fully examines and analyses scribal motivation, process, and influence, in addition to its collection of numerical data, can certainly move scholarship towards a more sociolinguistically realistic conclusion than any analytical method which minimises the importance of the processes of scribal translation in dialect study.

2.1. Selection of base text for study

Angus McIntosh's *LALME* questionnaire for differentiating language considered mostly very common words and features, which can be found in almost any text examined. In order to compare examples of Northern language in more detail, it will be necessary to examine a considerable number of additional linguistic features. One of the ways in which we might do this is by comparing two examples of the same text, where we can directly compare differences over specific lines and features.

Northern texts of the appropriate time period are not manifold. We might look to the *York Plays*, for example, or the *Northern Homilies*; but neither of these texts would provide an appropriate basis for a comparative study of different copies of the same text, and how dialect and scribal influence may have affected it. *The York Plays* we must rule out immediately, as they exist only in one manuscript.¹ The *Northern Homily Cycle* is perhaps of greater interest, existing as it does in twenty-one manuscripts; but where these manuscripts all contain some element or portion of the cycle, they do not all represent the whole of it.² To an extent, useful information could be gleaned from a comparative analysis of these manuscripts of the Cycle, but it is the *Pricke of Conscience* whose manuscripts are sufficiently lengthy and numerous for us to acquire the greatest amount of directly comparable data. As such, the core text used for this study is the *Pricke of Conscience*.

In the preface to his edition of the *Pricke of Conscience,* Richard Morris (1863, p. xiii) describes six of the ten manuscripts he discusses as 'evidently transcriptions of a Northern copy adapted more or less skilfully to the Southern, western and midland dialects. This is easily proved by the way in which the several transcribers have endeavoured to translate pure Northumbrian words into their own South, West and Midland English.' Morris presents this information as a straightforward result of observation, but in fact, the concept of considering the process of dialect 'translation' in medieval texts was to garner little support among scholars for a further century. In making comparisons between versions of the same text in a variety of dialects, noting as significant those words which scribes have substituted and altered, Morris's work is an early recognition of the potential applications of translated texts in medieval word geography, which were not acknowledged again until the 1960's.³

The term 'translation' is used here to refer to a work which, having begun life as a poem in one dialect, has since been consistently converted by a copyist into another – such that a poem originally written in a West Yorkshire dialect becomes a version of

---

[1] Richard Beadle's definitive 1982 edition of *The York Plays* was revised and reprinted in 2009. A discussion of the plays' dialect can also be found in Paul A. Johnston's Appendix in Davidson's edition (2011)

[2] These and other edited Northern texts are discussed more fully in Chapter Six of this thesis, where their data is utilised comparatively alongside that accrued through transcriptions from *The Pricke of Conscience.*

[3] See Hoad (1994).

the poem fully translated into, for example, the dialect of Lichfield.[4] The recognition of these dialect copies as 'translations' of an original is by no means a modern construct or misapplication of terms – Folio 197[b] of MS Cambridge University Library Ii.4.9 describes the final text in the volume, '*Informacion of Richard the ermite*', as having been 'translate oute of northarn tonge into sutherne that it schulde the bettir be vunderstondyn of men that be of the selve contrie (Benskin and Laing, 1981, p.55). During the twentieth century, however, 'most scholars seem to have accepted that although translation is possible in principle, as a matter of history it is unlikely and even implausible (Ibid., p.55). What consideration there was of specific scribal dialects before the 1960's was largely centred on the so-called 'AB Language', seen as representing 'an unbroken continuity of written language from Old English times' (Tolkien, 1929, p. 114). The idea that translation may have been generally common among ME scribes was not widely considered by scholars.

Margaret Laing and Michael Benskin credit the dialectologist Angus McIntosh as having been 'the first to realise the importance of such translation for ME philology in general [...]arguing that translation between dialects was sufficiently common, and sufficiently thorough, to yield a very large corpus of trustworthy material, much larger than had been previously recognised' (Benskin and Laing, 1981, p.56). Certainly, his complaints regarding the tendency of scholars to discard any version of a text removed from the perceived 'original' as 'debased' are fully justified: in the case of the *Pricke of Conscience,* such an attitude has led to a scholarly ignorance of any dialectal material that might be contained in Southern versions of the originally Northern poem, none of these having been considered fit for the attention of an editor. Morris's 1863 edition remained, until Hanna and Wood's 2013 revision, the only full printed text of the poem.

McIntosh, in his own consideration of the language of ME texts, acknowledges the language of the scribe as being as valid as that of the author, identifying three scribal *modi operandi* encountered during the compilation of *LALME*, as detailed in the preceding chapter. The 'translated' text is by no means a rare discovery for the

---

[4] See Chapter One for a full discussion of scribal translation.

medieval scholar: quite the opposite is true. It is no coincidence that Morris, in editing the *Pricke of Conscience*, found himself considering what benefit to us such translations might be, for this is the poem that might be said to best exemplify the tradition of translation in the Middle Ages and how far it could spread.

The *Pricke of Conscience* is a long poem, 9624 lines in Morris's edition, in rhyming couplets, composed anonymously in the north of England in about the middle of the fourteenth century. It contains a prologue, followed by seven books which describe, in turn, the wretchedness of man's nature, the world and its condition, death and the fear of death, purgatory, the Day of Judgement, the pains of hell, and the joys of heaven. It exists in 115 manuscripts, rendering it, if one judges by volume of evidence alone, the most popular poem of the Middle Ages – its nearest competitor is the *Canterbury Tales,* of which 60 manuscripts remain. 96 of the manuscripts of the *Pricke* are considered part of the 'Main Version'; within this group there is evidence of many different dialects, rhyme changes, length of text and rearrangement of material, but all derive ultimately from the original. 18 manuscripts form part of a Southern Recension, which expands some sections, compresses others, and rearranges and reworks substantial portions of text. The two remaining manuscripts represent an abridged and altered version, the *Speculum Huius Vite*. The dialectal distribution of these manuscripts is very wide: nearly three quarters of the counties in England have at least one copy, and there are even three manuscripts in Hiberno-English, which testify to the great distances the poem travelled (Lewis and McIntosh, 1982, p. 1 – 15).

Evidently, then, to restrict study to only the earliest copies of the *Pricke* is to cut oneself off from potentially hundreds of words and phrases of interest to both dialectologists and word-geographers. Translated texts have traditionally been held as suspect evidence by ME linguists, but as McIntosh describes, translating scribes were usually extremely thorough,[5] meaning that the resultant text serves as good evidence for the dialectal features of the scribe, quite independent of those of his exemplar. It is of course true that many

---

[5] For a discussion of problematic scholarly attitudes to translated texts and the evidence for the thoroughness of the translating scribe, see McIntosh (1989a,p. 39).

scribes hesitate to alter rhyming words, but where these words are inconsistent with the scribe's dialect outside of the rhyme – if 'mon', for instance, is retained in rhyme where the usual usage is 'man' – this practice is easily detectable, and can be discounted as evidence. *Mischsprachen,* or mixed dialects resulting from half-translated texts, are more problematic. We may point, for example, to the scribe Robert Thornton, whose texts copied from Lincolnshire exemplars often contain elements of Yorkshire dialect, notably in *Sir Perceval of Galles* (Braswell, 1995, p.2). However, even these texts can prove of interest to the dialectologist, for where the resultant text is a mixture of two dialects, it is often possible to separate the strands through careful study, thus providing the reader with evidence for both the dialect of the exemplar and that of the scribe. This is obviously simpler when the dialects are quite distinct, and would be more difficult when comparing two fairly similar Northern dialects; but it is possible provided the right questions are asked.

The *Pricke of Conscience,* as described, is of very great use as a dialectologists' resource, particularly in those areas where written material is scanty. What Morris began to remark in 1863 was the potential inherent in the *Pricke* as a system of translations, capable of providing the scholar with word-geographical information which could be obtained from no other source. In the first instance, the popular nature of the text, attested to by the sheer number of copies remaining, combined with its length, mean that the scholar can be fairly certain of finding a significant number of common words across the manuscripts. That these common words are likely to be those habitually used in the area of copying is also implied by the number of translations: texts like the *Pricke* were presumably often copied to be read aloud, as indeed its author anticipates in his conclusion, and would therefore have to contain word-forms commonly used, or at least commonly understood, by local audiences of 'lewed' men. Because the manuscripts extant are in LME, moreover, our scribes are sufficiently distant from the rather linguistically-constrained era of the period immediately following the Norman Conquest that local written vernaculars had already developed to the point where many scribes were accustomed to writing the forms characteristic of their own localities as standard.[6]

A close study of several translations of a text such as the *Pricke of Conscience* allows the dialectologist to move beyond the *LALME* conception of scribes almost as automata in three varieties — A: the literatim scribe; B: the translating scribe; and C: the scribe who combines translating and literatim copying – and to illuminate the issue through the discussion and integration of the scribes' possible motives in translating and their sociolinguistic situations. Where two scribes' renderings of the same line of text can be directly compared, it is possible to see not only variation in basic language features, but also in lexical choices. It is also possible to determine whether the line appears to have been altered for sense. As such, these determinations, in accordance with manuscript and other textual evidence about the scribe's sociolinguistic circumstances, can shed light on the different sorts of changes scribes made to texts, both those motivated purely by dialect variation and those related to other factors, such as training and ideology.

In a general sense, it is obvious why scribes might choose to translate a text that has come to them for copying into the local dialect, particularly where, as previously discussed, this text is of a popular nature, and a local vernacular would be the most appropriate. In such a case, it does indeed seem, as *LALME* posits, that to translate would be the most easy and natural thing for a scribe to do, rather than its being a conscious choice requiring a specific reason for taking 'the necessary trouble', as J.R.R. Tolkien (1929, p.114) maintained.

Comparison of one copy of a text with another copy of the same text, in a different dialect, formed the basis for the first major word geographical study, Rolf Kaiser's 1937 work, *Zur Geographie des mittelenglischen Wortschatzes,* which examined points of difference between a Southern and a Northern version of the *Cursor Mundi.*[7] Terry Hoad (1994, p.200) finds significant problems with this methodology, stating that it is always possible, for instance, that the

---

[6] For a discussion of linguistic conservatism in the period following the Conquest, see Laing and Williamson (1994, pp. 65–67).

[7] For a discussion of Kaiser's work as the first exploration of Middle English dialectology, seeHoad (1994, p.200)..

translator may simply have avoided a word because he thought it old-fashioned, or simply misunderstood the exemplar. For this reason, 'one text alone will not yield conclusive evidence for the dialectal distribution of a given word'. But this criticism is based upon the assumption that no further examination of contextual and sociolinguistic factors would take place, and also that the single-text comparison is a comparison of a single pair of manuscripts. Anne Hudson (1983) maintains, contrarily, that the use of a single text is the only way to ensure that any discrepancy in vocabulary is due only to dialectal differences, and not to differing interests between two texts. Where one is considering a text as rich in dialectally different copies as the *Pricke of Conscience,* the information that might be gleaned from such a network – about the scribes, their reasons for reproducing the text, and the motivation behind their every change – is of a sort that must come from comparison within one text. A vast, but shallow, network of localised dialectal information, based upon a questionnaire of common words, such as *LALME*, can tell us straightforward things about dialects, but it cannot serve to tighten what, in the Northern regions, is a very coarse net. Manuscript study of different Northern versions of the *Pricke of Conscience,* however, could incorporate questions of scribal influence, audience, and reception in order to ask deeper questions about dialect and sociolinguistic contexts. Ultimately, only non-linguistic localisations can enable us to plot this information onto a map, but with more data, not only would more be known about the extent of linguistic variation within this region, but we might also be able to identify patterns and connections between dialects based upon deductions about their scribes and their circumstances. Moreover, should further anchor texts be unearthed, it is easier to compare a single anchor text against a wealth of pre-existing data than to attempt to build a net for as-yet-unacquired data using only one or two anchor texts.

A comparison of one given manuscript text to other Northern copies of the *Pricke* allows direct identification of what changes have been made, and what sort of changes they are, from those evidently resulting only from dialect variation, to others suggesting more complicated scribal motives. In this way, a close study of the process of scribal translation can serve to shed some light upon the context in which the scribes were working, and upon how deeply and deliberately they may have influenced texts.

In their 1971 study 'A dialect word in some West Midlands manuscripts of the *Prick of Conscience*', Margaret Darau and Angus McIntosh give a brief illustration of what information can be gleaned from a study of only two or three altered words. They isolate the word *goben,* which features, in various forms, in six out of seven surviving Lichfield manuscripts (in the seventh, the passage is missing). *Goben* replaces *body* in the sense 'body of that tre', and is in fact the only example of this word in ME. The most straightforward motive behind word alteration by scribes – that of dialectal pressure – cannot be posited for so common a word as *body,* used many times elsewhere by this scribe. Darau and McIntosh (1971, p.21) posit instead that this change is representative of a general intention towards 'clarifying and sharpening the argument of [the] text'. They cite an example of a similar sort of change, where, in line 1871, this Lichfield scribe replaces *mon* with *degree:*

Deþ to no degree hath rewared –
Ryche nor pore hyȝe nor lowe.

Here again, the original word could hardly have been an unfamiliar one: the substitution can only represent an attempt to improve the clarity of the text's message. If this is the case, recognition must be made of the Lichfield scribe as a figure of far greater literary importance than has traditionally been accorded to scribes; moreover, it seems unlikely that this sort of 'sharpening' change should not have happened elsewhere, more or less regularly. As McIntosh and Darau point out, the so-called Lichfield Master often appears to be working with a stylistic ideal in mind, removing or altering words, on a number of occasions, to avoid repetition within the space of a few lines – obviously not a concern of the original author, as this happens very frequently in Northern copies of the *Pricke.* In the exemplar, *body* – itself altered from the more commonly found *bely* — is repeated in lines 678 and 679:

Þe body of þat tre þar-by
Es þe brest with the body.

In replacing *body* with *goben* in line 678, then, the scribe is continuing his trend towards the elimination of repetition, as well as sharpening the argument of his text. As Darau and McIntosh indicate, 'here, a part of a tree is being compared with the "corresponding" part of a man and throughout the rest of the passage different words are used for the arboreal and human items in the comparison (roots: hairs; stock: head)' (Ibid., p.22). The change to *goben* thus serves a number of purposes: it renders this passage more internally consistent, and thus more effective, and it clarifies the material. It is also stylistically more pleasing to the ear, in that, as McIntosh and Darau observe, this scribe appears to abhor repetition and eliminates it where possible, such that *goben* here prevents the word *body* from being used in two adjacent lines (Ibid., p.22). Evidently, if *goben* was chosen by a Lichfield scribe, it must have been a word recognizable to the inhabitants of Lichfield – which, given that this Anglo-French derivative is attested nowhere else in ME, is dialectally interesting in itself. What this study serves to demonstrate, however, is that close scrutiny of a single translated word can shed much light on the motives and reasoning behind a translation: it allows us, as nothing else can, to penetrate into the mind of the scribe and understand something of his context and motivations, and how far he felt himself personally responsible for what he copied. Reapplication of this methodology to Northern manuscripts of the *Pricke of Conscience* would allow similar identification of some non-linguistic reasons behind language variation, and consideration of these factors could prevent misidentification of words as being 'disused' or not recognized within certain areas.

Before any comparative methods can be applied, we must first have sufficient material with which to work. Given the very large number of manuscripts of the *Pricke of Conscience,* and the considerable length of the text, it would be unrealistic to attempt to compare the entirety of each manuscript, and such an endeavour would require a study of greater magnitude than this one. As my focus is upon dialectal variation, however, it would be useful to have evidence of the dialects of as many Northern manuscripts as is viable, the better to compare dialectal differences and identify any patterns or correlations between them. This being the case, I determined that the most appropriate method of collecting and organising the relevant data was to select a number of manuscripts and then transcribe tranches from each – that is, to transcribe the same section of text, or equivalent sections, should the content itself vary somewhat – from the beginning, middle and end of each manuscript selected. In order to ensure that results were as representative as possible, these tranches were taken at regular intervals across the manuscript. These transcribed tranches were then interrogated using an appropriate linguistic questionnaire, and the results compared, so that any clear patterns in basic items could be seen at once. In order to ensure that the tranches were indeed fully representative, the remaining text was also scanned. The questionnaire method as an initial step demonstrated immediately where the greatest variation lay. An alternative methodology might have been to reduce the number of manuscripts scrutinised to two, so that they could be considered in their entirety, but for my purposes, this seemed a less appropriate approach: the reason that the *Pricke of Conscience* represents such a vitally important resource is that it exists in so many manuscripts, thus giving a clear idea of the diversity of language at that time. Comparing only two manuscripts, even in greater depth, would not make the best use of this advantage, nor provide the level of dialectal data which could come from a comparison of multiple representations of the same sets of lines.

2.2. The questionnaire for data analysis: compilation

In *LALME,* McIntosh sets out a number of useful guidelines for devising a questionnaire for dialect comparison and analysis. In the following study, as in *LALME,* the term *item* 'will be used to denote the heading for a collection of different *forms* that are regarded as equivalent in function and/or meaning, and may therefore, potentially at least, differentiate dialects'(*LALME,* vol. 2, p.7). An item might be represented by, for example, 'the word for ARE', and 'ben, er, buth, etc', would be equivalent forms or manifestations of this item. Items fall into four different general classes of evidence: orthographic(i.e., *miʒt v might*); phonological (*stan v ston*), morphological (*rideth: rides*) and lexical (*dark: mirk – darkness*). Although it may sometimes be difficult to assign items correctly between the first two categories, it is quite clear that they are, indeed, distinct, and as McIntosh indicates, an investigation of written language will not be greatly affected, in any practical sense, by this uncertainty.

We cannot, of course, hope to investigate every possible word in a dialect for comparative purposes. For the study, we have available the computer resources to compare and contrast our tranches directly with each other, but without some form of selective interrogation, this does not especially benefit us. As a means of selection, then, we must consider the degree to which items display regional variation – that is, how likely it is that they will vary between dialects, and that variation will therefore indicate dialect difference – and the probability that these items will recur frequently. Where the *LALME* scholars, however, were constrained by the fact that they were working with many different types of text, the following study need not consider to the same extent an item's probability of occurring in most classes of text. The questionnaire therefore includes a significant amount of religious terminology which might not occur in, for example, a selection of comedic stories, as the core of our resource material has a religious basis.

McIntosh indicates that 'one may quite rapidly compile from [different versions of the same text] a list of items whose manifestations differ between one version and another', which may serve as a 'useful initial strategy for selecting criteria' (Ibid., p.7). As Gillieron noted in 1915 (p.45), 'l'etablissement du questionnaire...pour etre sensiblement meilleur, aurait du etre fait apres l'enquete',[8] but of course, this option is never available to the dialectologist in actuality. The next best option is to use a combination of McIntosh's proposed questionnaire and scans of tranches to identify which items show most obvious variation, and to tailor the questionnaire based upon these determinations.

As McIntosh indicates in *LALME* vol. 1 (p.8), the choice of items in a questionnaire will necessarily differ depending upon the region under investigation, for the simple reason that 'certain criteria provide crucial differentiations in limited areas, but none of any significance for the rest of the country'. As we are aiming for 'maximal differentiation within each area', we have no reason to investigate forms which a broader survey might consider important, if these forms do not show variation within the Northern dialect area. Consequently, although McIntosh's *LALME* questionnaire served as the starting point for my own, items which did not appear or did not seem subject to variation were dropped.

---

[8] "In order to establish the best possible questionnaire, we would have to do it after the study had been done."

In any study based upon written forms, orthographic or graphemic differences, even small ones, are, of course, of importance, in that they may indicate distinct different spellings of words dependent upon geographical area, even where they have no apparent influence upon perceived pronunciation. Thus, rather than querying whether ð or þ is used in a medial and final position, for example, one might preferably note a number of items, such as *earth* or *other*, from each manuscript, and observe differing behaviour for each. Conversely, it is sometimes more helpful to conflate items for a clearer representation of the whole, as where, for example, we are surveying grammatical endings such as the *-ynge/-ende/-ande* present participle ending question. To collect data for each present participle as a separate form dependent upon items in terms of single words, such as BEGINNING or RECKONING, would be unprofitable and potentially confusing. In this case, it is better to consider the present participle ending as an item in its own right, as more likely to make any patterns readily apparent.

The final questionnaire utilised in this project was based upon a combination of terms identified by McIntosh as useful for study, and preliminary observations made from the selected manuscripts. The questionnaire was completed initially from tranches, and each manuscript was subsequently fully scanned in order to ensure that the form noted as most common within the tranches was borne out by the rest of the manuscript, and also to locate items that did not appear within the transcribed tranches. An electronic copy of Morris's edition, containing the full text, was used to ensure that, when it seemed that a given item did not feature in the text at all, this was indeed the case. The questionnaire can be found in Appendix 2.

2.3. Approaching and using manuscripts to accrue data

One of the most unique and useful attributes of the *Pricke of Conscience* as a resource is, as has been established, the fact that it exists in so many manuscripts. Ideally, were we able to analyse and assess every single 'fully Northern' manuscript, it might be possible to draw up a very intricate and informative set of linguistic profiles and dot maps to help localise these manuscripts, ultimately resulting in an understanding of NME far more advanced than what currently exists. In practice, however, this would be a huge scholarly undertaking. One of the reasons that the *LALME* team found it so difficult to localise its Northern manuscripts is that there are far fewer anchor texts – texts already firmly localised to a particular place – extant for that area of the country, and a scholar specialising in the region would have to contend with this difficulty. What anchor texts do exist for Northumberland, Cumberland and Durham are, firstly, mostly restricted to the fifteenth century, and secondly, are often very short, such that the data contained was insufficient for *LALME* scholars to be able to localise any of the non-anchored NME texts based upon it. The only texts localised within the fully Northern region outside of Yorkshire are those anchored to a place by firm evidence within the text, such as leases, arbitrations, memoranda, signed letters and similar short documents. One or two texts have been localised based upon individual analysis of the manuscript, such as London, British Library, Harley 1260, judged by A.I. Doyle to be of Durham origin, but no text has been 'plottable' within this area based upon the evidence of linguistic features alone (*LALME,* vol. 1, p.193).

Consequently, one of the first things any study must do is recognise what are the true possibilities of its scope, and in this instance, it was determined that firm localisation should not be the ultimate goal. Rather, an assessment of the current scholarly situation made it clear that this study should concern itself more with interrogating the idea that NME is a single, homogeneous dialect, despite the broadness of the so-called 'fully Northern' dialect area. If the study could demonstrate that there were – or, indeed, were not – notable differences between the dialects of 'fully Northern' manuscripts of the *Pricke of Conscience,* this would be an excellent foundation upon which to build. Future studies could then be carried out towards the long-term goal of localising manuscripts firmly within the NME area, if it could be proven that the dialects could be differentiated.

Another major consideration that had to be contended with early in the research process was that of determining how many manuscripts could form part of the core study. I have discussed already how the massiveness of *LALME*'s scope has necessarily resulted, in some cases, in data that cannot really be called representative. The *LALME* study was undertaken by a team of people over a great many years; having assessed its capabilities, the study determined that only brief surveys would be possible in some cases. In the same way, this study had to assess its own capabilities. Having determined that the primary aim should not be localisation, my intention then became to determine, through assessment of a suitable number of manuscripts, whether any differentiation could be made between different forms of NME. In order to do this, it would be necessary:

1. To consider each manuscript's language in sufficient depth to ensure a coherent and accurate set of data, which would require tranches to be taken from, if possible, every extant book of the poem.
2. To consider the sociolinguistic factors impacting the manuscript's production, such as the scribe's intended audience and where he was trained, in order to help determine any possible connections between variation and training or circumstance.

This being the case, I judged, through a process of trial and error, that the most appropriate number of manuscripts to consider as base texts was four. This number was small enough to enable thorough analysis of each manuscript in its context, but also large enough to demonstrate whether the dialects could, or could not, be differentiated from each other.

2.4. The base manuscripts and their scribes

In order to select the best manuscripts for this study, a number of different criteria had to be applied. This study is, first and foremost, concerned with illuminating the little-explored Northern region, so naturally all the texts selected had to be classified as 'fully Northern'. But it is also important to consider, in any dialect study, the fact that diachronic variation – that is, variation over a period of time – must be accounted for, as distinct from diatopic variation (or variation by geographic distance). In order to simplify the study and prevent confusion, the best selection of manuscripts would all be from a similar point in time. It was necessary, therefore, to select a group of manuscripts all dated to within a century of each other, at the widest distance. The earliest of the manuscripts, **B,** has been dated to the second quarter of the fourteenth century, the latest to the first quarter of the fifteenth. It is significant that, if Lewis and McIntosh's datings of both **B** (second quarter of the fourteenth century) and **B2** (the end of the fourteenth century) are correct, then this span of time – up to 75 years – would fall within the working life of a single scribe, **B**.

It would also be necessary for the manuscripts chosen to contain sufficient material to enable us to compare, line by line, more than one tranche of identical text. As such, small fragmentary manuscripts could not be considered. **B2**, as detailed below, contains a more complete text of the poem than **A**, but, as will be described, this book has been identified by Ralph Hanna (2002, p.93) as having the same scribe as **B**. Ergo, although the manuscript was examined, it seemed less illuminating to use this as one of the core texts, as then we would have four manuscripts as evidence, but only three scribes. Using these criteria, then, the thirteen 'fully Northern' manuscripts of the *Pricke of Conscience* could be narrowed down to the following four as base texts, plus **B2**.

MS A: Oxford, Bodleian Library, Rawlinson C. 891 s. xv 1.

This is a parchment manuscript, 270 x 172 mm. It is written in double columns in four hands, all writing in anglicana, with the exception of Hand 3, the 'fully Northern' hand and the one with which we are concerned. This hand writes in textura throughout, and occupies the greatest part of the manuscript, from ff. 35 – 111v (of 127 ff). *LALME* localises the language to Yorkshire's West Riding. Latin quotations in this manuscript are written in a variety of anglicana formata by Hands 1, 2 and 4, to distinguish them from the slightly different anglicana script of the main text (Lewis and McIntosh, 1982, p.112). Hand 1 is a North East Midlands hand; Hand 2 central Midlands, and Hand 4 is in a mixed dialect but, notably, with a 'strong Fenland ingredient'.

The manuscript contains the *Pricke of Conscience,* followed by Richard Maydestone's paraphrase of Psalm 51 and brief annals of England from the Creation to 1377. Its text of the *Pricke of Conscience* is incomplete, and the book shows much evidence of having been revised, notated and corrected, with later scribes commenting on the work of earlier ones, while the 'fully Northern' section contains occasional notes and corrections in a hand other than Hand 3. All of these things, particularly the variant scribal dialects and additionally the judgement of Lewis and McIntosh (Ibid., p. 112) that the book must have made use of at least two different exemplars for the *Pricke of Conscience* text, make the book particularly intriguing.

B: Oxford, Bodleian Library, Rawlinson poetry 175 s. xiv 2.

This is a parchment manuscript, 268 x 190 mm. *LALME* localises it to the North Riding of Yorkshire. The book is written in what Lewis and McIntosh (Ibid., p. 116) judge to be a single, 'fully Northern' hand, entirely in textura. Hanna and Wood (2013, p. xxi) contend that the book contains two scribes, with the first copying only the *Pricke of Conscience,* and a second scribe, in very consistent language and near-identical hand, copying everything after this text. Within the *Pricke of Conscience,* the Latin quotations are not distinguished from the English except in that they are written in red ink, rather than the black ink of the main text. In some places, the black ink has rubbed off onto the pages, suggesting that the book was heavily used. The pages are worn in many places.

The handwriting and presentation of the book are very regular and neat, evidently written all at one time and with all the necessary material available to the scribes. So similar are the two hands that Hanna and Wood indicate they must 'share common training'. Possibly, the book was copied directly from an identical exemplar; or, possibly, the scribes had a list of items they had been asked to include, and ready copies of all these items. Either way, the scribes were evidently well prepared for their task.

The manuscript contains eleven items in English and Latin, including 'Passiones Jesu Christi', 'The Book of Penance', 'The Gast of Gy', *The Seven Sages of Rome,* and some other, shorter religious pieces. It seems likely that the book was produced for some kind of devotional use, and while it has been carefully handled, the wear indicates that it was used regularly.

The *Pricke of Conscience* scribe in this manuscript, referred to here as Scribe **B,** has been identified by Ralph Hanna (2002, p.93) as the scribe of a second 'fully Northern' copy of the *Pricke of Conscience,* in British Library, Harley 4196, where he is the fifth scribe, from quires 27 – 34. As such, this copy of the poem did not constitute one of the four core studied versions, as it seemed more useful to investigate the work of four separate Northern scribes. However, Hanna and Wood revise this opinion to indicate that there are, as noted above, two scribes in this manuscript, and that the second scribe of MS **B**, in fact, was the scribe of Harley 4196. The extreme consistency of usage between the two scribes of MS **B** is highly intriguing, and indicates two scribes of the same training and provenance, and a connection between the manuscripts. Consequently, Harley 4196 was investigated and some transcriptions taken from it, in order to gain further insight into the copying practices of these scribes and their language. It is described below.

B2: London, British Library, Harley 4196 s. xiv ex.

This is a parchment manuscript, 258 ff., 380 x 275 mm. The manuscript contains five hands, the last of which writes *the Pricke of Conscience* in textura (Lewis and McIntosh, 1982, p. 66). Having examined the hands, I concur with Hanna's conclusion that this is the same scribe as Hand 2 in the **B** manuscript, above, and that it is nearly indistinguishable from the hand of Scribe **B**. The *Pricke of Conscience* is written in double columns, 48 lines to the column, and there are catchwords between folios. The Latin is distinguished from the English text only in that it is written in red. The book does contain decorative capitals.

There is an omission of seven leaves between ff. 228 and 229, containing ll. 2593 – 3937 of the poem. Each book commences with an English title, except for IV, which is imperfect at the beginning, and VI (which is not). The manuscript also contains the expanded *Northern Homily Cycle,* saints' legends in verse, and *The Gospel of Nicodemus.* Its entire contents are classified as 'fully Northern' by Lewis and McIntosh, and it was owned, in 1622, by William Browne (Ibid., p.66). This manuscript serves as the base for Morris's edition for ll. 1538 – 729 and 6923 – 9210, where **C** was imperfect.

MS C: British Library, Cotton Galba E i.x s. xiv ex.

This manuscript formed the base text for the greater part of Morris's 1863 edition (see above), and is anomalous amongst our manuscripts in many ways. Morris (1863, p. 8) refers to it as a 'fine folio of Northumbrian poetry' and it is, indeed, more a poetry collection than a selection of religious and didactic texts, as the other manuscripts are, and moreover is far more impressive. It is a parchment book (Osberg, 1996, p.2) the original parchment sheets fused onto newer vellum sheets, 330 x 208.8 mm in size, making it larger than all of our other manuscripts.

The book contains eleven poems attributed to Laurence Minot, the Arthurian romance *Ywaine and Gawayne,* and *The Prophecy of the Six Kings to Follow King John* (*The Prophecies of Merlin*), as well as three devotional pieces found elsewhere in the *Cursor Mundi*. It also contains some more popular and widely disseminated poems: *The Sevyn Sages of Rome,* the apocryphal *Gospel of Nicodemus,* and, of course, the *Pricke of Conscience.*

The manuscript is written in textura, in double columns. It contains six hands, all Northern or North-East Midlands, with the fifth, referred to in this study as Scribe **C,** responsible for the *Pricke of Conscience* in its entirety. Its only known owner was Robert Cotton, although it does contain the name 'Richard Chawser', three times in an early modern hand on the last folio, possibly evidence of a sixteenth-century owner of the manuscript.

Despite the manuscript's impressive size, the texts themselves contain little decoration. We do find ornate blue capitals, picked in red (Braswell, 1995, p.2), where our other manuscripts contain only black and red ink, but there are no further, less common colours. Blue was generally considered the 'third colour' of medieval manuscript writing (De Hamel, 1992, p.5). The texts do not contain corrections other than minor ones in the main hand of each segment.

MS D: Wellesley, Massachusetts, Wellesley College Library, 8 s. xv. in.

This manuscript is similar in size to **A** and **B** – 210 x 150 mm – but unlike them, is written on paper rather than parchment. The *Pricke of Conscience* is written in anglicana, in single columns. The wooden boards of the book are covered in sheepskin, and the manuscript is paginated rather than foliated. There are catchwords throughout the manuscript, but not consistently. The manuscript consists of quires of eight. Although *LALME* describes this text only as 'fully Northern', Hanna and Wood (2013, p. xxv) theorise that it contains elements indicating a connection to the Vale of York.

The book contains, as well as the *Pricke of Conscience,* the *Stimulus Consciencie Minor,* a thanksgiving to Christ attributed to Richard Rolle, and the latter part of *The Book of Penance* (Lewis and McIntosh, 1982, p. 129).

Most of the Latin quotations are omitted, although there are brief running titles. The manuscript shows interlinear corrections in the main hand. On page 247, we find the inscription 'Iste liber constat Ricardo Gardner' in a fifteenth-century hand. On page 248, we find in a sixteenth-century hand, 'Wylliam Hotterbrim'. On page 252, we find the name 'Skeibey' and the date '1534'.

2.5. Limitations observed in the questionnaire method, and subsequent additional methodologies

In examining the results of initial applications of the questionnaire, it became clear that, while the questionnaire permits simple comparison of orthographical and, potentially, phonological differences between the manuscripts, it is not sufficient for a full dialectal investigation. Certainly, in comparing the results, patterns in orthographical differences could be seen. For example, one of the first major patterns to surface in the application of the questionnaire was in the differing forms of WHO and WHICH.[9] In Rawlinson C.891 (**A**), we find <q>, where Rawlinson Poetry 175 (**B**) and Cotton E i.x (**C**) prefer <wh>: **A** gives *qwo* for *wha* (**B, C**); *qwilk* for *whilk* (**B, C**), *whylk* (**B**), *wilk* (**C**). Already, it was possible to identify interesting differences: the spelling *qwo* is particularly notable for its juxtaposition of the initial <q> against the 'o' ending, while **B** and **C**, contrarily, retain the Northern <a> spelling, but use a more southerly-influenced initial <wh>. A similar pattern was also noted across the item WHEN, with **B** and **C** giving *when* to **A**'s *qwen*. The item SHOULD showed consistent differences which, again, seemed to group **B** and **C** together, while setting **A** slightly apart, dialectally. **A** uses *schulde* throughout, while **B** and **C** both prefer *suld*. Similarly, where **A** uses *agayne* for AGAIN, manuscripts

---

[9] Note that D and A2 do not feature here, as these preliminary observations were conducted before these manuscripts had been transcribed.

B and **C** both use *ogayne* consistently. This is also reflected in the word *ogaynst* in this manuscript, and no <a> forms of AGAIN or AGAINST appear in this first transcribed tranche of **B**.[10]

At other points, we see variation that seems to group the manuscripts in other ways. Scribe **B** emerges as a lone outsider when he uses the form *effward* for AFTERWARD, this form also used by Scribe **B2**, where **A** and **C** prefer *afterward* and *aftirward*, respectively. Elsewhere, we find *sepen* in **A**, where **B** has *sithen* and **C** *sythen* for the item SINCE. The use of 'þ' in **A** is not terribly informative here, indicating, most probably, simply some scribal preference, but the <e> could arguably suggest that this word was pronounced – or rather, mentally coded – differently by users of the **A** dialect. Likewise, **A**'s usage of *doun* for DOWN, where **B** and **C** give *don* and *donne*, respectively, would seem to indicate a possible difference in the pronunciation – or mental coding – of the vowel sound in this word. Potentially, these forms may have sounded different in speech and in the mind of the scribe as he wrote.[11]

Evidently, the questionnaire, used on its own, formed a useful starting-point for comparing the manuscripts of the *Pricke of Conscience*. The initial analysis demonstrated that the dialects of the three manuscripts considered at this stage are far more similar than they are different, as one would expect of any three manuscripts from the same extended geographical region. Syntactically, in particular, they vary very little. However, even this preliminary assessment usefully suggested that they are not indistinguishable from each other, and that some of the differences appear very regular. The first two tranches of text used in this analysis did not provide sufficient information to fill the questionnaire, from which I determined that another three or four of similar length would be required. As the poem comprises a prologue, seven books, and an epilogue, but with the epilogue or prologue often missing, it seemed logical to take an opening tranche from each of Books 1 – 7 of the poem, where these existed in the manuscript. The initial findings indicated that this would result in a fairly extensive catalogue of points of orthographical divergence between the manuscripts, as

---

[10] These examples are given here as illustration: the orthographical differences will be discussed at length in Chapter Three.

[11] For further analysis of these items, see Chapter Three.

indeed proved to be the case. It was also determined at this stage that, having used this preliminary analysis as a test run for time and resultant data accrued, it would be both possible and optimal for a fourth manuscript to be introduced into the study.

Dialect study, however, is not restricted to orthographical and phonological variation, as has been extensively discussed above. As such, I determined that the questionnaire would not be sufficient for my purposes; further investigative techniques would be required. In compiling the questionnaire, I made use of a number of spreadsheets, in which the tranches of text from the three manuscripts were arranged in columns alongside each other, such that Line 1 in **A** was immediately adjacent to the corresponding line in **B** and **C**. This arrangement of the tranches represented a fairly useful resource even in this basic format: it enabled me, for example, to see where one manuscript included an additional line not found in the others. Tracking the inclusion or exclusion of lines across manuscripts, while not always directly related to the question of dialect, can certainly have some bearing upon it, particularly where there seems to be some substantive reason for the change. If an included line illuminates the scribe's purpose or ideology in writing, this can often inform our interpretations of later examples of lexical or syntactical variation, enabling us to better judge whether they represent straight dialect variation or differences unrelated to geographic factors – paralinguistic and sociolinguistic differences, or the idiosyncrasies of a scribe seeking to emphasise a particular point or ideology. Line-by-line comparisons or collations enable us to identify these additions and redactions, and examples of lexical variation, while the questionnaire does not. This first investigation indicated to me that line-by-line comparison, while time-consuming, is a useful tool in comparing and analysing data. Although this process could not realistically be applied across a large number of manuscripts, the restriction of study to four core manuscript texts meant that it was possible to use it here.

2.6. Applications of selected methodology

There are a number of examples of lexical variation – the substitution of one word for another or a distinct difference in form

– visible in the line-by-line comparison. Where **A** uses the word *drede*, for instance, we find, in **B,** *fridlayke,* and in **C,** *ferdlayke*. Comparison of the section in which this word appears reveals a further difference in **A**, too, where the scribe has chosen to consider 'þe synful' in the singular – 'In grete drede he schulde be brouȝt' – rather than the plural, 'þai suld in gret fridlayke be broght' (**B** and **C**). Moreover, the sentences are syntactically different in their positioning of the prepositional phrase. Otherwise, it is not immediately clear as to why the scribe should have chosen *drede* here, rather than the word *fridlayke/ferdlayke* preferred by the scribes of **B** and **C**. The tranche at the beginning of Book VI, where this word appears in l. 6427, is missing from **D,** but the word also appears in l. 2917. This falls outside of the transcribed tranches, but a scan shows that **D** also utilises *drede.*[12]

This type of lexical variation could not be noted nor subsequent investigation conducted using only a questionnaire. The most thorough method to investigate lexical variation would be to transcribe the entirety of each manuscript, in such a way that it could then be searched electronically. This would require a huge amount of manpower; however, it is possible to search an electronic copy of Morris's edition for other occurrences of *fridlayke*, and then consult the other manuscripts, seeking out these particular lines, to determine in what form the item appears. This is less sound a method, but is rather more practical, and in this instance enabled us to see that MSS. **A, B** and **C** all use the same form twice, while **D** uses *drede* in the one instance available to us, the other line being missing. In any event, it is evident at this juncture that investigative techniques beyond the questionnaire are necessary in order to pursue and confirm analyses of variation in many cases.

2.7. Language dictionaries as aids to study

Another useful method for determining possible reasons behind the use, or non-use, of words such as *ferdlayke/fridlayke* would be to search for the word in the *Middle English Dictionary (MED)* (Lewis, McSparren et. al., 1952 – 2001; 2000 – 2018; henceforth cited: *MED)* . Admittedly, given that this resource can only list

---

[12] For fuller analysis of this variation, see Chapter Four.

occurrences of words in texts that have actually been transcribed, this is not of as much use to this study as it would be to a student of Southern Middle English. Many dialectally invaluable Northern manuscripts have never been properly studied, and so the *MED* cannot point us to instances of word-use within them. The entry for 'ferd(e)leik (n.)' lists the only two occurrences of this word as being found in Morris's edition of the *Pricke of Conscience* – in ms. Cotton Galba E.ix and Harley 4196. We know already, from our transcriptions, that this is not the case. However, it is interesting that our record of this word is restricted to this poem, since this indicates that it was not used outside of the Northern dialect area – or at least, was not commonly in use in the better-documented areas of the country. It may, of course, exist in unedited manuscripts.[13]

Due to the sparsity of information in the *MED*, it is also useful for the student of NME to investigate items, where applicable, through reference to the considerably greater library of resources available for students of Older and Middle Scots. NME is not the same thing as Middle Scots, but we have discussed already how difficult it is to demarcate the boundaries of the NME area specifically, and many of the signature features of 'fully Northern' English, such as the <a> for <o> and <q> for <wh> orthography, are also traits found in Middle Scots. The online resource, *Dictionary of the Scots Language (DSL)*, could not provide any results for the item *ferdeleik*. It is as well to note, however, that this resource exists. As stated, there is considerable crossover between the orthography and lexicon of NME and Middle Scots, so we might expect to find some words in the *DSL* that have been noted and studied in Scots texts, but not in ME scholarship, due to the predominant focus of most scholars upon Southern, rather than Northern, dialects.

It is problematic that so much modern scholarship should fail to treat the dialect boundary between NME and Middle Scots as unfixed and changeable. The concept of a distinct literary Scots had not emerged at this point in time; the Scottish Chaucerians, for example, characterised their own writing as being in English. In his poem "The Golden Targe", William Dunbar, invoking Chaucer, asks 'Was thou noucht of oure Inglisch all the lycht/Surmounting eviry tong terrestriall',(Dunbar, edited by Conlee, 2004) clearly

---

[13] This word is analysed in detail in Chapter Four.

indicating a sense of continuity between literary traditions and a common language. The imposition of an artificial boundary between Scots and English at this time seems therefore anachronistic and, for our purposes, certainly unhelpful. Exploration of Scots resources, where available, can only aid a study of NME.

A number of texts traditionally held to be in Scots, due to their presence in such notable Scottish manuscripts as the Auckinlech Manuscript, (National Library of Scotland Advocates' MS 19.2.1) have been determined to be of less clean-cut and definite origin by more recent scholars. For example, *Sir Tristrem,* a text in the Auckinlech Manuscript, was heralded by Walter Scott in his 1804 edition as a great Scots poem (scott, 1804, p.iv, xxii). Angus McIntosh, contrarily, in a 1989 article, argues that many of the forms earlier scholars had believed to be evidence of the poem's Scottish origin were actually more likely to be Northernisms, rather than features supporting the theory that the poem's dialect is Scots. He notes that the poem's dialect still needs further study, suggesting that it is indeed often difficult to discriminate between Northern and Scots texts based on linguistic features (McIntosh, 1989b, p. 94). If we look at the poem itself, we see that there are certainly many characteristic Northern forms: for example, the OE /ɑ:/ is retained in such words as *stan* (lines 115, 270) while we also find the forms *ta* and *tan* for *take* and *taken* (lines 607, 2767; 753, 895, and many further instances) (Lupack, 1994). However, although McIntosh's article assumes a NME or Scots origin for the poem, other scholarship indicates that we cannot even be certain of this. As early as 1941, Bertram Vogel notes that although there are many Northern forms in this poem, there are also a great many more that are not Northern at all. According to Vogel, the poem's dialect lacks, for example, the characteristically Northern <q> for OE <hw>, preferring <wh> instead (e.g., line 4, 101, 209). Vogel (1941, p. 542) also notes that 'the pronoun for the third person feminine singular is either *sche* [see lines 79, 99, etc.] or *hye* [see lines 101, 103, etc]. Nth. *scho* is not used' and 'non-Nth. *miche, michel* are used in 15 instances; Nth *mikel* is not found'.

The illustration of *Sir Tristrem* serves to demonstrate that further study in this area is necessary so that we can determine whether such 'non-Northern' forms as these are, in fact, actually observable in texts we know to be of Northern origin by this point in time. Certainly, not all of the core manuscripts of this study use initial

<q> for <wh>; nor do they all use consistent *scho*. It also illustrates that it would be a mistake for scholars of NME to cut off our list of potential resources at the Scots border. In light of this, employing the *DSL* as a possible alternative resource where the *MED* fails us seemed, and has proven throughout the course of the study, a logical step.

2.8. A further note on *LALME*

A brief survey of the Linguistic Profile given in *LALME* for Rawlinson C 891 (**A**), one of the first manuscripts whose data I began to catalogue, throws up some further points against scholarly reliance on *LALME* alone, particularly for Northern manuscripts. The LP (171) for Hand C, the Northern, *Pricke of Conscience* hand in this manuscript, is derived from analysis of ff. 35r – 74r. Compared to the tranche sizes given in several of the other LPs for the relevant *Pricke of Conscience* manuscripts, this is a sizeable section. This is possibly due to the fact that only one hand is being analysed for the profile. Nevertheless, as the segment itself is sizeable, this analysis would seem insufficient, as it does not confirm, for example, whether the same word forms were used at the beginning of the section as at the end of it, and so forth. The *LALME* team were of course not concentrating especially on NME manuscripts; the fact that this study does privilege them, and particularly this manuscript, means that it is able to consider a great many more tranches of Hand C's usage, taken at regular intervals across the section.

The *LALME* questionnaires, as stated, list all of the word-forms that can be found for each item within the analysed tranche. Sometimes, word forms found through a brief scan of the rest of the manuscript may also be included, but here, no mention is given of a scan. We must assume that all of the word forms given are those found between ff. 35r and 74r. I have already noted some of the shortcomings of an analysis based on so small a fraction of the text. Also problematic is the fact that no elaboration is given when listing the word forms. In my own analysis of this manuscript, which included a full scan, I found only very occasional forms of the word 'which' not spelled with initial <q>. The LP, interestingly, lists five alternative forms of this item, four of which begin with initial <w> – *qwilke, whiche, wiche, wilk, wilke* (*LALME*, vol. 3, LP 171). The fact

Methodological Approaches 65

that all of these alternate forms are in double parentheses indicates to the reader that they are lesser used variants, where *qwilk* is given without parentheses, as the dominant form – a finding consistent with my own. However, no notes are given as to when these alternative forms are used, and with what level of frequency (other than that they are less frequently used than *qwilk*). We cannot tell, for example, whether these forms are used once only, or if they are used multiple times each; close investigation of the particular positions of <w> forms within the text, along with the frequency of usage, enables the scholar, rather, to assess the reasons for these variations and what they might tell us about the manuscript, scribe, or both. In a study such as the current one, it is possible to note placement of words, in order to determine patterns. The *LALME* team, of course, could not be expected to make more than a brief survey of this manuscript as one among many, given that its aim is to consider as many chronologically appropriate manuscripts as possible, and not to focus upon the Northern manuscripts specifically. As an aid to the dialectologist, *LALME* represents an invaluable leap forward, but it is not a clean data sweep and it was not intended to do the scholar's work for him. As such, the lists of alternate word-forms are not sufficient for a scholar to draw real conclusions without further study. The lists of word forms are a starting point, but require close manuscript study in order to be useful. Where word forms vary, more extensive notes must be made of the circumstances of the variation, if we wish to determine why it may have occurred and what this might indicate. Reliance on the *LALME* lists alone would be to misunderstand the intentions and limitations of *LALME,* and could in fact point the scholar towards false conclusions.

By way of example, we might consider what the LP for Rawlinson C.891 manuscript indicates, and what my own survey, based upon a full scan and a number of tranches from different points in the manuscript, showed. We find that there are a number of instances of disagreement between the *LALME* analysis and my own. Where *LALME* gives *þese* as the most common form of THESE, I found that *þase* was more common across the tranches I surveyed, for both THESE and THOSE. *þese*, contrarily, was more rarely noted, although it does occur several times between ff. 34 – 75, the section scanned by *LALME*. Likewise, *LALME's* LP gives *þaim* as the most common form of the item THEM, with *þam* as a less frequent variant – accurate within the surveyed segment, but not what was indicated by my broader survey. The LP also finds *mikel* to be the most common form of MUCH, as opposed to *mykel*, which I determined to be considerably more frequent in this manuscript, although *mikel* is certainly noted too. These points of difference would seem to serve as an excellent illustration of why *LALME* can only be expected to form a starting point for manuscript study: anybody wishing to investigate the dialect of a little-studied region must analyse the manuscripts directly, and in greater detail than the capacity available to the *LALME*.

Similar issues can be found in the LP for Bodleian Library, Rawlinson Poet. 175 – LP 174. In this instance, the manuscript is written in one, 'fully Northern', hand, but the LP is based upon only ff. 1r – 13v. Again, this is a small tranche to use as the basis for a linguistic profile intended to describe an entire manuscript, and the dialectologist ought to be aware that it cannot be taken as fully representative, although the rest of the text has been scanned. A comparison of the LP's findings with my own shows a number of discrepancies. In the first instance, while the LP gives a number of forms found in the manuscript for AGAINST, it does not provide *ogaynes*, which my survey found to occur fairly commonly across this manuscript. Likewise, although the LP notes four separate forms of WORLD found in the manuscript, it does not give *worlde*, which I noted fairly frequently. The word-form *might* is given, further, by the LP as being uncommonly used – enclosed in doubled parentheses – which, while the case within the analysed tranche, is not true of the wider manuscript. While *myght* and *moght* are, as LP 174 indicates, in evidence, might is also fairly commonly used.

Evidently, then, the linguistic profiles, where such small tranches as this one are used, are insufficient for the dialectologist's purposes. It is true that *LALME* is an invaluable resource, but it affords considerably less attention to Northern-dialect manuscripts than to more southerly manuscripts, whose linguistic profiles appear to be based, in general, on far larger tranches. Close surveys of these Northern manuscripts yield more information than *LALME* is able to provide.

The fact that so little work is conducted upon Northern manuscripts undoubtedly stems, at least in part, from the fact that there are very few resources for scholars wishing to undertake such work. *LALME's* lack of attention to these dialect texts is part of a broader pattern within dialectal scholarship, where insufficient interest in the Northern dialects results in less attention being paid to them – which, in turn, means that would-be scholars of NME are discouraged by the lack of previous scholarship to build upon. Although a single study cannot hope to break such a cycle, this book seeks to demonstrate how far it is possible to uncover new information about the variety within NME dialects when manuscripts are studied closely, and set within their sociolinguistic and codicological contexts. In the following chapters, I will present what data has been accrued about the language of this study's core manuscripts, through a combination of the questionnaire and line-by-line comparison research methods. Later in the study, this data will be examined within its codicological contexts, but the first step is to analyse and compare the data to determine whether any patterns emerge, and, in accordance with our research questions, whether the dialects of these manuscripts are indeed homogeneous.

CHAPTER 3

Consistent Differences in Orthography

Fascinating though it is to note substantial differences between one version of the text and another, and vital as it is to explore the different manuscripts through line-by-line comparison, the dialect questionnaire, with its straightforward charting of orthographic variation, remains extremely important for any kind of dialect comparison. Where line-by-line comparison permits the scholar to analyse and speculate about the interaction between scribe and text, motivation and output, the questionnaire remains a fundamental weapon in the dialectologist's arsenal. If 'dialect' is, in terms of linguistics, the systematic usage of a group of speakers, with lexical, phonological and grammatical rules, then it is the questionnaire which allows us to see these rules at work on the most basic level. It is the questionnaire, and analysis of what it shows, that enables us to isolate and describe the systematic variation between the language varieties used in the manuscripts under scrutiny. Even taken alone, the questionnaire for this project shows a number of clear patterns within the orthography and phonology of each manuscript's language, marking each dialect as distinct while simultaneously demonstrating the many ways in which the languages are similar.

The pronoun forms used in a manuscript are often among the items that differ mainly between significant umbrella dialect areas, and accordingly, manuscripts **A, B, C** and **D,** all stemming from the same broad dialect area, utilise a generally similar set of forms throughout. A manuscript's preferred form of SHE is always one of the major indicators of its geographical origins in ME. However, the word SHE appears with extreme infrequency in the text – indeed, it occurs only six times in the entirety of the *Pricke of Conscience.* All instances are very late in the poem and outside of the transcribed tranches, so that the instances had to be individually searched for in each manuscript. As such, it is very difficult to determine what may have caused the two instances out of six of *sche* in **A,** alongside the more expected form, *scho*.

The *scho* form is the one found in the Northern and Scots record, while *sche/she* is more commonly used in the Midlands and

Southern areas. Simon Horobin and Jeremy Smith convincingly argue that *scho* must have been the earliest form, developed through close contact between Norsemen and native speakers in the North of England.[1] Northern dialect texts continue to prefer the *scho* form most commonly throughout the ME period. Where we do find *she* or *sche* forms in the manuscripts under scrutiny here, we might infer that there has been some contact with more southerly, Midlands, dialects, where *she/sche* was the more common form. There are a number of ways in which this could have occurred. We might find *sche* or *she* because Midlands features had begun to seep into the dialect area in which the manuscript was produced, meaning that the sometime-usage of *sche/she* in the written dialect reflected the dialect as spoken. However, infrequent usage of *sche/she* could also occur because the scribe had previously lived in an area where this form was used; or simply because the scribe had copied a number of manuscripts which used this form, and had been, perhaps unconsciously, influenced by it.

The presence of *sche* in the **A** manuscript is minimal. Two of the six uses of the item SHE appear to read *sche* in this manuscript. These <e>s could still, based upon this evidence, represent simple slips of the scribe's pen due to a history of copying manuscripts that did feature the *sche* form of the pronoun as described above, but the frequency is too small, in truth, to make such a statement with any confidence. Certainly, the pronoun does not appear often enough to suggest that the pronunciation of *scho* had begun to alter in the dialect area of **A,** or that the forms were interchangeably used. It might have been possible to infer that the scribe was translating from an *exemplar* that made use of the *sche* pronoun, converting each into his own dialect, and that these were simply instances where he had forgotten to do so. Given that the *Pricke of Conscience* originated in the Northern region and then spread southwards, rather than the inverse, this seems less likely in this instance, but it remains a possibility.

The instances of *sche* show no obvious logic – they do not, for example, appear at beginnings of lines, or at ends of lines, nor do they occur close together within the brief array of instances of SHE.

---

[1] For an overview of the current state of scholarship on SHE and its origins, see Horobin and Smith (2002, pp. 129–131).

Consistent Differences in Orthography 71

The sporadic usage could be a reflection of the fact that the scribe does sometimes write *sche* where the exemplar uses *scho*; but as stated, it is impossible to determine from so little data whether this is the natural tendency of the scribe, whether he is simply used to copying *sche* directly from other manuscripts, whether he perhaps has no strong feelings either way about the *sche/scho* question, or whether these are slips of the pen, where *sche* is the scribe's own preferred form and he has slipped in reproducing the exemplar's *scho*. These may simply be examples of constrained selection – the process whereby a scribe suppresses some of his own spellings in favour of those in his exemplar where these forms are familiar. Forms which are part of the scribe's passive repertoire – that is to say, forms used in neighbouring areas and with which the scribe is familiar, even if they do not form part of his own active repertoire of words – might be retained in this way. As Margaret Laing (2004, pp. 63 – 65) states:

> The resulting 'constrained usage' does not include exemplar forms alien to the copyist's own language; except for the occasional relict, such exotic spellings would normally be converted by a Translator into forms familiar to him. But when the copyist does encounter a familiar spelling for a particular word, he reproduces it unchanged, thus skewing the relative frequencies of forms that are functionally equivalent in his own repertoire.

This might certainly be an explanation here. However, the marked infrequency of usage of SHE in the text simply makes it very difficult to draw firmer conclusions about this variation. As such, the occasional *sche* instances in **A** seem to be anomalies about which we cannot suggest anything conclusive.

Otherwise, we find that pronouns and articles take identical forms from one manuscript to another: *he, it, þai, þe, þam*, each appearing in all four manuscripts. The exception to this rule of similarity is the pronoun YOU, which will be discussed later. When, however, we come to examine such items as WHO and WHICH, we do begin to note differences.

A makes consistent use of an initial <qw>, where the other three manuscripts employ a <wh>. This tendency makes itself very evident across the WHO/WHICH/WHEN forms – for example:

WHO   *WHICH*   *WHEN*

A	qwo	qwilk	qwen
B	wha	whilk/whylk (70:30)	when
C	wha	whilk/wilk (80:20)	when
D	who	whylke	when

As the table indicates, an examination of these three items alone gives some illustration of some of the ways in which the manuscripts' languages consistently differ. The *Middle English Dictionary* demonstrates that WHICH and WHEN are items which each have a huge number of possible forms in ME, listing sixty-five possible forms of WHICH and fifty-three of WHEN. While the twenty-two forms listed for WHO pale in comparison, they still constitute, relative to most words in the language, a vast number of known variants. The variants used here for each of these words all make notable points about the orthographical restrictions and phonological implications of each scribe's language. Interestingly, the most recent electronic update of *LALME* notes <q> forms of WHO *only* within East Anglia (Benskin, Laing, Karaiskos, Williamson, et. al, 2013). This form in **A** is potentially the result of dialect contact, but it is also possible that the scribe uses this form only by analogy with *qwilk* and *qwen*, both of which are widely attested all across the east of the country from East Anglia northwards. Further investigation of the manuscript, and further investigation for <q> forms of WHO in NME, will shed greater light on this matter.[2]

Initial <qw>, while an important and dialectally useful orthographical distinction, is not known to have indicated any kind of difference in pronunciation. The spelling of 'WHO', however, in **B** and **C,** does carry phonological implications, based upon the use of the traditionally 'fully Northern' [a] sound. If the scribes of **B** and **C** pronounce this word as /hwæ/ as opposed to the /hwō/ pronunciation implied by **A** and **D**'s [o] endings, then dialectal motivation can be inferred as the reason for this difference. The **B** scribe's *wha* form is also found used by scribe **B2,** the first example of many items demonstrating a high level of consistency in their language usage, both across the **B** manuscript and within MS **B2**.

---

[2] See Chapters Five and Six for a fuller discussion of this.

Indeed, the extent to which this shared language variety remains consistent across two copies of the *Pricke of Conscience* lends significant support to the idea that translating scribes did indeed transform their texts consistently. While both the exemplar for **B** and that for **B2** are classified by Robert Lewis and Angus McIntosh as belonging to the same group, line-by-line comparison indicates that they are not identical, a conclusion also shared by Ralph Hanna and Sarah Wood's (2013, p. lxv) stemma of textual descent. Therefore, the scribes did not simply make two literatim copies from the same manuscript. They could potentially have been copying literatim from two different exemplars, both sharing a consistent dialect, but it seems far more likely that scribes **B** and **B2** are consistent, translating scribes, trained in the same centre. The sociolinguistic implications of this idea will be discussed later on.

As Margaret Laing (2004) indicates, we must be conscious at all times that our only recourses for the study of ME are samples of text language, rather than of the language as spoken, and consequently our ultimate intent should be to privilege the written evidence as witnesses over any presumed connections between these written samples and what we imagine the correlating spoken language may have been.[3] Unlike in the case of a modern dialect survey, there is no viable way to firmly determine this, and although it can often be useful to note instances where phonological variation seems to be implied, this does not mean that orthographical variation without such implications can ever be rejected as potentially important. The 'text languages' with which we are working may 'manifest variations and variability in ways that can certainly be correlated with [...] regional factors [in the spoken dialect], but these correlations are not always simple and direct' (Ibid., p. 50). Consequently, we are looking for variation within text languages, and pure orthographical variation is a valid method of distinguishing one text language, one written dialect, from another. The orthographic variation in WHICH, then, although it need not necessarily indicate any phonological differences, does reflect an important orthographical trend that is borne out by many other items in the questionnaire (and observed when making line by line comparisons, as well as when consulting the questionnaire itself). The use of <y> where the

---

[3] For discussion, see Laing (2004, pp. 49–51).

other manuscripts use <i>, as well, often, as a seemingly redundant addition to a word-form such as a repeated consonant (*gyffed, fykell*) is something very commonly found in the language of **D**. Word-forms in **D,** moreover, are consistently longer than equivalent forms in other manuscripts, and will usually have final -e, even where the others do not. Where other manuscripts vary between the usage of <i> and <y> in similar positions in the middle of words (**B2**'s language showing the same patterns used by **B,** below)[4] the **D** scribe consistently employs the <y> spelling. Thus:

	THINK	*FIRST*	*WILL*	*MUCH*	*EACH*
A	þink	first	wille	mykel	ilk
B	thynk	first	will	mykell	ilk/ilka
C	thynk	first	wille	mykel	ilk/ilka
D	thynke	fyrst	wylle	mykell	ylke

And also the following items not included in the questionnaire:

	CONTRITION	*SALVATION*
A	--	--
B	contricion	salvacion
C	contricyon	salvacion
D	contryciowne	salvacyowne

The orthographical variations in CONTRITION and SALVATION make good illustrations of the tendency of the **D**-language variety to contain forms longer and more elaborate than those in the other manuscripts. Characteristic <y> for /i/ and final

---

[4] Because the B2 manuscript does not form part of the core study, and was not investigated in the same depth as the other manuscripts, but only examined for cross-referencing purposes, B2 usages are not tabulated here alongside the other manuscript forms. Broadly, the language of the B scribe is highly consistent in B2 with what is seen in B–the implications of which are discussed more fully later in the thesis, when the manuscripts are reviewed according to their codicology. The full data taken from B2 can be seen in the transcriptions in Appendix 1, and in the questionnaire in Appendix 2.

<e> are present, alongside another common element of **D's** language, the use of <w> as the second element in <au> or <ou> spellings. **D** frequently makes use of a <w> where the other manuscripts use either <u> or nothing, as in *sawle* (as opposed to *saul, saule, saul* in **A, B, C**) or *owre* (v. *our* in **A, B** and **C**). In the case of the <aw> spellings, it is a diphthong that is represented, and in the case of <ow>, what we see is simply a different orthographical representation of a monothong, but in instances of both diphthongs and monothongs, the **D** scribe appears to find <w> acceptable where other scribes would generally prefer <u>.

Although it is not demonstrated through any of the forms in the questionnaire, line-by-line comparison of the manuscripts has also shown that **D** often doubles letters, particularly <f>, <t> and <e>. For example:

	HERE	*FEEL*	*WELL*	*FOR*	*TORMENTS*
A	here	fele	wele	for	--
B	here	fele	wele	for	tourmentes
C	here	fele	wele	for	tourementes
D	heere	feele	weele	ffore	towymenttes

In the cases of HERE, FEEL and WELL, the doubled letter appears to represent a long vowel, as it might in Modern English. Positioning within the rhyme scheme indicates that 'wele' rhymes with 'fele'; Jeremy Smith (2012, p.40) notes the use of the silent final <e> in early Scots as a means of marking a long vowel, alongside the more commonly recorded <ei> in Scots. He suggests that this feature 'seems to have spread into Older Scots from Northern England'. This would support the idea that, in NME, FEEL and WELL would be mentally sounded as /fi:l/ and /wi:l/, in keeping with this pronunciation of WELL in descendant Northern dialects.[5] Alternatively, if these raised forms are later, it may suggest /fe:l/ and /we:l/. In either event, it would appear that the doubled vowel in **D's** orthographical representations of this item is an

---

[5] See, for example, traditional Tyneside folksong "The Keel Row", where 'well' forms a rhyme with 'keel', as described in Gregory (2010, p. 273).

additional means of representing a long vowel, where the <e> alone seems insufficient to this scribe, or in this scribe's particular dialect.

However, in the case of FOR and TORMENTS, it is not clear why the doubled consonant might have been used. The doubled initial <f> might conceivably represent a capital, except for the fact that this is found in places where there would be no need for capitalisation in **D.** It is possible that a phonological difference, some form of length-marking, might have been indicated by such a doubling in these particular placements; there is, however, no evidence to suggest that this is necessarily the case, and it does not seem a likely phonological development (Horobin and Smith, 2002, pp. 165 – 167). Where a doubled consonant may give guidance as to the length of a vowel that precedes it, it is not ordinary practice for a consonant to be doubled in order to indicate features in a vowel which follows, as would need to be the case in order for this explanation to be applied here. Horobin and Smith (ibid.) state that the practice of using a doubled consonant after a short, stressed vowel to indicate how it ought to be pronounced 'only applies after short vowels in closed syllables', such as in 'annd' or 'lanng', to denote sounds differing from that in 'land', for example. Consequently, this would seem completely inapplicable to the doubled initial <f> in this manuscript, and there does not appear to be any other commonly noted reason why consonants are doubled in ME. Even in the *Ormulum,* a late twelfth-century autograph manuscript from Lincolnshire whose highly idiosyncratic orthographical system makes frequent use of doubled consonants, we can find nothing that might serve to shed light upon the question. While the *Ormulum,* has been able to provide much information concerning the lengthening and shortening of vowels in ME, based upon its usage and placements of doubled consonants, we do not find any instances of initial <ff> within it. [6] *Forr* is noted in the manuscript, but not *ffor,* so we are unable to use it to determine any possible phonological indications of this feature. Richard Jordan (1974, p. 33) notes that initial doubled-f shows 'Welsh influence', and interprets it as indicating a capital when in initial position, but this, again, does not appear to be what is indicated in this instance. While *LALME* notes some items featuring

---

[6] See Guest(1968, p. 104) and Welna (1998, pp. 476–480).

medial or final doubled-<ff>, there is no dot-map for initial <ff>. Nevertheless, whether phonologically indicative or not, the doubling certainly marks a notable orthographical constant within the language of this scribe – such a constant, indeed, that it may well reflect a local scribal convention, perhaps of the house in which this manuscript was produced.

There are some other ME manuscripts where this doubling of <f> can be seen apparently performing a different function from that of capitalisation. Consultation of the *Piers Plowman Electronic Archive* (Duggan, Stinson, Turville-Petre et. al., 1994 - 2019), for example, demonstrates that doubled initial <f> is found commonly in the B Archetype of this text, in such words as *ffor* and *ffals*, often in the middles of lines, where we cannot assume a reasoning based upon capitalisation. Notably, the doubled <f> is not invariably applied when words begin with this sound, which may imply that it was not entirely meaningless – we find *forgiven, ful, fifty* alongside the *ffor* and *ffals*. Complicating the issue, however, is the fact that the form *for* appears alongside *ffor*, so it cannot be posited that the choice between single or double <f> necessarily bears any relation to the derivation or pronunciation of a word. Nor can we detect any pattern related to what part of speech the double-<f> words comprise: it is not applied, for example, to nouns only, or to adjectives. Ultimately, it seems impossible to positively identify the reasoning behind this usage of initial doubled <f>, but it is interesting that so similar a usage pattern should be found in a *Piers Plowman* manuscript – Oxford, MS. Laud Misc. 581 – whose dialect contains heavy West Midlands influence. Potentially, then, this feature in the **D** scribe's language could indicate some contact with West Midlands dialect, either directly or through copying of Midlands manuscripts. Searches of the *MED*, which contains data from manuscripts all across the country, show that the initial doubled <f> feature in the middles of lines is not at all common. Interestingly, however, we do find *ffor* in the middles of lines, with no apparent capitalisation purpose, in Oxford, Bodleian Library, Add. B.107 and Oxford, Bodleian Library, Eng. poet. a.1 (Vernon), both of which manuscripts are localised to Worcestershire, in the West Midlands.[7] We also see the doubled initial <f> quite

---

[7] See Horstmann(1892), and Oxford, Bodleian Library, Add. B.107.

commonly across three manuscripts of John Lydgate's *Pilgrimage of the Life of Man*: London, British Library, Cotton Tiberius A.7, London, British Library, Cotton Vitellius C.13 and London, British Library, Stowe 952.[8] Neither *LALME* nor Furnivall and Lockcock give possible localisations for any of these manuscripts, but as the feature is common across all of them, it may be authorial in origin. Lydgate was born in Suffolk, in the East Midlands, suggesting that perhaps this feature was found across the whole Midlands region (Simpson, 2002, p. 582). Some other features in **D**, such as the preference for <y> rather than <i> spellings, and the more prevalent usage of <k> in this manuscript than in the others, are arguably in keeping with the language of, for example the West Midlands *Pearl* poet of Cotton Nero A.x.[9]

Even if we cannot posit a decisive reason for this doubled-<f> feature, it certainly sets this language variety apart from the others, alongside the various other features described above. Orthographically, **D's** language shows a greater degree of variance from **A, B,** and **C** than they do from each other. **D**'s elaborate word forms enable us to identify them immediately as belonging to that particular manuscript, and while they may not indicate clear differences in spoken dialect, our overriding intention is not to connect written forms to spoken ones, a very difficult task when the language studied is no longer spoken. What they may represent is a geographically localisable set of orthographical rules, perhaps deriving from a particular house, which may be said to characterise a written dialect. Inasmuch as this dialect is notably different from the other three, then part of our hypothesis is already proven: these dialects may share many significant features, but they are not homogeneous. These examples from **D** alone serve to illustrate this.

Graphemically, it is the **A** manuscript that most obviously stands out from the others. All the manuscripts make use of thorn for a particular set of words: *þe, þase, þa, þam, þai, þair, þare, þan, þogh.* Only **A,** however, ever uses thorn within words that fall outside of this accepted thorn-containing set. Not all words beginning [θ] take thorn in **A,** but it is used consistently in *þink,* for example; and in the middle of *erþe.* **A** also makes use of yogh, which the other

---

[8] See Furnivall and Locock(1899).
[9] See Andrew and Waldron(1982) for more on this.

manuscripts do not – we find it, for example, in IF, ȝif, as opposed to *if* in **B, C** and **D**.

In this instance, the use of <ȝ> may have some phonological, and certainly a historical, implication. 'IF' is derived from the OE *gif* and, as the *MED* indicates, the word is often spelled in ways that suggest a possible initial [y] might be sounded by the scribe – many forms in <ȝ> and <g> but also a number beginning <yh> or <y>. Potentially, then, the **A** dialect sounds this word differently, as well as spelling it in a way that descends from the OE antecedent. There may no longer have been any pronunciation difference indicated by the time of this manuscript's production, with the <ȝ> only indicative of a conservative style. Nevertheless, it is an interesting feature specific to this manuscript among the four.

Elsewhere, the <ȝ> grapheme appears simply, but consistently, as a graphological variant, as demonstrated within the forms of the item YOU:

	YOU
A	ȝowe
B	yow
C	yhow
D	yhow

This set of forms represents the only notable instance of variation in pronoun-forms between these manuscripts. Initial yogh in **A** does not seem to represent any phonological distinction between it and **B's** *yow*, although it might be suggested that the final <e> – particularly since this is not rife in **A** the way that it is in **D** – might have been sounded.

Potentially, the <yh> digraph may be the result of interference from the traditional Latin orthography for Jesus: <ihesus>. As the <y> in this situation is performing the same task as the <i> in the Latin, it might be the case that a scribe who frequently copied Latin would infer a need for a <h> between the <y> and the <e> in this word, as between the <i> and the <e> in IESUS. The likelihood of this is, however, difficult to establish. Scribe **D** is very evidently some sort of scholar, to judge from his emendations to the text – as he appears to have studiously translated and removed Latin from the English text, we may assume a considerable knowledge of, and training in, Latin. Where removing Latin tags is obviously a conscious decision on the part of the scribe, a Latin influence on his orthography may have been an unconscious development over many years of study. Perhaps, then, we might make the suggestion of a possible Latin influence, regardless of this scribe's conscious attitude towards the existence of Latin within his English manuscripts.

More important is the fact that YOU is an extremely common word, for which conventions would most certainly have existed within any house that worked from any guidelines at all. As such, the fact that YOU varies in form between **A, B** and **C** makes clear, even without other evidence, that these scribes were working from different orthographical conventions, whether they were fairly loose conventions of local usage, or more tightly-imposed guidelines within a scriptorium. **D** is, on this occasion, in agreement with **C** upon the preferred orthography of this item, but **D,** as we have already seen, very clearly differs from the other manuscripts in manifold instances with regard to orthographical conventions. As such, we cannot doubt that each scribe is working under the guidance of a distinct set of conventions of his own – albeit not necessarily of his own devising.

Initially, as far as the questionnaire shows, there does not seem to be a clear pattern as to the degree to which that feature noted by Lewis and McIntosh as the most fundamental identified of NME dialects – the <a>, rather than <o>, for Old Norse and OE /ɑː/ – is used from one manuscript to the next. **D,** for example, uses *so*, as does **A,** where the other manuscripts, **B, B2** and **C,** all use the OE form *swa* exclusively for the item SO. This is consistent with these manuscripts' forms of WHO, as previously shown in the figure above: in all manuscripts, these two items rhyme with each other. Elsewhere, however, this a/o pattern does not continue.

BOTH

A	both
B	bath/both (50:50)
C	bath
D	bothe

The above example, to a considerable extent, supports the pattern set out by the items SO and WHO, with the Northern <a>

to be found in **B** and **C**. **B**, however, also contains a great many instances of this word spelled *both*, as does **B2**, which unsettles the pattern somewhat. Furthermore, for the item KNOW, we find the 'Northern' <a>-spelling to be the only one used throughout all four manuscripts, *knawe*. The manuscripts' forms of the item MORE, similarly, are all identical, and all 'fully Northern': *mare*.

What, then, is the logic behind this system of usage? It might be hypothesised that **A, B, C** and **D** all employ <a> where the sound falls within a word, but that the dialects of **A** and **D** have come to use <o> where it falls at the end. This is a fairly sound suggestion, apart from the fact that the form of ALSO used consistently in **D** is *alswa*, where it should, by this logic, be *also*. This word is noted a number of times in the middle of lines, as well as at the ends, so it could not really be assumed that any kind of rhyme-scheme reliant upon older Northern <a>-spellings could be responsible for this apparent anomaly. There seems, indeed, to be no obvious reason for it at all, but it certainly serves as a particular marker of this **D**-language, as a sole example of final <a> within a system based mostly upon final <o>. It could be that *alswa* is the form found in **D's** exemplar and has been retained, but the language of **D** in general indicates consistent and fairly systematic translation is the norm. It would seem unusual, then, for such a common word to have been left unchanged; it is more likely that *alswa* is **D's** preferred form – perhaps a word which, for whatever reason, resisted the otherwise systematic shift from final <a> to final <o> in like positions.

It is rare to find a questionnaire item for which every manuscript has an entirely separate common form. For the most part, at least two of the manuscripts will use the same preferred form of any given item, most commonly **B** and **C**, which are linguistically the most similar two dialects of the four. However, there are certain instances where no two scribes agree.

The most obvious example to be found in the questionnaire is the item SINCE. The preferred forms of this item are recorded, in **A, B, C** and **D** respectively, as: *sepen, sithen, sythen, sytthen*. While there is no obvious reason for this particular item to be one over which scribes would differ, closer examination of the various forms highlights the fact that this word contains more than one of the common points of contention already described.

In the **A** form, for example, we see the use of thorn within a word. As indicated earlier, **B, C** and **D** only ever use thorn within a certain accepted 'set' of words; here again, we see this point of common variance arising, with **A** the only scribe to implement this grapheme in its form of SINCE. Note also the shifting vowel across the forms. The pronunciation of <i> and <y> in this position – and, indeed, in any position where <y> represents a vowel – can be assumed to be identical, especially as many manuscripts interchange these two letters indiscriminately. The use of <e> stands out as potentially representing a different sound, but it is possible that this, taken alongside the already catalogued <i> and <y> forms, simply reflects a reduction of this vowel to schwa. The fact that so many different vowels are used in this position could imply that this is a low stress environment. As such, it seems fairly likely that the differences in vowel between these forms of the word may not have carried any major phonological implications.

Orthographically, however, there are points of interest here. The use of <y> in this position in **D** is a common tendency already discussed. The variance on this issue between **B** and **C,** while less striking, does occur elsewhere, as in their respective forms of the item MIGHT – for which **B** uses an <i> form, as here, while **C** prefers *myght,* again in accordance with its form of SINCE. Meanwhile, the doubled letter in **D** is another common trait of this manuscript. Thus, although the item SINCE does not carry any particular meaning or significance that would cause it to vary in this manner, it does contain a combination of features which vary particularly, elsewhere, between these manuscripts. As such, it serves as an indication of some of the most commonly noted differences between the languages of the manuscripts. If the manuscripts are written along guiding conventions which emphasise these points found in SINCE, then there is no special reason that SINCE should be a highly contested form, other than that it happens to contain a number of notably contested features.

RECKONING

A	rekennyng
B	rekenyng
C	rekennyng
D	reckenynge

Another item that varies quite widely across the manuscripts is RECKONING, although **A** and **C** do share a common preferred form, *rekennyng*. **B** gives *rekenyng*, while **D** prefers *reckenynge*. Superficially, these are not enormous degrees of variation, particularly given that all scribes prefer the *–yng* ending for the item. The suffix is, ordinarily, the part of a gerund in which we might most expect to note dialectal divergence, where the *-and* suffix (in fact, traditionally a 'fully Northern' suffix for a present participle) is sometimes appended by analogy in Northern texts, although the OE gerund form always ended in *-ung*.[10] In southerly dialects, the *-ing* form is used both for the present participle and for the gerund, so there would be no reason to make such analogous alterations. Here, there is no variation in this aspect, where we might be most inclined to look for it.

Nevertheless, it would be remiss of the scholar to dismiss this as a form that can tell us nothing. There is much that is of interest in the letter combinations each scribe selects. We know that the scribe of **D** is given to doubling of letters, but the usage of the French-influenced <ck> is notable, particularly as none of these other manuscripts show a preference for it. In a similar way to the **D** scribe's tendency towards lengthier word forms, as in the orthography of such items as CONTRITION, this type of usage colours the language of **D,** separating it from the curter, more traditionally Northern-dialect preferences of the other three manuscripts. The French colour to the **D** language is unique among the manuscripts we are considering, where more usually we see spellings that show the influence of Norse on the phonology of English in the north of England.

Other gerunds in the manuscripts generally utilise forms in the following suffix pattern:

BEGINNING
A   bigynnyng
B   bigynnyng
C   bygynnynge

---

[10] For example, Fowler (1889, p. iv) observes this occasionally in London, British Library, Arundel 507.

D   begynnynge

C, in this instance, utilises a final <e> where one is not found in, for example, its preferred form for RECKONING, but this is in accordance with the occasional tendency of C to append final <e>, apparently as a flourish only, in situations not concurrent with its use in OE – as opposed to D, which uses rather than omits it almost as default. The significant factor here is that the *yng* core of the suffix is always present in all noted gerunds across all manuscripts. This is, of course, fully in accordance with the *-ung* suffix found in OE gerunds, and, as noted earlier, the substitution of <y> for the <i> is of little linguistic consequence.

The present participle forms in the four manuscripts generally follow this pattern:

	Suffix
A	-and/-ande
B	-and
C	-and
D	-ande

Again, the variation between these suffixes is so minimal as to be unworthy of remark, except to note that all four manuscripts adhere to the general NME tendency to use the *-and* ending here, as opposed to the more southerly *-ing* or *-yng*. None of the manuscripts make analogy with the gerund forms to make an *-yng* or *-ynge* suffix here, as is sometimes the case. In this area, the manuscripts are all in agreement.

As we might expect, given that these dialects come from the same umbrella dialect area, many of the commonest building blocks of the language take identical forms across the manuscripts: AS, for example, exists in the *als* form in each manuscript, while TO, before an infinitive, is always *to* in all manuscripts. Before a noun, the preferred form of TO is still *to* in all manuscripts, although we do find sporadic use of *til* in A, *till* and *tyll* in B and C, with *tyll* and *tylle* making appearances in D. TILL is a word of probable Old Norse origin, more frequently found in manuscripts originating from areas within the Danelaw, which included the entire NME dialect region. It is consequently unsurprising that its usage is common to all of our NME manuscripts, regardless of specific dialect. The orthographical variations between the forms of TILL we see here are not apparently significant beyond a further note that they continue the linguistic tics noted elsewhere in these manuscripts with regard to doubled consonants, <y> for <i> usage, and addition of final <e> in the case of **D**. The frequency of their usage, in relation to the usage of TO before a noun, is approximately the same across the manuscripts, with some form of TILL appearing 30 – 40% of the time. This makes it difficult to ascertain what occasions the scribes to use a form of TILL as opposed to TO, despite the fact that each scribe appears to make such a decision approximately as frequently as each of his brothers. Even having examined the usages in context, there does not appear to be any immediately obvious logic behind the scribes' decisions to use either *til* or *to*.

In some instances, we may be able to make inference from context – let us consider, for example, the usage of *til* before a possessive pronoun in l. 90: 'God made til his awen lyknesse' (orthography from **C**, but the TILL form is found here in all four manuscripts). If we consider this line out of context only, it is difficult to see why *til* has been used – it does not fall before a vowel that would have made enunciation difficult after the 'o' of TO. However, the context of this line is as follows:

> And if he be til God bousom
> Til endeles blis at þe last to com,
> And if he fraward be, to wende
> Til pyne of helle, þat has nan ende.
> Ilk man þat here lyves, mare and lesse,
> God made til his awen lyknesse,
> Til wham he has given witte and skille
> For to knaw bothe gude and ille,
> And fre wille to chese, als he vouches save,
> Gude or ille whether he wil have;
> Bot he þat his wille til God wil sette...' (ll.84–94)

Evidently, this usage is not isolated, and this seems to be a theme among instances of TILL before a noun in the manuscripts: they fall in clusters, often in close proximity to a possibly significant usage of TILL which may have influenced the scribe. Here, for example, we find a very large number of assonant words in the passage: *skille, ille, wille,* some repeated; directly prior to the passage quoted, we find yet more instances of all of these words, as well as the pararhymes *dwelle* and *felle* in ll. 81 and 82. Could it be, then, that an earlier scribe in a common ancestor manuscript, however far up the tree, was simply influenced by this overwhelming number of assonant words on the poetic level, making the use of TILL for TO here unconscious? It was apparently a permissible usage in this context in the dialect area, but there seems to be no common factor to unite the items it precedes here. One might tentatively suggest that there is some sense of UNTIL included in the phrases 'til endeles blis' and 'til pyne of helle'. Between 'his awen lyknesse', 'wham' and 'God bosom' there seems no possible connection. It may therefore be the most defensible theorem that TILL forms were used in this context purely when they best matched the sound of the passage. The usages do occur in clusters, and they do occur across all manuscripts, suggesting that this was a valid usage in all of these dialects, and that it was used unconcernedly and without any firm systematic rationale. What rationale we may apply to it is possibly more analysis than the scribes themselves ever applied in the writing of it; nevertheless, while there is intra-manuscript variance here, there is not, as stated, any observable inter-manuscript difference. As such, this can be categorised as another feature acceptable across the broader umbrella dialect to which the four belong.

The figure below shows variance between manuscripts of some very commonly-used modal verb forms:

	SHALL	*SHOULD*	*WILL*
A	salle	schulde/suld	wille
B	sall	suld	will
C	sal	suld	wille
D	salle	solde	wylle

Most of these forms represent simple extrapolation of tendencies shown elsewhere in these manuscripts, and while the consistently different forms are useful to us in systematising the dialects separately from each other on an orthographical level, the only item here that stands out as particularly notable is **A**'s preferred form of SHOULD in <sch>.

The use of <h> as a diacritic to indicate modulation of the letter it followed is a result of French influence, a developmental outcome of the adoption into English of a number of techniques used for writing French (Brown and Ogilvie, 2009, p. 352). It is interesting that **A** alone should use this form, as it represents a development of OE <sc> in the opposite direction from the <s> forms used in the remaining three manuscripts. SHOULD is, according to the *MED*, one of those items that varies most widely in ME, with forms of the verb *shulen* taking every conceivable form in <sc>, <sh> and <s> (*MED*, 2000 – 2018). The grapheme <sch>, which later became <sh>, is a result of French influence upon the OE <sc> (Melzer, 2008, p. 11). Forms in <s>, such as *sulde, solde, sud* and *suuld*, are those generally noted only in NME, whereas <sch> forms, although found widely dispersed across a great many dialects, are not typically Northern forms.

It is unusual that it is in **A** that we see in this item the influence of contact with French orthographies. It is **D,** as previously noted, that most commonly shows evidence of French influence, albeit not in ways which, as here, could be attributed to changes filtered through more southerly dialects and developments, where elements such as <sch> are found commonly. However, it might be pointed out that this is not the only instance in which the **A** manuscript utilises a specific orthography that sets it apart from its brothers. The <qw> diagraph and the use of yogh are the two other most notable instances of this in **A,** with the two indicating rather opposite things with regard to origin. <q> did not exist in the OE alphabet, and is, as such, a graph borrowed from French, although its usage in such words as 'qwo' does not reflect its usage in French at all. Conversely, the standard yogh digraph is a letter form commonly used in OE, but which is found less and less frequently as the ME period progresses.

Interpretation of this tendency of the **A** manuscript towards orthographical peculiarities of this sort is difficult. One might, perhaps, infer from it that the **A** manuscript differs diachronically, as well as diatopically, from its brothers, but the *Descriptive Guide to the Pricke of Conscience* indicates that, in fact, the diachronic difference between the manuscripts is not large, as has been discussed in the presentation of manuscripts in Chapter Two. These are all manuscripts of the early era of *Pricke of Conscience* manuscript production in the NME area, produced within a span which is unlikely to be responsible for any great degree of graphemic variance, although it could be responsible for some. Barring this explanation, we might be inclined to suggest that the combination of factors indicates a higher degree of contact with more southerly dialects than that of the other manuscripts. The <sch> and <qw> forms do suggest this, given the *MED*'s record of them as more frequently found outside of the NME area. The yogh usage is anomalous in this regard, but its consistent usage as a graphological variant in the **A** manuscript nevertheless is useful to us as exemplifying a consistent rule within this dialect. It does not seem to demarcate any phonological difference when it appears, as opposed to the <y> or <yh> forms preferred by the other manuscripts, but it might be a trained preference based upon the guidelines of a scriptorium, given the consistency with which the scribe makes use of it.

When we consider those forms which do vary notably between the manuscripts – and there are certainly many of them – the forms used in **B** and **C** are the most similar of the four, and often identical. It must be emphasised, however, that this is not always the case. The instances of variation between the items BOTH and YOU might be cited as examples of important and frequently used items that do differ between **B** and **C,** serving to remind us that **B** and **C** are not written in the same dialect, although there is a high level of overlap. They are the dialects closest to each other of these four, but they are not identical.

D is unquestionably the most distinct dialect of the four. While it and **A** often share points of divergence from **B** and **C,** they do not usually diverge in the same direction, except with regard to the difficult question of <a> versus <o>, where both seem generally to adhere to the same conventions. As such, while they are each more removed from **B** and **C** than **B** and **C** are from each other, **A** and **D** are not necessarily any closer, dialectally, to each other than to the other two manuscripts. **A** does contain a number of very distinct features of its own, such as the use of <qw> for <wh>, and, as discussed, it is the only manuscript whose grapheme usage is significantly different from that of the others. It is **D,** however, that shows the most variation in word forms, particularly with regard to its use of final -e and <y> for [i], both of which features permeate the manuscript. Likewise, the **D** scribe also has a tendency towards the doubling of letters and insertion of <w>-digraphs into words like *sawle*. These constitute further examples of the **D**-dialect's bent towards longer and more elaborate word-forms. Many of these features evidently derive from scribal convention, which is interesting in and of itself, but some may also suggest phonological features in the **D** language which are not found in the other manuscripts – notably consistent final -e, and the w-based digraphs. Let us compare the manuscript forms for the item ANGEL, in illustration of a place where **D** prefers a <w>-containing digraph:

ANGEL

A	angels
B	aungels
C	angels
D	awngels

In the above figure, one might query the reasoning behind the usage of the <aw> digraph in **D**. It may simply be an orthographical tic in line with other forms in **D**, but it is notable that **A** and **B** seem content with a lone <a> while **A** and **D** both use a digraph here. The complicated etymology of ANGEL itself makes this item particularly intriguing. According to the *MED*, ANGEL – in ME, commonly *aungel, angel, ongel, engel* – is rooted both in the OE *engel* and in the Old French *aungel*. Each cognate form would have been differently sounded, and the descendant form *angel* presents difficulties in that it has the same orthography and composition as another word which already existed in OE and persisted into ME with the meaning of 'fish hook' or 'carpenter's ruler' (*MED*, 2000 – 2018). The digraphs in **B** and **D**, then, perhaps make explicit to the reader that this word is to be pronounced in the French fashion, with the <au> and <aw> being sounded as in Modern French *ange* [ɒnʒ]. This would be fully in accordance with the French influences seen elsewhere in the orthography of the **D** scribe. Complicating the issue, however, is the fact of the word *angel* existing already in English with a different meaning, which leads us to query whether it does, in fact, connote a pronunciation difference. Possibly, this is simply an example of an orthographical convention intended to make distinction between two homonyms, similar to the development whereby a doubled final 'd' came to demarcate *god* from *godd* in many dialects.[11] The form *angel* is also recorded in the Old French, denoting the same item as *aungel*, and so what we see here is not an instance of two of our manuscripts using a French form of the item while two use an English – these are all French forms, where other dialects use the OE-consistent forms *ongel* or *engel*.

Comparison of the ANGEL forms to those for SOUL presents a further question:

	SOUL
A	saul
B	saule
C	saul
D	sawle

As may be seen, the vowel sound in the form for SOUL does not in every case correspond directly to the way the vowel in ANGEL is written in that same manuscript. One would presume that in **B** and **D**, where the same digraph is used for both items, the vowel sound is mentally sounded identically by the scribe – such that *saul* makes a half-rhyme with *aungel* and *sawle* with *awngel*, creating assonance.

SOUL is an OE-derived word, whose recorded forms were in OE manifold – for instance: *sawel, sawol, saul, saule*. The use of the <w>-digraph here recalls OE usage, although the OE forms indicate two syllables with the use of a vowel before, rather than after, the <l> – and, moreover, the <w> grapheme is here replacing OE <ƿ>. We may suggest that scribe **D**'s unusual spelling of ANGEL is based upon analogy with SOUL, indicating that the pronunciation of the vowel sound is the same – that is, clarifying that ANGEL is to be sounded in the French fashion by analogising it with an English word that has a similar sound already, SOUL. Scribes **A** and **C** do not do this. Potentially, this is simply that these words did not sound similar in these dialects, where 'angel' had come to be pronounced also in English fashion, like its OE homograph: /ˈæŋ.gəl/. Without a straightforward example of an <au>-containing

---

[11] See Laing (2008, p. 11).

word set against an <a>-containing French word as part of a rhyme, it is difficult to determine whether or not this is true. Possibly, however, the language of **A** and **C** simply assumes an understanding that *angel*, a French word, is to be sounded in French fashion, and *saul*, an English word, in English fashion, whether or not the readers did possess this understanding. It is not at all out of keeping for the **D** scribe to attempt to guide his readers more authoritatively than any of the other scribes.

What we can state, however, is that **D's** *awngel* is a rarely recorded departure from the more usual *aungel* and *angel*, and that it is in accordance with the scribe's use of *sawle* elsewhere. As a preferred form, this is interesting because of the sheer infrequency of its occurrences across the transcribed ME corpus in the *MED*, unlike **B**'s oft-recorded *aungel*. The insertion of the <w>-digraph represents a very distinct form of the word, visually speaking, which might suggest a Francophone pronunciation, despite the fact that it does so using a digraph based on English expectations of graphemes. The use of <w> makes the digraph unambiguous, unlike <au>, which has a different connotation in OE words from French ones. The orthographical pattern across the manuscripts here is consistent with the same pattern found elsewhere, and it enables us to draw up further rules about orthography within these dialects. We can see, moreover, a number of features used consistently in these manuscripts which are not in accord with the usually stipulated range of 'fully Northern' features. For example:

1. The use of <o> rather than <a> for OE /ɑ:/ is noted consistently across three of these four manuscripts, contrary to the idea that <a> for /ɑ:/ is the defining marker of a 'fully Northern' text. It was observable that <a> spellings were retained in the items KNOW, MORE, ALSO, even where <o> was elsewhere the preferred orthography, suggesting that potentially the existence of <a> spellings for these items might be a more reliable indicator of a dialect's 'fully Northern' provenance. Meanwhile, it is evident that, as <o> forms are part of the natural consistent usage of three of these four scribes, these are not anomalies in NME texts, but are an attested linguistic variation in this region.

2. Question words in Northern texts may begin with initial <qw>, as well as initial <wh>. Many more versions of WHO are found than simply *wha*.
3. Pronoun forms across the YOU item in particular vary considerably across these manuscripts. There is evidence of the form *sche,* alongside more commonly attested *scho*. Moreover, there is considerable orthographical variation identifiable in the pronoun forms specifically.

As the above assessment demonstrates, it is already clear, from the comparison of four manuscripts, that the languages of these 'fully Northern' texts are not homogeneous and identical, a fact which further material can only serve to emphasise. These are dialects working within a similar overriding structure, and, as such, many of the major features are the same. Modal verbs are normally formed in similar ways; infinitives are introduced in the same way. However, even across far wider dialect areas than that usually classified as 'Northern Middle English', these are the features that change least frequently. Variation is most frequently found in lexis and orthography, where sufficient systematic differences suffice to make a dialect identifiable by examination of them, and we certainly find that here. In some cases, the variation is simply the addition or removal of an <e>, but this is by no means always true. As noted above, the variation in digraphs, graphemes and word-length across the manuscripts seems to indicate that, at times, there were phonological differences at work, and even if not, the levels of orthographical variance are enough to imply the existence of more than one set of dialectal features, some of which overlap, but some of which are unique, among these four, to the dialect in question.

It is not necessary to connect a written dialect directly to a spoken one in order to study it as a dialect. The AB Language of the Katherine Group manuscripts, for example, is now assumed to be a written standard only, which, while obviously based in the spoken dialect of its area of origin, is most usefully studied as a set of orthographical and graphemic features.[12] The dialects of these manuscripts do not vary hugely – in that they, like all ME dialects,

---

[12] For a basic summary of AB Language and scholarship in this area, see Blake (1992, p. 11).

share certain characteristics common to a broad area, in which several dialects might coexist — but they are certainly distinct enough to render suggestions of homogeneity quite spurious. Benskin (1992, p. 23) defines a dialect thus:

> A dialect, whether broadly or narrowly delimited, can be regarded as an assemblage of linguistic components. Each component — each form — has its own distribution. Some may be confined to the dialect in question, but unless the dialect is defined in very broad terms, most of its forms will be found in some of the neighbouring dialects as well.

Previously, the Northern dialect area always has been defined, as Benskin says, in 'very broad terms'. It is not at all surprising that manuscripts written in 'neighbouring' dialects to each other will share many forms. These manuscripts are evidently related, in the way that all manuscripts within a broad dialect area are related. However, this does not mean that the very broad dialect area cannot be narrowed down. While there are features shared between these manuscripts, there are also points of divergence, as would be expected of dialects which, while neighbours to each other, are not identical. What the evidence indicates is that the traditional idea of the Northern region as home to a single broad dialect with a single set of features can be improved upon; there is more variation of feature than is usually suggested, and it is possible to detect patterns in this variation. While these manuscripts share many forms, this similarity of linguistic components is consistent with dialects within the same broad area, and once we begin to move beyond the 'broad terms' picture of the NME region, we can see that there is, alongside these similarities, considerable variation, and evidence of features outside the range of what is commonly maintained. Where such features as <o> for Northern <a> might usually be considered the result of contamination or *Mischsprachen,* the consistency with which this feature are recorded in three of four manuscripts suggests strongly that it is a valid part of more than one NME dialect. The more data is collected and studied in this way, the more we are able to uncover such evidence — and the more we know about the scribes themselves, the more accurately we are able to assess consistency of usage, and the implications of these discoveries. Consequently, we will now consider the textual transmission of the *Pricke of Conscience,* and scribal behaviour within these manuscripts.

CHAPTER 4

The Textual Tradition of the *Pricke of Conscience*

Analysis of raw data collected from the core manuscripts proved sufficient to provide general answers to a number of important questions, notably: what sorts of differences can we identify between different Northern copies of the *Pricke of Conscience*; what reasons might we posit for these differences; and what, then, is the importance of considering scribal influence in differentiating dialects? What analysis of data also made clear, however, is that these questions cannot be fully answered without an understanding of textual scholarship and how it applies to these manuscripts of the *Pricke of Conscience,* their transmission and their potential inter-relation. Due to the scarcity of anchor texts from within the 'fully Northern' area, the methodology of this thesis relies heavily upon intensive study of scribes, scribal circumstance, and scribal behaviour, making analyses about language and variation from scribal handling of the text. As such, it is necessary to consider scribal behaviour and textual transmission, in the context of these manuscripts, in order to properly illuminate the data collected.

At the time of initial data collection, the use of a questionnaire proved helpful as a means of charting major differences between manuscripts in a clear and organised way. As detailed in the assessment of methodology, however, it swiftly became clear that, while the questionnaire permitted simple comparison of ortho-graphical differences between the manuscripts, it was not sufficient for a full dialectal investigation. As such, my consideration of later data placed a greater emphasis upon the line-by-line text compar-isons available to me – this being, indeed, one of the greatest advantages of analysing dialects across different versions of the same text, rather than simply across similar texts which appear to differ dialectally. The findings below reflect the patterns and points of interest I noted through reference both to the updated question-naire, and to straightforward comparison of manuscript contents. Line numbers are given with reference to the numbering used in

Morris's 1863 edition of the *Pricke of Conscience*. Where there are lines additional to those in the Morris edition (taken from the **C** manuscript), or where there are lines displaced or missing, this is also noted.

The data available for direct comparison comprises identical tranches of Books 1 – 6 of Rawlinson Poetry 175 (**B**), Cotton E.ix (**C**), of Books 1 – 5 of Wellesley 8 (**D**), and of Books 5 and 6 of Rawlinson C.891 (**A**). Additionally, the same tranches of Books 2 and 6 were transcribed from MS Harley 4196 (**B2**), for cross-referencing, although these were not used as part of the core data comparison. The **A** manuscript, as noted above, is written by non-Northern scribes prior to the commencement of Book V; the other manuscripts, however, are 'fully Northern' throughout.

In comparing the tranches of Book III transcribed, we find some interesting examples of divergence between the **B**, **C** and **D** manuscripts. This book, in each manuscript, offers a number of cases of scribal eye-skip, with all of the manuscripts omitting lines, or inadvertently collapsing two lines into one, causing unfortunate breaks in the metre as couplets transform into single lines. For example, **C** and **D** give the following two couplets – here cited from **C**, but with only minor orthographical variation between the two manuscripts (Morris, 1863, p. 47):

> Bodely ded, þat es kyndely
> Es twynyng betwene þe saule and þe body
> And þat ded es full bytter and hard
> Of whilk I sall schew yhow afterward.

In **B**, however, we find:

> Bodily ded þat es kyndely
> Es twynyng bitwene þe saul and þe body
> And þat ded es full bitter afterward.

The final line quoted here is an interesting conflation of the latter couplet, as found in the other two manuscripts. It makes sense, which is possibly why it has not been corrected by the scribe – the most logical inference is that eye-skip has occurred here, causing the scribe to conflate the lines inadvertently as he copied them, without afterwards noticing his error due to the fact that what he has written is an acceptable sentence. This sort of scribal error must be expected occasionally, and usually occurs where the exemplar is particularly small or ill-written: variations of homeoarchy, or eye-skip, are naturally more frequent where lines are closer together and more difficult to read, in the same way that it is easier for modern readers to quickly and accurately scan double-spaced text than single-spaced fine print. It seems likely that for the scribe to have failed to notice the loss of his metre here, he may have been struggling with his exemplar for some distance, preventing him from concentrating properly on the poem itself, so much as simply the words as shapes to be discerned. Even with a good exemplar, speed or carelessness might cause such errors, but the handwriting in this part of the manuscript is neat and practised – the page does not look as if it has been hurriedly or carelessly written.

In the **D** manuscript, we find that the scribe has omitted l. 1683 – '*This manere of dedes are þat men dredys*' – but has then reinserted it later, following l. 1691. As in the previous example of eye-skip in the **B** manuscript, the new configuration of lines does broadly make sense, but again, the rhyme scheme is disrupted. It is perhaps understandable that the scribe did not notice the incomplete couplet where the line should have gone, due to the similar endings of several lines in that section – what we see in **D** is (Ibid., p.47):

> For als þere clerkes fyndes wryten and redes
> [omitted line]
> One es badely dede þat thrugh kynde es
> Another es gostly þe thredd endeles.

The reintroduction of the line, slightly later in the section, reads oddly, disrupting the rhyme scheme and rhythm:

> Gostly dede es a twynning thorgh syn
> Be twene godd and man sawle within
> This manere of dedes are þat man dredys
> Ffor als þe sawle es lyf of þe body
> SSo þe lyf of þe sawle es godd alle myghty

This is particularly unusual behaviour for Scribe **D,** who is elsewhere so meticulous in his attempts to improve the text as he copies it, as will be discussed in more detail later. However, it may be noted that, again, the line-endings here are similar for a stretch – *dredys,* as it is spelled in the **D** manuscript, does end <ys>. This may perhaps have made it easy for the scribe to insert it alongside lines ending in <y>. There is certainly no logical reason for the scribe to have deliberately removed the line from its original position and then reinserted it here – it does not alter the sense of the passage at all, except to disrupt the rhyme scheme. The jump of five lines is not too great a distance for eye-skip to occur, especially where the exemplar has more than one column and the eye skips across, but this would be more likely if the exemplar were, indeed, untidy or closely-written. Moreover, it is possible that the exemplar itself gave this line as marginalia, where the scribe had omitted it and then added it, such that Scribe **D** could only guess at where it might fit.

In none of the manuscripts I examined did I find Book III, as recopied, to be especially small, or badly laid-out, compared to the books on either side of it, and the fact that all these scribes found difficulties with it does raise interesting questions. Beyond the above-discussed errors, noted in the transcribed tranche, scans of the remainder of Book III demonstrated further such errors in each manuscript. None of these scribes demonstrates such a high level of inaccuracy elsewhere, particularly with whole lines. The lines omitted are not the same lines from one manuscript to another, which suggests that the common prevalence of errors in this book is not due to a single shared untidy exemplar, but nevertheless, the observation is intriguing.

The evidence, then, draws us towards the question of textual scholarship, and its importance as a basis for accurate and full analysis of the variation between these manuscripts. In this instance, the exemplars, or manuscripts from which the scribes of **A, B, C** and **D** copied the poem, are hypothetical, in that they are unidentified. Having made reference to these hypothetical manuscripts, however, in order to suggest explanations for examples of errors common to the manuscripts under consideration, it is necessary to explain further what exactly textual scholarship is, and how it can aid us.

The individualism of scribes, and the ways in which they translate, amend, misunderstand, and otherwise make alterations to the texts they copy, have already been discussed at length.[1] Traditional textual criticism is concerned with the identification and removal of these perceived errors in manuscripts, and with an attempt to reconstruct the original text, or archetype, for example

---

[1] See Chapter One.

for an edition of a poem or other work. Obviously, as Robert Lewis and Angus McIntosh (1982, p. 77) point out, 'this unenthusiastic reaction to what (textually speaking) is often a depressing process of decay down the chain of descent from one manuscript to the next is not normally shared by the dialectologist, for from his linguistic point of view there is not necessarily any degeneration at all, still less the menace of progressive degeneration.' Dialectologists are not concerned with reconstructing 'original' texts, but rather, are interested in precisely these examples of variation between manuscripts which traditional textual critics perceive as examples of degeneration. To the dialectologist, they represent our greatest resource for the study of dialectal and sociolinguistic variation. Nevertheless, the processes employed by the textual critic to reconstruct an original can also be of use to the dialectologist, where an understanding of the recensions of a text, the proposed stemmata, and the possible relationships between manuscripts, is relevant to the discussion, as it is here.[2]

There are, of course, a great many criticisms to be levelled at the stemmatic method. In the first place, it assumes that every manuscript is descended from only one exemplar; if a scribe refers to two exemplars in the production of his own copy, then the resultant manuscript will not necessarily fit into a single branch of the stemma. Secondly, stemmatics assumes only that scribes will make new errors, and does not make allowances for the fact that many scribes, in fact, do attempt to correct the errors of their predecessors, and to 'improve' upon the text in their exemplars. Furthermore, stemmatics assumes that all witnesses are ultimately derived from a single source. This does not account for the possibility of the 'author' himself producing more than one copy of the work at once, nor, more importantly, for the idea that he may have revised his own work, thus enabling more than one 'authoritative' copy of the text to coexist, as in the case of Wulfstan's *Sermo Lupi,* which was apparently revised by its author to reflect changes in the political situation at the time of writing (Whitelock, 1939, pp.1 – 5). This idea of 'authorial revisions' is of course somewhat simplistic, and can

---

[2] For good concise discussion of stemmatics in Middle English, see Hanna (1996, pp. 83–99). Hanna especially discusses the problem of assuming 'errors' and an ultimate exemplar.

become hazardous when scholars are focused upon the idea of a single authorial figure, as in the case of Chaucer scholarship. As Ralph Hanna (1996, p.159) has indicated:

> Since 1912, when Root attempted to show that T and C exists in three authorial versions, a large number of Chaucerian textual critics have become obsessed with the issue of revisions. Following Root's apparent demonstration that inclusion of extra passages and substantial manuscript variation in local readings should be attributed to the author and not to his scribes, critics have painstakingly amassed further instances of "Chaucer at work" from elsewhere in the canon. Yet I think a great many of these efforts have been pursued without consciousness of the very real methodological differences involved.

Nevertheless, the basic idea of stemmatics has still proven useful to scholars of texts, such as the *Sermo Lupi*, that seem to fall outside of the strict parameters it expects, provided that scholars are conscious of the potential pitfalls.

In the case of the *Pricke of Conscience*, actual stemmata have been proposed only very recently, the most thorough being Hanna and Wood's revision of Derek Britton's proposed stemma.[3] Hanna and Wood feel that MS C and B2 derived from an identical exemplar. This hypothetical exemplar is termed d, and derives from c. Copies a, b and c represent three early copies, each an independent rendition of the authorial one, from which the *Pricke of Conscience* tradition descends. According to this stemma, D derives from a, MS B derives directly from *c*, and MS **A** falls under the 'general manuscript tradition' group deriving from *b*.

In his work on the poetic techniques of William Langland, George Kane sought a preferred version of his text through his identification of not only a 'Langlandian' style within the text, but also examples of a second, scribal style. In this case, the scribal style was seen as 'a series of disruptive and degenerative choices' (Hanna and Wood, 2013, p. 159), which Kane chose to eradicate and exclude as part of his process of editing. A similar process, however, might be used to remark a number of scribal styles which, rather than being degenerative, seem to improve the structure and focus of

---

[3] Both Britton's original and the revision are given in Hanna and Wood (2013), pp. lxiv–lxv.

the *Pricke of Conscience*. This was not a poem for which any named author took credit, nor attempted to control. As such, it proliferated in a communal tradition within which scribes did commit common errors, such as simple homeoarchy, but also, in many cases, felt able to amend and improve, for reasons of style or context. None of the major splits within the *Pricke of Conscience* tradition – for example, that which resulted in the Southern Recension, or the *Speculum huius vitae* – is 'authorial', in the way that Gower's second recension of his *Confessio Amantis* is flatly authorial, and separate from instances of scribal 'degenerative' activity. All of these splits within the tradition are, rather, scribal.[4]

In their *Descriptive Guide to the Manuscripts of the Pricke of Conscience*, Lewis and McIntosh explain the textual tradition of the *Pricke of Conscience* as comprising five main parts: the Main Version; the Southern Recension; Extracts; the *Speculum Huis Vitae;* and the Latin translation. All of the manuscripts studied in this thesis are part of the main, or oldest, tradition of the poem, which comprises 97 manuscripts and appears to have originated in north Yorkshire. Lewis and McIntosh (1982, p. 5 – 13) note that:

> [...] it is clear from what little work has been done on these ninety-seven manuscripts that subgroupings can be made on the basis of varying length of copies, rearrangement or addition of material, and line by line textual revision, but that, in comparison with the more radically and thoroughly revised Southern Recension, they are all, to a greater or lesser extent, variations of one and the same poem.

These subgroupings, of course, are a far looser set of guidelines than the traditional stemma later proposed, and posit only major points of connection between manuscripts. The first classifications of *Pricke of Conscience* manuscripts were made by Percy Andreae, using the eighteen British Library manuscripts of which he was aware, and these groupings were followed and expanded upon by subsequent scholars. Lewis and McIntosh construct their own 'refined and corrected' groupings, concluding that the 97 manuscripts 'appear to divide themselves tentatively into four groups' (Ibid., p.6). But according to the Lewis-McIntosh groupings, three

---

[4] For a discussion of Gower's authorial revisions to the *Confessio Amantis*, see Nicholson(1984, pp. 123–143).

of the manuscripts under discussion here – **B, C** and **D** – belong to the same group, Group I, while the Northern hand in **A** is placed under the heading of Group II. This is not in accordance with the later stemma, which would place **D** as descendant from a quite separate hyperexemplar, *a*, to the *c* manuscript that ultimately anteceded **B, C** and **B2**, so we must use caution in using these groupings. If **B, C** and **D** do not derive from the same hyperexemplar, we cannot then posit that any single manuscript contained a very closely- or untidily-written Book III which created confusion further down the line. Rather, we must assume that the errors across Book III in all of these manuscripts are simply coincidental.

Nevertheless, the fact remains that Book III provides many linguistically interesting examples of divergence. At one point, for instance, the scribe of **D** has altered the pronoun in a sentence, from 'where þai er, will God noght dwelle' to 'where he es'. We may assume that the scribe, for reasons of his own, objects to the word *þai* being used to refer to the dual threats of 'syn' and 'the devil', choosing, instead, to narrow down the focus simply to 'the devil', *he*; but why might this be, and what could it indicate about the other two scribes, in comparison to scribe **D**? It could be the case that the scribe of **D** thought the syntax unclear with regard to whom, or what, 'they' referred; whereas the other two scribes were less scrupulous, simply recopying the sentence without detecting any ambiguity in the syntax. However, this seems fairly unlikely – the fact that two scribes whose manuscripts are otherwise not identical copied this section faithfully would suggest that the reading seemed to them unproblematic. Neither scribe appears to have taken issue with the structure, and subsequent clarity, of the sentence. What other reason, then, might there be for Scribe **D** to make his alteration?

At this juncture, we must question whether Scribe **D,** rather than taking exception on a dialectal, or general grammatical level to the sentence, was instead objecting to it on a level of content or of style – an idea to which we have already alluded. Upon first glance, one might query whether Scribe **D** was overly concerned with the suggestion that God cannot exist where sin exists, as the sentence implies in **B** and **C**. After all, as the poem states elsewhere, sin is a fundamental part of all human beings, and thus one might take issue with the implication that God cannot ever exist alongside sinful humans, whether living or dead. However, closer examination reveals that, in fact, Scribe **D's** revision leaves this potential theological pothole quite intact – that is, he does not seem to have considered this to be a difficulty, and his revision does not clarify or remove it. Scribe **D's** comment that 'whare syn es es þe devel of hell' still places the devil firmly wherever sin is found – including, potentially, on the earth, among living men. Scribe **D,** then, is not objecting to the content of the sentence so much as to its style. Where **B** (Morris, 1863, p.47) has:

> For whare syn es es þe devell of hell
> And þare where þai er God will noght dwell

D prefers:

> For whare syn es es þe devel of helle
> And þare where he is Godd wyll noght dwelle.

We must assume that although the **B** version of this couplet is clear enough – as suggested by its retention by both **B** and **C** scribes – Scribe **D** found it stylistically jarring. Certainly, the use of *þai*, while arguably correct, is also rather redundant: if sin is wherever the devil is, then one can state that God cannot dwell alongside the devil and safely feel that the further statement – that God cannot dwell alongside *sin* – is contained in, and implied by, what has already been said. If one follows the internal logic of the couplet, the use of the *þai* pronoun is unnecessary, and Scribe **D's** version of events is neater and more stylistically pleasing. His rearrangement of words gives the couplet a better sense of overall balance. The phrasing 'þare where þai er will' is far clumsier in its sounds than the smoother 'þare where he is Godd wyll.' Certainly, if the book was intended to be read aloud, the reader of **D's** line would be far less liable to stumble.

This may seem an unnecessarily lengthy exposition upon a seemingly small variation, but it is precisely this sort of variation that allows us to begin to see our scribes in context, leaving us better placed to analyse and understand other changes they may make. Use of a questionnaire alone would have completely elided this variation between the manuscripts, as there are no notable orthographical differences – certainly none that are not found elsewhere – and no lexical substitutions. However, line by line comparison has allowed us to identify both a notable divergence between the manuscripts, and to posit a probable reason for it. The outcome of this is that we know that Scribe **D** is liable to exercise a level of authority over the text in order to reshape the text for stylistic reasons. This knowledge may well be useful in determining the likelihood of other differences being due to dialect variation, or simply to stylistic impact.

In his essay on the subject of style in Chaucer's works, John F. Plummer (2003, pp. 414 – 27) comments:

> If the author...is demoted in contemporary reading strategies ('dead' in some theories), his intentions no longer regarded as the source of meaning in a literary text, then it follows that we will be less interested in style, the revelation in the text of those unique habits of thought and expression.

This observation, arguing against the importance that has historically been placed upon the author, is fascinating in light of the current study, which seeks to consider the potential importance of the scribe as contributing author. Thus, in accordance with Plummer's statement, we naturally become more interested in style as illustrative of the scribe's intentions and the meanings he may have wished to bring to the text as he transformed it. If we are able to establish a strong engagement with style as typical of a particular scribe, such as Scribe **D** here, then we place ourselves in a stronger position when it comes to understanding that scribe's work and the motivations behind his alterations. The dialectologist must always interrogate any scribal amendments before deeming them likely to be dialectally based, and further information on a scribe's stylistic practices can be a means of ensuring that too much is not attributed falsely to dialect variation. Hanna (1992, p. 160) concurs that:

> Although scribes typically produce predictable sorts of minor errors, they are also capable both of improving the texts they copy and of extensive rewriting of their exemplars. Such changes can occur for various reasons, ranging from simple incomprehension of the authorial lection all the way to a desire to join in the fun and write some poetry too.

In the manuscripts of the *Pricke of Conscience* with which we are concerned, it is evident that something, whether it be incomprehension or stylistic objection, has motivated the lexical and sense changes such as those discussed above. The results of these changes are texts which, although of no interest to a scholar seeking an 'authorial' text, are deeply relevant to the dialectologist, or the student of scribal method. If we can detect that a scribe, or scribal school, seems commonly to amend for stylistic reasons, then, as stated, we can use this to analyse the likelihood of dialectal factors in changes he has made. If we can track similar changes from one manuscript to another, however – discerning manuscript inter-relationships, to a certain extent, through comparison of content differences – then we can also track whether or not there seem to be dialect changes even between recopyings of new material. For example, if we know that manuscripts **A, B** and **C** are all part of the same group, we know that there is a similarity of content between them, on a level that is not found elsewhere. If a clearly amending scribe has drastically revised a line, we may be more likely to wonder whether that revision could be attributable to stylistic motivations, rather than because a particular word was not in use in his dialect (although this would of course depend on a proper analysis of the revision in question).

It is evident that medieval writers had a firm understanding of the concept of style, and that each author could have his or her particular own. Plummer (2003, p.420) illustrates this by reference to Chaucer's *Troilus and Criseyde*, in which the author expresses a hope – addressing his book itself – that 'non myswrite the/Ne the mysmetre for defaute of tonge'. He notes that 'Chaucer felt he had written and "metered" his verse in a particular way, that he had a sense of his own style, that he quite naturally wanted it preserved intact and feared that it could well be reproduced wrongly.' The core scribes of this study are not archetypal authors like Chaucer, but this in no way implies that they could not have felt a similar pride in and attachment to those works to which they contributed in recopying, particularly those scribes who did take close note of metre and rhyme as they worked. Scribe **D** appears to be exactly such a scribe.

The rules of medieval rhetoric descended directly from those that had governed classical orators, although the system was now more concerned with effective communication in written contexts than in speech-making, even if there remained an oral dimension. Consequently, medieval writers had set 'rhetorical expectations of decorum or fit between subject, speaker and audience' (Ibid.), to which scribes would have wanted their work to conform. An engaged scribe might wish to make amendments to bring the text closer to these expectations; but he might also alter the text to conform to certain idiosyncratic stylistic tendencies of his own. M.H. Abrams (1961, p. 94) defines style simply as 'a characteristic manner of expression', which can colour whole poems. Raymond Oliver (1970, p. 74) notes that style 'varies with diction, which varies according to the poet's intention', with style and meaning being not two separate entities, but co-factors which support each other: a poet concerned with style will wield and exercise his own style in order to present better his intended meaning.

There are other indications that the scribe of **D** felt able to exercise some level of authority upon his text for stylistic reasons. Perhaps the most notable point of divergence between **D** and the other manuscripts considered is its continued use of Latin introductions to the books, where the other manuscripts contain English ones. Thus, where **B** has: 'Here bigyns þe ferth part þat es of purgatory', in **D** we find 'de purgatorio peo quarta'. This sort of basic substitution is made consistently across all the books of the poem, with every English introductory rubric being quietly translated into Latin, making the introductions generally much briefer. Of course, we cannot be sure, without the evidence of the exemplar, whether or not Scribe **D** himself made these conscious changes. What the preference for Latin indicates, however, is that the manuscripts in **D's** family became, at some point, more concerned with a certain type of scholarly style and finesse than **A**, **B**, **C** and related manuscripts. Consequently, any stylistic alterations within the text for metre, structure, and so on, would accord with this tendency, confirming the need to interrogate the reasons behind any idiosyncrasies found in **D**.

One of these idiosyncrasies is represented by scribe **D's** frequent tendency to omit altogether those Latin quotations within the text which are then given in English, too. For example, in Book IV, **B** and **C** give 'Minima pene purgatorii est major maxima pena mundi', prior to giving the translation. **D**, however, simply provides the English: 'He says þe leste payne þat es þare/In purgatory es weele mare' The same thing is found on almost every occasion where a similar construction occurs. For example, in Book I, **B** gives:

> Pat pruves þe gospell þat sais us
> How god said till his disaples þus
> Nisi efficiamini sicut parvulus, non intrabitis in regnum celorum.

Bot yhe he said be als a child...

C, barring differences in orthography consistent throughout the manuscript, gives the same four lines. In **D,** however, we find simply:

þat prwfes þe godspell þat sayse us
How godd sayde tyll hys dyscyples thus
Bot yhe be he sayde als a chylde...

Had this tendency been encountered independently of the **D** scribe's preference for Latin introductions to his books, we might have considered whether it constituted a simple attempt to eradicate Latin from the text entirely, rendering it more suitable for a lay audience. However, viewed in conjunction with the introduction or retention of other Latin rubrics elsewhere, we must examine it more closely. It is true that the scribe may have felt that the introductions to each book existed more for the information of clerics navigating within the book than for lay people: it is possible that the scribe was writing a book to be read aloud, in which case it would make sense for the Latin to be eradicated from within the text, for the sake of the audience. This still does not seem sufficient explanation for the addition of other Latin, however, as a cleric would be equally well able to navigate using English introductions and rubrics. While the removal of Latin from within the text would aid a lay audience, the introduction of it in the rubrics would not necessarily help a clerical reader, even if it would not hinder him either. Both forms of alteration, however, could be seen as stylistic changes. The Latin quotations within the text interrupt the metre and rhyme of the poem. Without them, the reader can simply continue reading in the same metre and form; the Latin, from this perspective, does nothing but disrupt the poem's beauty, while adding nothing to its meaning. The Latin at the beginnings and ends of books, similarly, eradicates clumsy incidences of vernacular prose, replacing it with far briefer Latin tags which lend a sense of gravitas to the poem's openings and closings. As such, it would appear likely that both of these sets of alterations were part of a kind of stylistic reform visible throughout the **D** manuscript, although it is equally likely that the scribe was considering the needs of a potential lay audience.

The **D** manuscript also consistently demonstrates the most substantial alterations to the text of the poem. In the transcribed tranche of Book IV, for example, we find, in **B** and **C,** the following (orthography from **C**) as part of a description of which souls find themselves in purgatory:

> And er noght parfytely clensed here
> Of all venyele sinnes sere.

In **D,** however, we find:

> And war noght parfytely clenssed heere
> Of bodely and venyale synnes dere.

There are of course a number of basic orthographical differences, which fall into the patterns noted in the questionnaire. It is not these, however, which constitute the biggest point of variation between the two versions of this couplet. In the first line, we find that the scribe has altered the tense of the sentence, one must presume for reasons of style – while it is grammatically permissible to say that souls which are not fully cleansed on earth do end up in purgatory, scribe **D** clearly preferred to discuss them as souls which were not cleansed on earth, and thus are now in purgatory. This, most probably, simply reflects idiosyncratic scribal logic. More notable are the changes made to the second line of the couplet, into which the scribe has actually inserted an additional word: *bodely*.

Consultation of the *MED* entry (bodilich, also bod(e)ly) gives the meaning of this word as very similar to that of its contemporary descendant, 'bodily'. The *MED* (2000 – 2018) defines it as 'Of human beings, their behavior, and their wants: pertaining to or affecting the body (as distinct from the 'spirit'); physical, corporeal'; or possibly 'Of things and states: physical, material'. This being the case, it is difficult to see any way in which additional meaning is added to this sentence through the incorporation of this word. The term 'venial' itself was then, as it is today, a theological term referring to a minor, forgiveable sin – that is, one which does not stain the soul; indeed, a sin 'affecting the body (as distinct from the spirit)' and whose taint can be cleansed in purgatory. The scribe's decision to include an additional word here, then, does not seem to have stemmed from any theological objection to the content or implication of the sentence.

This being the case, we must assume that the scribe's concern was with the metre of the poem, and that the extra word was intended to correct a perceived imbalance in the couplet. In texts that use the spelling *veniel*, as does **B,** this line does seem very short, which might perhaps explain the scribe's decision. However, when the lines are read aloud, there is no violently objectionable difference in length between the two lines of the couplet, even in version **B,** which appears the shortest when written. Consider the scansion:

B:

∧ / ∧ / ∧ ∧ / ∧ / ∧
And er |noght parfytly | clensed | here

∧ ∧ / ∧ ∧ / / ∧
Of al | veniel |syns | sere |

The fact that only Scribe **D** saw any difficulty here is interesting. In Scribe **D's** presentation of the lines, the second one is much more in keeping in physical length with the first. Furthermore, the addition of *bodely* would seem to equalise the balance of metre between the first line and the second of the couplet, such that scribe **D**'s lines would be parsed in a rhythm such as this:

D:

∧ / ∧ / ∧ ∧ / /
And war |noght parfytely |clenssed heere

∧ / ∧ ∧ ∧ / ∧ / /
Of bodely |and venyale | synnes| dere

The second line in **D** has an equivalent number of major stresses to the first line: the scansion is thus improved. The line also looks longer, on the page, than the equivalent line in **B,** because of the increased number of final -e flourishes found in **D's** language. As Donka Minkova (1991, pp. 45 – 47) indicates, many dialects retained the final -e in etymologically motivated positions long beyond the point where evidence suggests that it had a phonological value, so it need not have been the case that the instances of final -e were still sounded in any of these manuscripts. In **D,** this addition is made whether or not it is historically motivated, so we can assume that its addition does not contribute to the stress pattern of the line. As such, it appears likely that this addition of *bodely* was simply an alteration for style, lengthening a line which felt overly short according to the particular pronunciation and emphases of a scribe who seems quite confident of a certain degree of authority over his text.

In ME lyrics, the purpose of sound figures was to bind words together for emphasis, making the poem as suitable as possible for public recitation (Oliver, 1970, p. 86). As such, assonance and alliteration were important: one might argue here that a degree of assonance has been created between *war* and *parfytely, noght* and *bodely,* which the arrangement of lines in B and C does not possess. As the assonance spans the whole couplet, the first line therefore leads more naturally into the second, the assonance lending the couplet cohesion. The 'sound-texture' of a poem was intended to help its audience to understand it, and might effectively use alliteration, rhyme, assonance and metrical stresses together to aid meaning. The poem 'Alysoun', in MS. Harley 2253, provides an excellent example of these devices all being used in perfect conjunction. Here, it appears that Scribe **D** has attempted to improve the 'sound texture' of his work as he copied it, in terms of metrical balance and, potentially, assonance; in turn, this can indicate to us that this scribe was evidently of a certain level of education, well-versed in how best to improve the impact of a work.

Another notable substitution in **D,** is that of the word *dere* where we find *sere* in the other two manuscripts. The *MED* (2000 – 2018)tells us that *dere,* in this sense, descends from the OE *deor,* and has the meaning 'Of persons, devils: fierce; of a judgement, a wound: severe; of a blow: hard; of poison: deadly.' In **D,** then, this word serves to describe the venial and bodily sins as, effectively, severe or great. *Sere,* however, can have two possible meanings within this context. The *MED* states that it is a word from the ON cp. OI *ser,* and is found chiefly in NME texts. It can mean 'extraordinary, great', making it similar to *dere,* but it can also have the meaning 'Different, various, diverse.' The quotations in the *MED* show overwhelmingly that the word is far more frequently used to mean 'various' than to mean 'great', giving only two examples of its use in the latter context.

Why we find *dere* in **D** instead is therefore a question of some complexity. It appears that *sere* was used in Northern manuscripts for both of the above purposes, so we cannot simply assume that only the latter meaning was common in NME, such that scribe **D** naturally took it to mean this – the equivalent of *dere* – in this context. Indeed, the *Pricke of Conscience* – in manuscripts **A, B, C,** and **D** – uses *sere* to mean 'various' at many other points within the poem. Only a few lines later, in Book IV, for example, **D** gives the following:

for þe leste payne of þe paynes þare seere
Es more þan es þe moste payne here.

On this occasion, Scribe **D** differs from **B** and **C** only orthographically, and *seere* is most probably used to mean 'many'. However, it is interesting that here, again, it could be argued that the word might be used to mean 'severe' – severe, rather than many, *paynes*. This may in fact be considered an illustration of some of the issues Scribe **D** may have had with this word, as will be expounded upon below. In l. 3261, however, we find another usage of the word *sere* apparently in the sense of 'diverse':

Þus sal þai on seere-wyse pyned be,
Sum many wynter for þair syn.

'So shall they in many ways be pained'. The *MED* (2000 – 2018) gives only a single definition for *sere-wise*: 'in a diverse way, variously', which makes good sense in this context. Clearly, Scribe **D** (or his exemplar) was aware of both possible meanings of 'sere', having used it elsewhere to mean 'various' and then translated it as 'severe' or 'great' in this instance: '*Of bodely and venyale synnes dere.*' The greater question is why this has been done. On the one hand, it could simply be a further example of the drive, in **D**, towards neatness of style, to the extent that words with possibly confusing multiple meanings be reserved, as far as possible, for only one of those meanings. On the other, it could be that, while **D** recognised the word 'sere' in this context, he felt that his audience would not – that is, it was not a term commonly used for this purpose in his dialect area, although it existed within the category of words the scribe knew, but would not commonly use. This is not an altogether ridiculous suggestion, given the evidence of the *MED* as to the infrequency with which this word was used with the meaning of 'severe', or 'great' as a modifier for such negative ideas as 'pain' or 'need'. This, however, brings us to the question of how the scribe knew that this was the intended meaning in this instance. Grammatically, we are given no guidance as to which sense was meant, and contextually, both are equally likely. Indeed, it might be said to lend something to the poem to have the ambiguity present, the sense that either, or indeed both, meanings could be contained within the line.

Scribe **D**, however, was not, as we have seen, particularly tolerant of ambiguity or what he apparently views as a lack of clarity. It is not unthinkable that he simply decided to settle upon a meaning and make it explicit through the substitution of *dere*, to avoid possible questions and confusion. This is still more likely if the scribe also felt that *sere* was not widely understood to mean 'severe', particularly if he felt that this was the most important of the two potential meanings conveyed by *sere*. On consideration, then, while it is very likely that the scribe's stylistic vision for the poem played a part in this decision – he may have felt, indeed, that two rhymes of *sere* and *dere* occurred within too close proximity of each other within this passage – it does seem possible that there were some issues of dialect difference also at work.

Later in Book IV, we find yet another instance of Scribe **D** substituting one word for another. It should be noted that, for the most part, although there are consistent differences in orthography between Scribes **A, B, C** and **D,** which render their languages all, to a certain extent, distinct, it is not very common for these scribes to differ over lexical choices. Given that all of these texts come from the same general area, and thus would certainly have been comprehensible to scribes from other places in the same broad region, this is not surprising. As described elsewhere, scribes would usually retain words they felt were understandable to their audience, whether or not they would have been the first word of choice within the local area, unless they had some particular reason to make an alteration.

Because lexical differences are quite infrequent, line-by-line comparisons of the manuscripts make them abundantly obvious and easily notable where they do occur. In Chapter Two, we briefly discussed the item *ferdelayk*. This item appears in **B** (*fridlayke*), **B2** (*ferdlayk*) and **C** (*ferdlayke*) in l. 6427, at the beginning of Book VI, where **A** uses the word *drede*. This section of Book VI is missing from **D,** but as an electronic copy of Morris's edition enables us to search within Book **C,** it could be determined that the word appears also in l. 2917, although this falls outside of the transcribed tranches. As such, investigation for this word specifically showed that **D** gives *drede,* while the other manuscripts again use the same forms of the *ferdlayk* item. Comparison of the Book VI section in which this word appears reveals a syntactic difference in **A,** where the scribe has chosen to consider 'þe synful' in the singular – 'In grete drede he schulde be brouȝt' – rather than the plural, 'þai suld in gret fridlayke be broght' (**B** and **C**). Otherwise, however, it is not immediately clear as to why the scribe should have chosen *drede* here, rather than the word *fridlayke/ferdlayke* preferred by the scribes of **B** and **C**.

The line-by-line comparison method enables us to see, for example, that the scribe of **A** will occasionally alter words for sense, or to emphasise certain elements. Following on from the line previously cited, we find that **A** gives 'Ffor þe mynde of þaim schulde him fere'. **B** prefers 'For þe mynt of þam might men fere', while **C** has the similar 'For þe mynde of þam myght men feer'. The notable difference is the use of *schulde* in preference to *might*, an alteration which would seem to change the meaning of this line subtly, but distinctly. Where **B** and **C** allow that the generic 'synful men' might be fearful, **A** carries a greater sense of immediacy in its statement that this 'synful', he, should be fearful. It is almost an exhortation to the audience to identify themselves with the faceless man in question, and, furthermore, to recognise that they most certainly should be afraid. This brings into question the scribal decision to use the singular in the first place. It is possible that he simply felt it to be grammatically unwieldy to continue to apply the plural, here, as manuscripts **B** and **C** do – which might indicate either personal preference, or the natural tendency of a particular dialect. Given the *schulde/myght* variation, however, we must also consider whether all of the variations in this section are connected, all of them combining to affect the sense and emphasis of the passage.

The knowledge that the scribe of **A** was capable of such alterations for sense requires us to look more closely at his use of *drede* for *fridlayke/ferdlayke*. Where we find questions like this, one of the soundest methods of investigating further is to find out whether or not the scribe has used the discarded word elsewhere – that is, if it can be determined that he has used some form of *fridlayke* in the manuscript, one can probably assume that his objection to it here is not an objection to the word itself, but to its application in this particular context (notwithstanding the possibility that the scribe may have failed to spot any occurrences of the word later on, or changed his opinion of its suitability). This could suggest that the word had a narrower meaning in the dialect of **A** than in that of **B** and **C,** such that it could not be used in this instance; perhaps that he felt *drede* to better convey the required meaning, as he understood it. However, in this instance, informed scans of the manuscript based upon the appearance of *ferdlayk* in **C** did not find any appearances of *ferdlayk* in **A,** or indeed in **D,** a scribe still more inclined to exercise some authority over his text. As such, it is simplest to assume that this is some sort of straightforward dialectal variation, where the word *fridlayke* would not be used by the scribe of **A** or of **D.**

Overwhelmingly, the instances of lexical variation are determined to occur in the **D** manuscript. In Book IV, just prior, in **B** and **C,** to the first of many Latin quotations omitted by Scribe **D,** we find:

'Als says a gret clerk þus shortly
In a buke of þe payns of purgatory.

The above is Scribe **B's** version, from which Scribe **C** differs only in minor questions of orthography. In **D,** however, we see instead:

Als says a grete clerke þus sleghly...

Again, this is the sort of lexical variation that could not have been detected using only a questionnaire comparing word-forms, and it is an interesting substitution. The *MED* (2000 – 2018) tells us that *shortly,* in this context, has the following possible meanings:

(b) briefly, in few words; concisely, in abridged form;

(c) to put it briefly or concisely, in short

The word is of OE derivation. It is not, by any means, an uncommon word: it is found in everything from Chaucer to Rolle's Psalter and the *Cursor Mundi,* transcending the divide between the language of NME and its more southerly counterparts.

Sleghly, meanwhile, is of Old Norse derivation, and has the possible meanings of '(a) Of workmanship, technique, treatment, etc: skilful, careful; (b) cleverly made, written, or said; well-wrought; effective; of a reflection: artfully contrived, ingenious; **wordes** ~, wise words' (*MED,* 2000 – 2018). Again, this word is found in manuscripts localisable to all areas of the country, and its Old Norse origin does not appear to have made it more popularly used in the NME region.

The reasons for this lexical substitution, then, are rather unclear. It does not seem likely that there could have been any dialectal motivation behind it; nor, truthfully, is there any great change in content occasioned by the substitution. It is true that *sleghly* is nuanced more towards congratulating the cited scribe's skill, and thus emphasising the pithy nature of the quoted saying; but contrarily, the *MED* (2000 – 2018) also notes that 'wordes slegh' could connote 'deceptive language', with *slegh* carrying overtones of 'cunning, crafty, sly'. Evidently, this is not what the scribe intended to suggest in this instance, but it seems strange that he should have made a substitution which could invite such an interpretation for the sake of attempting to highlight the usefulness of a quotation that is surely already underlined as relevant through the sheer fact of its being cited here.

A possible explanation might be that this word, in Scribe **D's** exemplar, was partially obliterated by damage, or written semi-illegibly, for whatever reason. *Sleghly* is approximately the same length as *shortly*, and begins and ends with the same letters. Each word contains a long upstroke after the initial 's', and another before the final 'ly'. As such, substitution of one word for another could not have been occasioned by any attempt to improve metre or rhyme; it is conceivable, though, that one word could have been misread as another. If Scribe **D** were faced with a semi-illegible *shortly*, it is perfectly possible that he may have guessed from the context that the word intended was *sleghly*. The words are so similar to each other – in length, meaning in this context, cross-dialectal frequency, and physical appearance on the page – that there really does not seem to be any other reason for the scribe to have substituted one for another, except through pure accident. It is possible, of course, that Scribe **D** did choose to substitute *sleghly* in some attempt to improve the meaning or style of the sentence: we cannot determine for certain that he did not. But it is important to recognise that, although we do know that Scribe **D** has a tendency towards stylistically-motivated alterations, we need not, and cannot, posit this as the reason behind every non-dialectally-motivated substitution. Scribes misread, make errors, and struggle with difficult exemplars, and where there is no obvious reason behind substitutions such as this one, we need not assume that the variation is of consequence.

Line-by-line comparison of texts, however, and analysis of scribal habits and motivations, enable us to make these sorts of determinations on a case-by-case basis, equipped with information about scribe and manuscript. Without this level of manuscript study, it is impossible to suggest whether any instance of lexical variation is of any more consequence than another, whereas, having compared the usage of these scribes against one another, we now know more about the behavioural tendencies and apparent concerns of each scribe. This, in turn, provides information about the possible differences in training between each scribe, which can help illuminate the circumstances in which the scribes were working. Where textual evidence is useful on its own, however, it is still more so when viewed in conjunction with extra-textual manuscript evidence, which can aid us in setting the scribes and their languages in context, connecting language variation to sociolinguistic circumstance and, potentially, place. Consequently, we will now assess the codicological evidence of the manuscripts.

CHAPTER 5

Codicological Evidence and Sociolinguistic Contexts

It is sometimes tempting to envision the medieval writing community, a place largely without named authors, in the same way that Graham Pollard (1970, pp. 193 – 2018) described the fifteenth-century book-binding community: 'a strange world...it has no real people in it...it lacks the coordinates of place and time.' And yet, as this study has noted, this view of the medieval world as an anonymous place, driven by the anonymity of its manuscripts, is not one that can be maintained if texts are to be fully explored and understood. It is not only the key base manuscripts and their texts that are important, but also the men (or women) who wrote them. The manuscripts are physical, rather than purely theoretical or textual, witnesses, produced in real places by real people. Language is a product of these people and their circumstances, and one of the major concerns of this study is with the influence scribes could and did have upon the texts they copied. The more we know of scribes' sociolinguistic circumstances, the more data is available to us in analysing and explaining the linguistic variation, and differences in textual transmission and behaviour, we have seen.

The size, composition and other features of a manuscript can suggest a great deal about the scribe, or scribes, who wrote it, their places of origin, their training, and their motivation for writing. Three of the four core manuscripts used for this study are modestly-sized books of religious texts without illustrations. Close investigation of the codicological evidence and scribal behaviour, however, suggests a number of notable differences in the manuscripts' methods of production. Knowledge of these differences enables us to infer provenance and, to some extent, intended audience. The basic manuscript descriptions can be found in Chapter Two. Codicological examination of these manuscripts, however, can point us towards a number of inferences.

5.1. Codicological review of manuscripts

MS A: Oxford, Bodleian Library, Rawlinson C. 891

To briefly summarise the features of this manuscript: it is parchment, in double columns, written in four hands. All write in anglicana with the exception of Hand 3, the A scribe, who writes in textura and whose dialect is identified by *LALME* as of the West Riding of Yorkshire. Hand 1 writes in a North East Midlands dialect, Hand 2 central Midlands, and 4 a mixed dialect with Fenland features. The manuscript contains an incomplete *Pricke of Conscience*, Richard Maydestone's paraphrase of Psalm 51, and annals of England to 1377. The book shows evidence of revision, notation and correction, and Lewis and McIntosh (1982, p. 111) feel that the book must have made use of at least two exemplars for the *Pricke of Conscience* text.

Our primary question here is to ask why there should be four hands, each writing in a different dialect, within the same manuscript. Why might a manuscript be passed around from a North East Midlands, to a Central Midlands, to a 'fully Northern' hand, to be concluded by one that is 'dialectally very mixed but with a strong Fenland ingredient' (Ibid., p. 112)? De Hamel (1992, p. 35) points out that 'there was evidently a surprising amount of travel between one monastery and another, and a great deal of carrying about of manuscripts' usually for the purposes of providing scribes with exemplars to copy. Parkes, in his discussion of student copying of manuscripts, identifies a number of known instances of manuscripts being transported from one place to another for the purpose of copying. Durham Priory, for example, appears to have sent two fourteenth century manuscripts to Oxford to be copied – namely, Durham Cathedral, B II 19 and B II 28, copies made from Durham Cathedral B IV 8 (minor works of Augustine) and B II 26 (Augustine's *De Trinitate*) respectively (Parkes, 1991, p. 301). These are Latin works, but there is no reason to assume English manuscripts were not transported in the same way, to be used for exemplars. Parkes also identifies New College, MS 116 (Aquinas, *in I Sententiarum*) as having been copied on Oxford parchment from an exemplar in forty-one *peciae* apparently produced by the *pecia* system in Paris, suggesting that this manuscript, too, travelled for copying. Equally, it is possible that the manuscript remained in one place, accessed by a succession of scribes who travelled to work on it.

The main hand, **A** (Hand 3), is highly competent, as are the corrections throughout this section, apparently written in either Hand 1 or Hand 2. Lewis and McIntosh (1982) note – and this, as will be discussed later, is borne out through the codicological evidence – that Hands 1 and 2 must have been working from a different exemplar from Hand 3. Hand 4 copies a text which exists in no other manuscript, so we can make no comment on its possible exemplar.

When we look closely at the codicological evidence of this manuscript, we find more evidence in the construction of the book itself as to its means and order of production. It appears that Hand 3, the *Pricke of Conscience* section, was the first written, despite its position in the middle of the manuscript. This section of the manuscript is in the hand of a competent scribe. Indeed, it is very neatly and scrupulously written, showing evidence of careful planning with its perfect quires of eight folios, clean textura script and use of catchwords at the end of each quire. More notably still, the folios are signed: ai, aii, aii, bi, bii, etc. These signatures exist so that the quires would not be mis-ordered, but moreover, the fact that they begin at 'a' suggests that this was, at the time of writing, the beginning of the manuscript. Hands 1 and 2 are written on parchment of a slightly different size from the folios in the Hand 3 section, and contain a fly half-sheet and a stub, evidence of new material being slotted in as best as could be managed.

The Hand 4 section, similarly, is clearly not part of the same production process as the Hand 3 part of the manuscript, if only because the quiring is so different. In this section, we find Quire 16 to contain 10 folios; Quire 17 contains seven, plus two cut pages; Quire 18 is a quire of 5, of which two of the pages have been cut. Evidently, these pages, too, have been added later by a different person. This was not a book put together by one person and then passed around several dialectally variant scribes to write in for training purposes. This was a book put together over a period of time, with new pages added in different ways and according to different customs on every occasion.

Transportation of the book from one centre to another might serve to explain the change in exemplars, as a second institution would have meant a second copy of the *Pricke of Conscience*. In this instance, however, it seems more likely that the main section was copied first from a *Pricke of Conscience* text that only began with Book IV. While the scribe must have known this was not the beginning of the entire text – it is, after all, labelled 'Book IV' – we might assume that no copy of the earlier part of the text was available to him at this time. At a later juncture, then, in this scenario, the owner of the book decided to have the earlier sections of the poem added, presumably because an exemplar containing this part of the poem was now available to him where it had not been before. It could be that the initial exemplar was the second volume – beginning with Book IV – of a copy of the *Pricke of Conscience* in two volumes, where the first volume was not at that time available. Potentially, whoever chose to have the first half of the poem added to this manuscript was not the original owner. The A scribe may have copied the first half of the poem, too, in a separate volume now lost. Either way, it seems most probable that the Prologue – Book III segment of the manuscript came to join the book, rather than the book being transported somewhere and then added to.

Lewis and McIntosh were unable to find any markings or suggestions of names anywhere in the text that might help us to determine to whom this book belonged, or for what purpose it was written. However, I was able to identify the name 'Thome Whyttes', apparently as part of an obituary, written among the final leaves of the book, along with a date: mcccxxii, or 1322. I could not find any record of this person in the National Archive (www.nationalarchives.gov.uk).

B: Oxford, Bodleian Library, Rawlinson poetry 175

In brief: another parchment manuscript in two extremely consistent, almost identical, 'fully Northern' hands. The first hand, B, copies the *Pricke of Conscience*. The remaining items are copied by Scribe B2. The dialect was localised by *LALME* to the North Riding of Yorkshire, although based on an extremely small tranche. Latin quotations are in red ink; black ink has in some places rubbed off, indicating heavy use. The book is very neat and regular, evidently written all at the same time by one person whose materials were all readily available to him. The manuscript contains eleven items in English and Latin, including 'Passiones Jesu Christi', 'The Book of

Penance', 'The Gast of Gy', *The Seven Sages of Rome,* and some other, shorter religious pieces.

This book may well have been produced for the personal use of a clergyman of some kind, either commissioned by an individual or simply one of several similar books produced by a production house of some sort, for general clerical use. Likewise, it may simply have been produced for pious lay use. The level of skill and professionalism with which the materials have been pre-gathered and the texts written suggests a practised production centre. The *Pricke of Conscience* contains no other hands, and few corrections, suggesting that the scribe was used to copying parts of similar collections of texts and was experienced enough not to require his work to be checked over by a colleague. That the scribe was very efficiently trained in consistent language usage and transformation of texts is evidenced by the incredible similarity of both language and hand between Hands 1 (B) and 2 (B2) in this manuscript, a consistency of feature and presentation which continues into MS B2, a second copy of the *Pricke of Conscience* in this same language variety. Unfortunately this does not help us to determine whether or not Scribe B was of monastic origin, as skilled and experienced scribes, used to copying large collections of texts, could have originated equally from monastic houses or from lay production centres.

The manner of copying, however, may be of some use to us here. The manuscript is written in double columns, with pricking at external margins and catchwords at the end of quires, lending further evidence to the theory that it was produced by skilled and practised scribes, probably within some kind of production centre, rather than as an amateur production. This theory is further substantiated by comparison of the scribe's language usage in the B manuscript to that in B2, which is a larger and more impressive manuscript, very neatly and professionally written, and consistent in its language features with B. Evidently, then, these scribes are no home copyists. Rather, we might place these scribes in some sort of commercial centre. The fact that we have two existing copies of the *Pricke of Conscience,* one by Scribe B and one by B2, in an identical hand and language, suggest that both these scribes, between whom there is a demonstrable connection, may well have copied more. Both B and B2 are placed in Group I by Lewis and McIntosh, but the varying content and structure of the poem in each manuscript suggests the use of more than one exemplar. The existence of these two professional copies of the same text, by scribes apparently trained and working in the same centre, demonstrates the existence, in real terms, of some form of commercial copying of the *Pricke of Conscience*. This begins to illuminate a network of *Pricke of Conscience* copying, beyond the idea of its dissemination simply between households and amateur scribes seeking their own copies of the text.

Edwards and Pearsall (1989, p. 257) suggest that 'although firm evidence is lacking, it seems reasonable to assume that the texts of the South English Legendary, the Northern Homily Cycle and the Prick of Conscience made before 1400 were mostly done in religious houses.' Certainly, vigorous activity did continue in monasteries throughout this period with regard to book production, as is implied by the existence of the Vernon manuscript (Bodleian MS English Poetry a.I) 'with its vast range of texts and access to exemplars' (Pearsall, 1989, p.3). However, the evidence of scribes B and B2 does not necessarily point to this conclusion. From the thirteenth century, more and more manuscripts were being produced in university towns and large urban centres, increasing the likelihood that one or several of this study's core manuscripts may have been produced outside of the traditional monastic setting. Denholm-Young (1954, p. 46) states that 'from perhaps the second half of the thirteenth century monasteries were ceasing ... to produce their own manuscripts', preferring to purchase their books, like everybody else, from the secular production centres that were springing up to satisfy the needs of the ever-growing literate public, and Doyle (1989, p. 111, 116, 119) notes that religious 'authors were not necessarily over-concerned with reaching a large audience, as we tend to assume they must have been', with 'a very large amount of writing by religious [...] limited in audience or readership to the immediate brethren or pastorate of the authors, and to their successors through the inheritance of their manuscripts.' Evidence for monastic use of commercial book producers can be found in many of the sixty manuscripts of the *Mirrour of the Life of Christ* based on the psuedo-Bonaventuran *Meditationes Vite Christi* by Nicholas Love, first prior of Mountgrace Charterhouse. Friedman (1195, p. 31) notes that this decline in monastic production was particularly evident in the north of England, where very few accomplished scribes can be attested at work in any monastery with the exception of Durham Priory by the mid fourteenth century.

Documentary evidence for urban centres and physical evidence of surviving books indicates clearly the amount of manuscript production that happened outside of monasteries throughout the Middle Ages. We find peripatetic artists, scriveners, editors and illustrators travelling between numerous centres in this period (Michael, 2008, p. 169). Although this evidence is rather scanty, Michael notes that it is certainly sufficient 'to suggest that lay centres of book production grew around the emerging university centres, first at Oxford in the late twelfth century and a little later, less actively, at Cambridge, but also around the law courts of London and St Paul's Cathedral' (Ibid., p. 169).

Documents indicate the existence of a large number of scribes and illuminators living in Catte Street, beginning in the thirteenth century and continuing until the fifteenth – an Oxford charter of 1355 records 'the necessity for taxing scribes, illuminators and parchment makers', indicating the extent to which the trade was thriving at this time (Ibid., p. 180). A contemporary parallel can be drawn with London where we see documents to suggest a community of artisans existing near Fleet Street around 1200. However, it is clear 'that the law courts and schools of London did not create the same intellectual climate as that found in Paris and Bologna, or, in the case of England, at Oxford' (Ibid., p. 175). Christianson (1989, p. 99) has identified 'at least 254 citizens who were professional manuscript book craftsmen and stationers at work in London between 1300 and 1520', but, notably, almost all of the recorded payments to London stationers 'involved service to royal commissions, schools, churches or civic and governmental accounts'. As such, we might infer that the London book trade, although clearly large, had more of a legal bent than was found in Oxford, where the primary stimulus was the University.

Intriguingly, the quires in B are all twelve folios long, with the exception of the tenth and final quire, which is 13 folios, plus four stubs and one end leaf. This use of the twelve-folio quire is unusual, with an eight-folio quire far more common, and is especially significant because B2 also has twelve-folio quires, lending further credence to the idea that these manuscripts were produced in the same place.Da Rold (2014, p. 114) notes that 'research into English medieval literary manuscripts is frequently hamstrung by lack of evidence about their place of production', where features beyond dialect, hand and annotations are rarely taken into account.

However, da Rold has identified the twelve-folio quire as a feature which can indicate much about the production of a manuscript. She indicates that several manuscripts with an Oxford origin, produced after the middle of the thirteenth century, are made up of twelve leaves. This need not, of course, localise these particular manuscripts B and B2 to Oxford; Doyle (2008, pp. 246 – 50) notes that Neil Ker recorded this practice becoming more widespread towards the end of the thirteenth century. However, given the suggestions that the manuscript was produced in a commercial centre, and given what we know of book production in Oxford at this time, it would not be out of the question for the B scribe to have been based in a large and thriving centre of production such as Oxford, London, or York, rather than in a rural setting.

This manuscript does contain a name at the top of f.1: 'Thomas Gyll'. Lewis and McIntosh (1982, p. 116) suggest that this person 'may have been a chantry priest somewhere in Yorkshire in the early 15th century'. However, they offer no evidence for this claim. Thomas Gyll is an extremely common name in this period, according to the National Archive (www.nationalarchives.gov.uk), found as far apart as Devon and Yorkshire. If the claim is true, it could suggest that the book may have been produced for the use of clergymen, but it goes no further towards telling us who produced the book or where. A simple collection of religious texts of this sort might have had a great number of uses. It could have been produced for the use of a monastery, either for the use of the monks directly or as a means of educating the local populace. It may have been produced to be used in this pastoral way by clergymen, rather than by monks, or indeed for the personal study of either a clergyman or a pious layman. The fact that the book does not contain any romances or other non-devotional texts does not stand against the idea of its being one of a run of commercially-produced books for general consumption. Many books of this kind 'maintained a bias towards religious material' (Boffey and Thompson, 1989, pp. 279 – 80), and the *Pricke of Conscience* was enormously popular, to judge by the number of manuscripts that remain to us. Evidently, this was a poem in demand by more than simply clergymen and monks, and the ubiquitous nature of it within the literate world of medieval England makes it still more difficult for us to determine where, or for whom, this book was produced, based on content alone. It is for this reason that examination of specific codicological features can be helpful in establishing the sociolinguistic circumstances in which the scribe was writing.

MS C: British Library, Cotton Galba E i.x

This is a large manuscript that formed the base text for most of Morris's edition. It is a poetry collection rather than selection of religious texts. Its original parchment sheets are fused onto newer vellum ones. Written in textura, in double columns, the manuscript contains six hands, all Northern or North-east Midlands, of which the fifth, the *Pricke of Conscience* scribe, is Scribe C. Its only known owner was Robert Cotton, but we see the name 'Richard Chawser' noted three times in modern hand on the last folio. The texts contain little decoration, other than ornate blue capitals, picked in red. The texts contain no corrections other than minor ones in the main hand of each segment. Interestingly, Ralph Hanna and Sarah Wood believe this manuscript to be descended from the same exemplar as B2, although, given that both exemplars and scribes were capable of journeying from place to place for copying, this need not indicate any strong connection between the two manuscripts.

The book contains: eleven poems attributed to Laurence Minot; the Arthurian romance *Ywaine and Gawayne;* and *The Prophecy of the Six Kings to Follow King John* (*The Prophecies of Merlin*) as well as three devotional pieces found elsewhere in the *Cursor Mundi*. It also contains some more popular and widely disseminated poems: *The Sevyn Sages of Rome*, the apocryphal *Gospel of Nicodemus*, and, of course, the *Pricke of Conscience*. Osberg (1996, p. 2) notes:

> In this aggregate of romance narrative, political prophecy, and devotional material, with its notes on horses and inventory of linen, Cotton Galba E.ix resembles "household miscellanies" like National Library of Scotland Advocates MS 19.3.1 (perhaps owned by the Sherbrooke family) – single-volume libraries that provided information, devotional materials, and entertainment for the instruction and recreation of the family.

Certainly, the content of the manuscript is in accordance with what one would expect to find in a household miscellany, with the *Pricke of Conscience* alongside not only other devotional material, but also romance and pragmatic material.

There are strong indications that this book was produced professionally for the everyday use of a family or household, with the *Pricke of Conscience* forming part of a general arrangement of texts felt to satisfy the requirements of ordinary laypeople in both their devotional and recreational lives. As we know, the *Pricke of Conscience* was a popular and oft-copied text, so it is not surprising that it should have been included in a miscellany as a text that a family might think important, or desirable, to have as part of a book meant to fulfil many literary needs. The changes in hands, in particular, given that the hands never switch in the middle of a text, suggest a sophisticated system of production by experienced scribes, probably in a lay centre. A scribe very familiar with copying *Ywain and Gawaine* would have copied this poem, and any others with which he was well acquainted; other scribes might then have copied their own particular texts on separate quires, with all the quires brought together after everything had been copied and arranged, by a compiler or bookseller, into the order we now find them in. This would also serve to explain why this copy of the *Pricke of Conscience* is so clean a text: the scribe had probably copied it a great many times before, and was thus unlikely to make many errors.

This idea also underlines a number of salient points about Scribe C and his method of copying. As discussed earlier in the thesis, Scribe C has never appeared to be a great revising scribe like Scribe D, from study of the texts themselves; if he has copied the text a great many times, it may be that he copies literatim from a familiar exemplar, or simply has no interest in revision, given that his commission is simply to copy the presented exemplar. Furthermore, the poem's popularity makes it fairly likely that even the original exemplar with which the scribe was working may well have been in a dialect very close to, or identical with, the scribe's own in the first instance. Certainly, there would be no benefit in producing a household miscellany in a dialect that would not be generally understood by lay people, making it more likely that code switches were made at some point, where necessary, to ensure that most of the poem shared an active repertoire with the people for whom it was written, but not necessarily by this scribe.

MS D: Wellesley, Massachusetts, Wellesley College Library, 8

Similar in size to A and B, this manuscript is, unlike them, written on paper. Lyall (1989, p. 12) writes that data evidence from the catalogues of Andrew Watson and Neil Ker's *Medieval Manuscripts in British Libraries* indicates that 'the use of paper was very rare (but not entirely unknown) about the turn of the fifteenth century, that the proportion of all manuscripts written on paper rose to about 20 percent by about 1450, and that it had reached 50 percent or more by the final decades of the century.' Notably, 'liturgical manuscripts[...]continued to be written on parchment throughout the period', and Lyall notes that only three of the manuscripts of the *Pricke of Conscience* from before 1450 are written on paper, although he feels that the reasoning behind this is purely chronological.

The *Pricke of Conscience* is in Anglicana, in single columns; the manuscript is paginated rather than foliated, and contains occasional catchwords. The quires are of eight. The book contains, as well as the *Pricke of Conscience*, the *Stimulus Consciencie Minor*, a thanksgiving to Christ attributed to Richard Rolle, and the latter part of *The Book of Penance*.[1] Scribe D makes a great attempt to excise the Latin from the manuscript, so there is rather less red ink here than in A and B, as most of the Latin quotations are omitted, although there are brief running Latin titles. The manuscript shows occasional interlinear corrections, but these are in the main hand, so do not suggest that the manuscript was written by a trainee scribe being corrected by a more experienced one. Again, this is a book of devotional poems, indicating that it may have been written for the personal use of a clergyman or common pious layperson. The book's modest size and lack of decoration might suggest this, rather than that it was commissioned by a pious nobleman. It is possible, of course, that it was simply produced cheaply by a lay organisation for general consumption, but the particular collection of poems we see here is not a common arrangement, and there is no evidence that more than any other identical collections were produced. Moreover, the single-column arrangement is unusual, and the hand irregular compared to those in the other manuscripts.

---

[1] For more information on the rather obscure *Book of Penance*, see Trudel (2005).

This book also contains a name inscription: 'Iste liber constat Ricardo Gardner', on p. 247 of the manuscript. This is, however, written in a later, fifteenth-century hand. On p. 248, we find another name in a still later (sixteenth-century) hand, 'Wylliam Hotterbrim'. These names, particularly given that they are far later in date than the original, early fourteenth-century hand, do not help us greatly. On page 252 of the manuscript, we find the name 'Skeibey' and the date 1534. Lewis and McIntosh (1982, p. 129) suggest that this refers to Skeeby, near Richmond in the North Riding of Yorkshire. It is tempting to leap upon this as evidence that the manuscript was written in this area, its dialect therefore localisable to the North Riding. It must be remembered, however, that books, like scribes, can travel easily across great distances, and the fact that the book may have been in Skeeby a century after it was written does not tell us much about its provenance, or the provenance of Scribe D. Likewise, the fact that Hanna and Wood (2013, p. xxv) have posited that there are Vale of York features in the scribe's language does not mean that the book was actually produced in this area. Certainly, the book may never have moved very far from the area in which it was created, but we cannot be sure of this, and there is an ever-present danger in scholars connecting a dialect falsely to a scribbled place name. In such cases, it is usually advisable to be cautious.

5.2. Scribal training and education: linguistic and orthographical features and what they indicate

As has become abundantly clear over the course of this study, it is the **D** manuscript that shows the highest frequency of orthographical preferences specific to itself, not shared by any of our other scribes. The most notable and unusual aspect of the **D** language is its French influenced orthography – which, alongside the scholarly bent of the scribe himself, as demonstrated through his treatment of the text, must surely indicate something about his training and education. The list of Scribe **D**'s French-influenced usages has been enumerated already in Chapter Three, including such things as a preference for longer spellings of words that are otherwise spelled more concisely, without Scribe **D's** penchant for final <e> in every case and for doubled consonants. For example, note the preference for *contryciowne* in **D**, as against *contricion* in **B** and *contricyon* in

C. These orthographical differences enable us to make inferences about the nature of a scribe and his training, the more so when they are examined *en masse* and in conjunction with the other ways in which a scribe's text differs from the other versions of the text we have examined.

However, it is in the graphemic choices a scribe employs that it is easiest to see indications of training and style preferences, be they ideological or part of a house style. One of the notable differences between **D** and our other three scribes is that this manuscript uses the French-influenced <ck>, for which none of the other manuscripts show a preference. In the **D** manuscript, for example, we see *reckenynge,* as opposed to *rekennyng* in **A** and **C**. <k> in itself was very rarely used in vernacular script during the OE period, but became much more widespread in ME as a means of representing a verbal plosive, probably encouraged by the Northern French tendency to use <k> before a front vowel, while retaining <c> before consonants and back vowels (Horobin and Smith, 2002, p. 60). Words from Norse, too, often display use of <k>, as in the Northern variant *kirk* for CHURCH. Consequently, we see a considerable amount of usage of <k> in ME texts, but the further development of it into <ck> was a more recent Northern French shift, not so readily or widely adopted in English (Scragg, 1974, pp. 50 – 51).

It is interesting, then, to see such a graphemic choice in a manuscript whose language is very decidedly Northern. We might query why we do not see, instead, orthographical and graphemic choices that show the influence of Norse on the phonology of English in the north of England. Something, it seems, in the training of Scribe **D** has made him more multi-regional in his influences than the other scribes under consideration. It is not only the French influence in **D** that seems out of the ordinary for a manuscript whose language is 'fully Northern'. While no real explanation could be found for the strange doubling of <f> in the **D** manuscript, it is interesting that, as detailed earlier, a very similar pattern can be seen in Oxford, MS. Laud Misc. 581, a *Piers Plowman* manuscript which, though 'certainly produced in London'(Hannah, 2005, p. 42) contains 'South West Worcestershire relict forms' (Hannah, 1993, p. 40) and other language features that can be localised to the West Midlands. Potentially, as I have posited, this could indicate that the <ff> was a West Midlands feature, and that Scribe **D** has therefore come into contact with the West Midlands dialect, either through having spent time in this area or simply through having copied a number of West Midlands manuscripts. We also find this doubled <ff> feature in other West Midlands manuscripts such as Oxford, Bodleian Library, Add. B.107 and Oxford, Bodleian Library, Eng. poet. a.1 (Vernon). Other potential West Midlands features, such as the preference for <y> over <i> spellings and prevalence of <k>, are noted in Chapter Three. The combination of these orthographic factors with what else we have learned about Scribe **D** – his clear scholarly bent; the fact that he is evidently familiar enough with Latin to translate easily into English, rather than simply copying; his tendency to correct and improve upon the texts – set both scribe and language distinctly apart. Scribe **D,** evidently, is a scholar. Part of the reason that the literary world of England had changed so much between the eleventh and fourteenth centuries was the rise of the universities, and it seems logical to consider the possibility that an apparent scholar such as the **D** scribe may have been a university-educated man.

Various sources indicate that West Midlands features are a common anomaly sometimes found in the language of scribes from outside of the relevant dialect area, where the common factor can tentatively be suggested to be an Oxford education. Interestingly, Samuels (1992, p. 5) notes that in many early manuscripts of Chaucer, Gower and Langland, c. 1400, we find 'pronounced western features', even in manuscripts clearly copied in London. He argues that south-west Midlands features differed from Northern features in that where texts have been copied literatim by Northern scribes, we see only 'isolated and sporadic Northern forms', as in Harley 7334 of *The Canterbury Tales*, because the Northern scribes are clearly so conscious of the fact that their usage is not appropriate for London. However, 'the fact that the north-south linguistic divide was recognised as far greater than any of the more gradual and less pronounced differences between east and west' means that 'westerners would feel less obliged to copy literatim', seeing their usage as less noticeably different from the standard, 'hence the very high proportion of western spellings' found in London texts at this time (Ibid., pp. 3 – 5). This may connect to the fact that, while the immigration pattern would not suggest a lot of Westerners moving into London, it is likely that many London scribes may have been educated in Oxford, where they may have picked up on Western features which are now more identifiable to us than they would have been to the London audience (not being radically different from London dialect spellings in the way that Northern spellings would have been). Potentially, we could argue that South West Midlands, or 'Oxford' features, are seen to be fairly acceptable and unobtrusive in any dialect, and that the scribe, if trained in Oxford or that area, whatever his actual origins, would not especially note his own usage of them or regard it as something to watch out for (Ibid., p. 4).

It is not out of the question, then, that Scribe D may have been an Oxford scholar. The potential West Midlands traits could put this scribe in line with a number of others whose languages contain West Midlands features, despite being largely localisable to places outside of the area. Oxford is certainly in the correct vicinity to bring a scribe into contact with West Midlands features, being geographically on the edge of the West Midlands dialect area. It is also the sort of place that might have produced a scholar like scribe D at this time, with his knowledge of Latin and French and his authoritative handling of the text. More importantly still, when we consider in detail the university's history, a number of facts become clear that might indicate that an Oxford connection may have been not only possible, but likely.

We have touched already on the idea that, while monasteries were no longer the primary producers of books in Britain by the time our manuscripts came into being, there are a number of features suggesting that Scribe D may yet have had some kind of monastic connection. His changes to the text betray a high level of education and, at times, an apparent desire to alter the sense of lines slightly, as if to bring them more in line with his own religious interpretations. In the Northern dialect area at this time, the main seats of ecclesiastical power were Durham and York. In *The History of the University of Oxford*, we find the following remarks (Dunbabin, 1984, pp. 565 – 607):

> The founding [...] of Durham College in 1286, followed in 1330 by the ruling of the order's general chapter that two monks from each house should attend a university, focused attention on the poor standard of Benedictine education. Strenuous efforts at improvement were made by some houses in the fourteenth century [...] Since the main justification for Oxford University was that it provided an educated clergy, the part played by Oxford University in raising monastic standards is noteworthy.

Evidently, then, it is quite possible that Scribe **D**, if he was indeed connected to a monastic house, could have been one of those invited to attend the University of Oxford, with the understanding that he would bring back his new knowledge and conventions to enrich his house. Even without a monastic connection, evidence attests a number of Northern men attending a University: Friedman notes that several Popiltons – a Yorkshire family that appears to have produced many scribes – went to Oxford, and that, furthermore, some, such as John de Popilton and Adam de Popilton, then returned to the North (Friedman, 1995, p. 43). Scribe **D's** high levels of scholarly adroitness would certainly support the idea of his having been University educated. However, even if Scribe **D** did not attend the University, this does not mean that he did not derive some manner of education from it nonetheless. According to Dunbabin (1984, p. 601):

> [...] outside the universities and the schools of friars or monks, probably the cheapest way for a cleric to acquire some basic grounding in theology was by attending lectures at his cathedral ... Although other bishops played some part in maintaining these schools, Oxford trained bishops, for example Simon of Ghent and Ralph of Shrewsbury, are conspicuous for their systematic interest, for their insistence that courses should be properly conducted and that the chancellor of the cathedral, on whom the responsibility for organising the school usually fell, should be highly qualified, preferably a doctor of theology or of canon law [...]

Such schools would certainly have operated across the NME region. Dunbabin (Ibid., p. 601) states that Cathedral schools of this kind are known to have operated in York and Lincoln, while probably a great deal more were in existence of which we no longer have sufficient records for proof. If Scribe **D** received an education, either at home or away, from a man who had been trained in Oxford, it is likely that some of the teaching scribe's Oxford-West Midlands features might have found their way into Scribe **D's** dialect – along with French features, a high level of religious understanding, knowledge of Latin, and so forth. There is certainly no reason to deny the idea that the University might have had some influence upon a scholar like Scribe **D**, if only because there are so many ways in which this could have happened during this period.

Dunbabin (Ibid., p. 602) states that, while Oxford's teachers 'wrought no revolution in the standards of clerical education...they undoubtedly helped to raise the general level among both the secular and the regular clergy.' Attending a university was of course not the only way for laymen at this time to acquire learning, provided that they were literate. However, it is true enough that the layman must nevertheless 'often have owed a debt to an Oxford schoolmaster or an Oxford-trained clerkly companion, and more often still have learned his grammar from a textbook written by one such.' In such a textbook, Oxford dialect features, or orthographical preferences, may have been detectable in the English glosses. Laymen learned from men of education, and the facts indicate that many of the best educated men in even the furthest-flung regions of the country would have been educated at Oxford or Cambridge. When we are discussing scribes from within, or close to, the dioceses of Durham and York, this seems still more likely, not least because Oxford had 'a statutory obligation to favour candidates from...Durham' and had also a discernible link with the town of Holderness in South-east Yorkshire (Aston and Faith, 1984, p. 290). This scholarly scribe may have learned his erudition and linguistic skill directly, having been, perhaps, sent to the university in a monastic capacity. If he was, despite his piety and knowledge of scripture, a layman, he might have attended the university independently; or, in either case, he might have been educated in one of the Oxford-influenced Northern dioceses by a man who had himself been educated there. In light of these facts, the idea that Scribe **D** may have been somehow Oxford educated is supported not only by some of his variants, but also by some of what we find in the history of the university.

The other most orthographically divergent scribe is Scribe **A**. Scribe **A** does not seem to have Scribe **D's** knowledge of, or flair for, languages, nor is he so infused with the urge to correct and improve upon his manuscript as he copies. Without overspeculating, however, in considering the usage of Scribe **A,** we do still find graphemic variants not echoed by the other manuscripts, which would seem to indicate some difference in training or practice that would set the scribe's dialect apart from the more similar **B** and **C**. Notably, scribe **A** makes use of *þ* within words, where **B**, **C** and **D** all decline to use this grapheme except within a 'set' of words in which it is acceptable to them. **B, C** and **D** will utilise thorn in the following places: *þe, þase, þa, þam, þai, þair, þare, þan, þogh*. Only **A**, however, ever uses thorn within words that fall outside of this accepted thorn-containing set. Scribe **A** also makes use of the yogh grapheme, ȝ, where **B**, **C** and **D** prefer the straightforward <y> or the combination <yh> in **D** – which could, perhaps, be an indication of some analogy to the Latin <ih> in IHESUS, as posited in my chapter on orthography, supporting the idea of Scribe **D** as a scholar much-exposed to Latin texts.

Scribe **A** also uses <ȝ> in places where **B**, **C** and **D** use no grapheme at all, as in 'ȝif'. While this usage might indicate a pronunciation difference between the dialects, with **A** sounding this word differently as well as spelling it in a way more closely connected to its OE antecedent, it might, too, simply be further evidence of the conservatism of **A**'s style. The old-fashioned nature of the spelling could indicate that the scribe had been trained in a style longer-established, less recently changed and developed, particularly if no pronunciation difference is implied. The large number of graphemes retained by **A** alone would seem to support this, and could perhaps increase the likelihood of **A** having been produced by, perhaps, an older scribe, using an older house style. The hand is clearly highly competent, but the way in which this book was put together, out of order and at different times, suggests that it was not the product of an urban commercial centre, but rather, commissioned by one or more owners of the manuscript who wished to add to it at various points.

5.3. Collating textual and manuscript evidence

Manuscript B

Manuscript B was evidently written all at once, by two identically-trained scribes writing in the same language variety. It was copied either from one exemplar or from a set of materials laid out for inclusion in this manuscript, which were, nevertheless, clearly all readily available to the scribes at the time of writing. The fact that the book has also been heavily worn indicates that it was produced for the daily use of one or several people. It is a very neat manuscript, with pricking at external margins and catchwords at the ends of quires, indicating that it was produced by a very practised scribe, but there are no illustrations, so it would not have been an extremely expensive production.

One of the most notable things about this manuscript's codicology, however, is the size of the quires themselves – unusually, they are twelve folios long, with the exception of the tenth quire, which is thirteen folios, four stubs and one end leaf. The twelve-folio quire is a feature that has been found in a number of manuscripts thought to have been produced in Oxford. Significantly, **B2** also has twelve-folio quires, suggesting that these two scribes were connected to some form of operation, however loose, that produced copies of the *Pricke of Conscience* commercially. As such, although the twelve-folio quire does not necessarily connect it to Oxford in this period, we can surmise that this book was probably produced in a thriving centre of book production, such as a university town. The fact that more than one copy of the *Pricke of Conscience* was produced in this identical Northern dialect, apparently in the same production centre, suggests a greater likelihood that this town was Northern. However, evidence for the commercial production of less elaborate vernacular books in York, for example, is considerably scarcer than in other towns. Michael notes that 'as in London and Oxford, there seems to have been a movement for guild organisation during the fourteenth century, and by 1377 the scriveners, text-writers, limners, tourners, flourishers and noters were incorporated' (Michael, 2008, p. 192). But it is notable that the larger proportion of books produced in York at this time seem to have been luxury liturgical books, such as the Percy Psalter-Hours, the De la Twyere Psalter. John Friedman has noted the large number of Psalters and other Latin texts recorded as having been ordered by the diocese of York in the late fourteenth and fifteenth centuries; that the scribes of these books were not monastic is indicated by their names, and that the books were extremely elaborate is indicated by the number of artisans commissioned for each (Friedman, 1995, p. 35). Many of the scribes based in York appear to have been unusually likely to sign their work in colophons, such that the work of such scribes as Ellerker and Robert de Popultoun – primarily elaborate, primarily in Latin – is known to us. The copies of the *Pricke of Conscience* this survey is based upon are far from luxury editions, although 'the existence of the Hours made c. 1405 – 1415 for the Bolton family[...]suggests that vigorous local production of books for the laity in York continued well into the fifteenth century' (Michael, 2008, p. 192), and luxury books, while the largest proportion of what survives, are unlikely to have been the only ones produced. It is clear that nearly every commercial centre and cathedral town would have needed artisans capable of producing its diocesan service books; the question is simply of which places were more productive than others, and more committed to the production of a wide range of books. Scribes and illuminators did not require large 'workshops' from which to work, although where there was a large demand for books on a regular basis, as in university towns, more permanent relationships between book artisans became established (Ibid., p. 194). But the peripatetic nature of scribes makes it difficult to judge the origins of a book based purely on its language alone, or its codicology. The factors are best considered as a whole.

In this case, it may also be possible that the books were produced by a Northern scribe, in a non-Northern town for Northern customers, either to be transported back to them or because the customers were part of a Northern enclave in the commercial centre. We know of 'a Psalter almost certainly made for the Augustinian nuns of Iona which also, unusually, contains two feasts of St Frideswide; there is every likelihood that it was made in Oxford for the Scottish community' (Michael, 2008, p. 176). Also interesting for our purposes is the fact that texts are known to have travelled from Oxford to the North, particularly via cathedral libraries. At Durham 'they arrived through Durham College Oxford and the donations of men like Alan de Chirden (fellow of Merton College c. 1291 – 1323) and Bishop Robert Greystanes (1333)' (Ibid., p. 181). Alan de Chirden was also vicar of Northallerton, relatively close to Durham. If **B** was produced outside of the Northern area and then travelled north in this way, it might be posited that Scribe **B** copied literatim from Northern exemplars provided, although the consistency of scribal language features between Scribe **B** and Scribe **B2**, and the fact that **B2** and **B** are not exact copies of each other as regards the content and structure of the *Pricke of Conscience,* would seem to stand against this. It is more likely that the **B** scribe consistently transformed whatever exemplars he was given into his own dialect.

Manuscript A

In this study, we have so far paid attention only to the 'fully Northern' hand in this manuscript. However, in taking into account the codicological evidence, it becomes clear that we need to consider the manuscript as a whole in order to make deductions. This includes taking note of the other hands, their dialects, and what this could tell us. To reiterate: Hand 3, the Northern hand, writes the major part of this manuscript. Hand 1 is a North East Midlands hand; Hand 2 central Midlands, and Hand 4 dialectally mixed but, notably, with a 'strong Fenland ingredient' (Lewis and McIntosh, 1982, p. 112).

The beautifully ordered 'fully Northern' section, written by Hand 3, the **A** scribe, was clearly the first part to be written. As discussed earlier, this fact is borne out by the cleanness of the text, the perfect eight-folio quires and their signatures, beginning 'a.i' at the start of Book IV. What comes before in the manuscript, the earlier books of the *Pricke of Conscience* in Midlands dialect, is evidently later material. It might be a logical assumption, then, that the owner – or, at least the first owner – preferred the Northern dialect of the original section; that is, he or she was of Northern origin. As I have noted, it would not have been unusual for later folios to be brought to join the original manuscript, but the dialect changes between Hand 3 and Hands 1 and 2 are interesting – particularly when one considers also the 'Fenland' dialect of Hand 4. While we might posit that the Hands 1&2 sections would not have had to travel too far to join the original manuscript, we know that the manuscript is now in Oxford, so it might be equally plausible that the manuscript itself travelled. This becomes more likely when we note that the later, final section is in a Fenlands hand – perhaps indicating that it had travelled to the Fenlands area, although of course, a scribe from the Fenlands area may have travelled north to add to the book. Interestingly, this manuscript does utilise a feature, *qwo,* attested by *LALME* as belonging solely to East Anglia. As such, the idea that the **A** scribe had a Fenland connection, and had come into contact with East Anglian dialect, seems more likely. Potentially, this scribe may have worked, or been trained, in East Anglia, from which region a large number of illuminated books survive, with rolls and deeds suggesting the existence of scriveners and scribal communities in Norwich, Lincoln and Cambridge

(Ibid., p. 188). The <qw> forms may then have been a concession to the Fenland region in the scribe's repertoire, but given the consistency of the otherwise strongly Northern dialect, it seems more likely that the scribe was copying for a Northern audience, and had simply acquired some East Anglian forms. It is also possible that **A**'s *qwo* is merely natural analogy with his *qwen* and *qwilk,* not unusual in the north, but the East Anglian connection is intriguing. Documentary evidence for Cambridge as a centre of book production at this time is considerably more scanty than it is for Oxford, but what exists does suggest that some form of trade was ongoing there at this period. The accounts of the Bishop of Ely, which document the summoning of scribes from Cambridge to Ely, 'confirm the importance of Cambridge as the major centre from which skills and materials could be brought' within East Anglia (Ibid., p. 189).

We have already discussed the often conservative nature of the language of **A;** the codicology and content of the manuscript, however, seems to rule out the idea of its having been produced in a monastic setting. When we consider the full content of the manuscript and the codicological evidence, it seems quite likely that this manuscript was produced on an ad hoc basis, with its owner (or owners) commissioning new sections as he came to need them.

Manuscript C

This manuscript is a 'household manuscript', or commonplace book. One of the most studied household manuscripts, noted above, is the Auchinleck Manuscript (NLS Adv MS 19.2.1). Like **C,** the Auchinleck manuscript is largely in NME dialects; like **C,** it is a 'household book' containing a mixture of secular and religious material by a number of different scribes (in this case, six) (Shonk, 1985, p. 72). Like **C,** too, the manuscript, while large, is relatively plain and lacking in decoration, and uses English almost exclusively. Potentially, then, much scholarship on the Auchinleck manuscript is applicable here.

In her 1942 analysis, Loomis posited that the Auchinleck manuscript was a product of a London bookshop. This idea was mainly based upon the fact that the romances in the manuscript appear to parallel each other closely, suggesting that the manuscript was conceived as a whole. Later scholars, such as Pearsall, however, have rejected Loomis's idea that the Auchinleck manuscript was conceived as a whole, largely due to some awkward transitions between the scribes' work and variations in format and style (Pearsall, 1979, p. ix). Moreover, there has been widespread objection to the concept of the sort of 'bookshop' she envisions. Scholars such as Pearsall and Edwards have accepted Doyle and Parkes' (1978) conclusions that there is no evidence for this sort of organised scriptorium.

In their study of a manuscript of the *Confessio Amantis* written by five scribes, Cambridge, Trinity College, MS R.3.2, Doyle and Parkes demonstrate that 'the activity of collaboration [...] was so unsystematic and disorganised that it can hardly have taken place on the same premises under supervision' (Doyle and Parks, 1978, p. 199). Rather than assuming a central scriptorium or place of production in a bookshop, they suggest that books such as these may have been ordered by a patron from a bookseller who would then farm out parts of the requested manuscript to various independent scribes for simultaneous copying. Doyle and Parkes (Ibid., p. 199) conclude that there is

> [...] no evidence for centralized, highly organized scriptoria in the metropolis [London] and its environs at this time [c. 1403] other than the various departments of the central administration of government ... We believe it is wrong to assume the existence of scriptoria or workshops without evidence of persistent collaboration.

According to Doyle and Parkes, without evidence of the same scribes' collaboration across two or more manuscripts, one cannot posit a central scriptorium with regular writing staff, of the sort that Loomis is suggesting. The more likely picture appears to be one of a trade in which books are produced to order, where a bookseller or stationer would supervise the production process through the supplying of paper to a commissioned scribe, and subsequent binding of the pages. Edwards and Pearsall (1989, p. 261) note that there is 'no reason to doubt the very high quality of editorial attention given to the preparation of exemplars for copying, whether by the scribe, his employer or literary advisers brought in from outside, in manuscripts like the Ellesemere MS of the *Canterbury Tales* or Huntington MS 137 of *Piers Plowman*, where no question of a "shop" has usually arisen.' However, the picture of book production indicated by the documentary evidence in such centres as Catte Street in Oxford at this time does not rule out the suggestion that some permanently-based scribes did exist, many of whom would have established interactions with each other. As such, whether or not all the parts of a book were produced on the same premises as part of a routine, it might be suggested that stationers and booksellers commissioned the same scribes over and over again.

The differing dialects in the **C** manuscript might support the idea of its production by a number of different scribes known to a central *stationarius* figure – scribes who lived and worked in areas close to the bookseller, but not necessarily all within the same precise region. It might serve to explain why the *Pricke of Conscience* scribe writes in such a clearly 'fully Northern' dialect, while other parts of the manuscript have strong North East Midlands traits. These are dialect regions geographically close enough to each other that a bookseller in a central location might know of an experienced *Ywain and Gawain* scribe in one of them, slightly to the south of him, while his nearest experienced *Pricke of Conscience* scribe was located in a more northerly town. This idea is also supported by the fact that the scribes do not, at any point, share the copying of the same item. In analysing and attempting to localise the dialect of Scribe **C**, I have suggested in earlier chapters that some of the scribe's peculiarities of orthography may be due simply to a house style. Ostensibly, the idea of the **C** manuscript as a product of a bookseller makes it more difficult to posit 'house style' reasonings behind any of the scribe's particular features – until we recall that all of these scribes, whatever their occupations at the time of writing the *Pricke of Conscience,* must have been trained somewhere. The language of Scribe **C** is most similar to that of Scribe **B**, and while the books in which we find their writing is very different, this is not to say that these scribes could not have been trained in similar centres, within the same dialect area, even if their paths later diverged.

Plain manuscripts such as **C** or the Auchinleck manuscript are unlikely to have been produced for the sorts of noble households that commissioned deluxe editions of Chaucer. However, in the era of the ever-expanding middle class, it is fairly probable that **C** may have been produced for 'a wealthy bourgeois public...who could have welcomed or commissioned the...enterprise' (Doyle, 1983, p. 65). As Shonk (1985, p. 90) states of household miscellanies and commonplace books:

If we can accept that an order by a bourgeois client was the likely impetus that put the wheels of production into motion, we must also conclude that the contents of the book were probably established before the copying began – in short, that the whole compilation followed an agreed upon plan. Perhaps the client was seeking a single volume which would fulfil the reading needs of his family and himself, much as people today order collections like The Harvard Classics. He would probably have asked specifically for some of the major romances popular in his day, like those Chaucer pokes fun at in Sir Thopas.

Given the mixed nature of the collection of texts in **C**, many of them fairly popular pieces, some devotional and some for entertainment only, this seems very likely to apply as well to Cotton Galba E i.x as to the Auchinleck manuscript, and, consequently, sets this manuscript aside from the others as definitely emerging out of a literary culture that was not monastic, nor primarily devotional. While the other, smaller manuscripts may be better suited to monastic or clerical use, large household manuscripts such as **C** were very common by this point in time, and while they contained many devotional texts, these texts would probably not have been altered in ways appropriate to any particular spiritual bent. Accordingly, Scribe **C**'s version of the *Pricke of Conscience* shows no special evidence of his motivations or religious orientation, unlike some of what we find in, for example, the production of Scribe **D**, as has been discussed both earlier in this chapter and in previous chapters of this study.

Manuscript D

The codicological evidence for **D** shows us nothing as illuminating as what we can find in this manuscript's textual evidence, but the manuscript itself is still a valuable witness whose physical traits bear out much of what we have suggested above about this book. **D** is similar in size to the **A** and **B** manuscripts; like **A**, it is comprised of quires of eight folios, but unlike **A**, it is paginated rather than foliated, and written on paper. The irregularity of the catchwords indicates that the production was not, perhaps, as neat or practised as that of Hand 3 in the **A** manuscript, or the entirety of **B**. This fact is borne out by the script in **D**, which is less regular and more idiosyncratic. However, the manuscript was evidently written all at one time, by the same scribe, and apparently from one exemplar. While the scribe made changes to the text as he wrote, he appears to have had available to him everything he would need to copy. This supports the idea of his having been associated with a university, where many texts would have been available, if not with some kind of monastic centre.

The manuscript does contain the word 'Skeibey', perhaps a reference to the town of Skeeby, near Richmond in Yorkshire. However, the fact that the manuscript may have been in Skeeby at some point in the sixteenth century – to judge by the date accompanying this inscription – does not make the theory of **D** as Oxford scholar any less plausible. As noted, manuscripts often travelled great distances, and, moreover, we must take into account the connections between Oxford and its Northern properties, notably in Yorkshire. We know that there was sharing of skills between Oxford and Northern centres. For example, 'a Durham copy of the works of Anselm and Augustine was clearly illuminated by an artist who also worked on the Secretum Secretorum' (Michael, 2008, p. 181), a known Oxford manuscript. Consequently, the 'Skeibey' annotation could easily accord with theories earlier proposed about this manuscript.

5.4. Conclusions

This thesis is a study of language in the medieval period, but it is also, fundamentally, a study of the writers and preservers of the dialects we are studying, and the witnesses they left. A survey of the codicological evidence, in its historical context, has proven very useful in cementing some of the ideas the textual evidence had already suggested, as well as suggesting many new ones. Codicological evidence is a vital means of illuminating dialects and their differences, particularly where no anchor texts are available, because it enables us to connect manuscripts and dialects to their possible contexts through other means. Through a combination of orthographical and textual evidence with codicological, we have been able to determine which manuscripts are likely to have been produced in urban centres, which may have university connections, and which appear to have monastic connections or otherwise. Context tells us that, of the Northern monasteries, only Durham is known to have retained a scriptorium at this time, and the codicological evidence of the manuscripts supports the idea that they were probably produced outside of a monastic setting, despite suggestions that the *Pricke of Conscience,* due to its content, may have been mostly a clerical production. Codicological evidence enables us to see which language features within these manuscripts seem to fall in accord with which sociolinguistic contexts. We are not, however, restricted to observation of these connections across the core manuscripts. In order to fully appreciate the data gleaned from these manuscripts, we can also set our findings alongside data taken from the broader context of Northern literary material to determine what patterns arise.

CHAPTER 6

Setting Data in Context

The bulk of this study investigates four manuscripts, **A, B, C** and **D**, using codicological approaches as well as textual study to identify what variation exists and to propose possible reasons for these differences. I have discussed at length why it is useful to base a study on different manuscripts of the same text, which, in this case, becomes a key to unlock much linguistic information. What has now been accrued is a significant basis of new data, demonstrating the considerable flexibility in language across this area, beyond what traditional models of the NME region have suggested. Were we to set these data in context, alongside some basic data from other manuscripts that are similar diachronically and diatopically, it might be possible to determine how far our speculations are supported, or otherwise, and to identify new patterns in the evidence.

This is particularly true where other texts and manuscripts have received more scholarly attention than the *Pricke of Conscience,* or have been more reliably localised to time, place and production centre, enabling us to bring sociolinguistic factors firmly to bear on the question of language variation. Comparing these data could enable us to ask, and answer, further questions: are there, for example, any visible patterns to the language variation we see? Is there any identifiable pattern behind the differing development of dialects across this region? If so, can we correlate it with any of our suppositions concerning the areas of university influence in the North, as at York and Durham? Can we establish a relationship between sociolinguistic setting and rate of language modification? The process of transcription and analysis of **A, B, C** and **D** has resulted in a valuable thumbnail picture of variation within the NME dialect area. Setting it now in its wider context puts us in a better position to illuminate both the larger and the thumbnail picture.

Obviously, it is not feasible at this stage to consider further manuscripts with the same degree of thoroughness afforded to our investigations of **A, B, C** and **D.** As a preliminary option, we might look at *LALME* reports, but we have discussed already why the use of *LALME* is not necessarily adequate for manuscript study in the NME region. However, there do exist editions of other Northern texts from which basic linguistic data can be taken, especially to compare those features which we found to differ most widely across **A, B, C** and **D**. With the addition of further data, we might be able to determine whether our suggestions concerning the language development of **A, B, C** and **D** can be further substantiated, or contradicted, when we have information from outside of the *Pricke of Conscience*.

It would seem untenable and, indeed, inefficient to run the entire questionnaire on these edited manuscripts when **A, B, C** and **D** have already told us which of the items are of greatest use to us in our investigations. In an attempt to find contextual patterns into which those indicated by **A, B, C** and **D** might fit, it is most logical to look for data in those areas where these main manuscripts showed an abundance of variation for comparison. Consequently, in studying these further manuscripts, we will restrict our investigations to the following features:

1. Pronouns
2. Question words beginning 'wh' in Modern English: WHO, WHAT, WHICH
3. Presence or otherwise of Northern <a> in such items as BOTH, MOST and SO.
4. Present participle endings
5. Grapheme usage with regard to the use or otherwise of þ and ð

The tables below show a selection of representations of each of the above features by the manuscript in question, intended to convey the manuscript's general trends.

In order to be able to apply sociolinguistic approaches to our investigation, it is necessary to consider not only raw linguistic data, but also a brief overview of each text we are studying and what is known of its manuscripts and potential origins.

6.1. The *Northern Homily Cycle*

The first text I have selected as likely to yield useful contextual data is the *Northern Homily Cycle*. The original *Northern Homily Cycle* comprises about 20,000 lines in octosyllabic couplets, and was intended to be a vernacular rendering of the Sunday Gospels for the benefit of laymen who did not understand Latin or French. In subject matter and ostensible purpose, this text is broadly similar to the *Pricke of Conscience,* and therefore is likely to contain many of the same words and language features for comparison. Many of the words I have considered might be common in any text of notable length, but religious texts are particularly likely to yield items such as ANGEL, SOUL and similar.[1] Margaret Deansley believes that the *Northern Homily Cycle* was originally composed in the Durham area, probably by an Austin canon or parish priest (Deansley, 1920, p. 149). Carver (1938, p. 260) believes the author to have been a friar, and argues that the original text of the Cycle, known as *U,* to have been written between January 1295 and July 1306. This would set it diachronically level with **A, B, C** and **D** (Nevanlinna, 1972, p. 2). More recently, Heffernan (1985, p. 296) has corroborated Deansley's view that the author was an Austin canon. The oldest manuscript in the *U* stemma is held to be Edinburgh, Royal College of Physicians (Pref.MS).[2]

Few editions of this work have been undertaken. The two most recent have been Thompson's *Northern Homily Cycle* for TEAMS (2008), and Nevanlinna's edition (1972) of the Expanded Version in MSS Harley 4196 and Cotton Tiberius E. The latter work, although informative on the background and transmission of the Cycle, will not aid us, as it deals with the V version of the Cycle, which consists of manuscripts which have been translated into Midlands dialects.

The original, unexpanded *Northern Homily Cycle,* or *NHC,* survives in sixteen manuscripts, of which only nine are reasonably complete. Thompson's edition is based upon two principal

---

[1] It is also important that the texts considered be all literary in order for comparisons to be viably drawn. See Horobin (2009, , pp. 24–25) for a discussion of how scribes' treatment of literary and non-literary documents may differ and affect the scribe's language. Horobin uses the example of Hengwrt and Ellesemere (CT) and the Petition of the Mercers' Guild of 1386, suggesting that 'as the vernacular began to be used for a variety of different functions, so scribes experimented with the kind of language that was appropriate for these functions.'

[2] Described in Cunningham, Ker and Watson (1977, pp. 539–40).

manuscripts. The first of these is Edinburgh, Royal College of Physicians (Pref.MS), which dates to the early fourteenth century but contains only the Prologue and the first thirteen homilies.[3] Where Edinburgh leaves off, Thompson's online edition (2008) continues with Oxford, Bodleian Library MS Ashmole 42, which 'offers a relatively early, good, and nearly complete text of the entire collection (fols. 216–223 are missing)' (Ibid). Thompson identifies the single hand in this manuscript as dating from the mid-fourteenth century, putting it, potentially, slightly later than **A, B, C** and **D**. The clarity of Thompson's edition as regards which manuscript is in use at which point is beneficial; however, she silently emends þ to <th>, which makes it impossible for full graphemic assessment to be conducted using her edition alone. The other edition of the *NHC*, Small's 1862 publication *English Metrical Homilies of the Fourteenth Century*, takes as its base text the Edinburgh manuscript, but 'the portions wanting are supplied ... by extracts from the Cambridge MS. Gg V.31 and the Ashmolean MS. No. 42' (Small, 1862, pp. ii – iii). However, Small has also silently emended the graphemes and, furthermore, his text gives no indication of which manuscript it is using at any one point, beyond the point where Edinburgh ends. Consequently, data is here taken from Thompson's as the most useful edition for our purposes.

As stated, neither Edinburgh nor Ashmole is thought to be the 'original' version of the text, the oldest in the stemma, of which no record remains. However, both are relatively early and strongly Northern in character; indeed, Thompson (2008) states that she chose to begin with the fragmentary Edinburgh version because of its 'highly distinctive Northern features', as well as because of its tendency to retain a large Latin rubric, as later manuscripts did not.

The editors of *LALME* (1986; 2013) have identified the dialect of the Edinburgh manuscript as generally characteristic of Yorkshire. Ker (Cunningham, Ker and Watson, 1977) indicates that McIntosh specified northwest Yorkshire. With regard to MS Ashmole 42, Sprouse (2003, p. 105) has attempted to pinpoint a precise geographical location and has concluded that the manuscript was copied in the West Riding of Yorkshire, close to the Lancashire border.

---

[3] See Cunningham, Ker and Watson (1977, p. 540).

Thompson (2008) gives a list of typically Northern features which characterise both manuscripts:

1. OE /ɑ:/ is mostly retained, e.g. nan (none), stan (stone), ga (go)
2. Verbs: The suffix -s is used in the third person present tense, both singular and plural: *saise* (he says); *tase* (he takes); *heres* (they hear); *dryves* (they drive). The present participle ends in -*and*: *wonand* (dwelling); *livand* (living). The infinitive normally appears without final -n: will *knawe* (will know); *walde do* (would do). The preterite plural loses its final -*n*: *we herd* (we heard); *we wend* (we thought).
3. Pronouns: Third person feminine singular: *scho* (she); third person nominative plural: *thai* (they); third person accusative plural: *thaim* (them); demonstrative plural pronoun: *thir* (these).
4. Vocabulary: *kirk* (church); *mikil* (much); *swilk* (such); *kythe* (show); *sal, suld* (shall, should); *til* (to).
5. In addition, Edinburgh shows the following unique Northern features:
   1. *qu-* for *wh-*: quat, qua, quil, quen, etc. (Ashmole: what, wha, whil, when, etc.)
   2. Edinburgh also occasionally uses the form *ic* or *ik* for the first person singular pronoun (Ashmole 42 always has *I*).

The *LALME* team appears to have assessed these manuscripts, particularly the Edinburgh MS, more thoroughly than **A, B, C** or **D,** and as noted, several scholars have attempted to localise them through the use of extralinguistic features. This study has demonstrated how far language variation can be usefully analysed without recourse to any firm localisations at all. However, where sound localisations do exist, this is information that can be useful to us, in that it can enable us to explore possible patterns of language variance across the Northern region in relation to known sociolinguistic contexts.

In order to usefully compare Edinburgh's and Ashmole's languages to those of **A, B, C** and **D,** we must compare the specific variant features discussed above. Because Thompson has used the Edinburgh MS for a certain portion of the edition, and then continued with Ashmole from a known point, I have been able to use her edition to collect data for both manuscripts – although, of course, this is not as rigorous a dataset as one which could compare two identical tranches of text, or take several tranches from each manuscript for full accuracy, as is possible with the *Pricke of Conscience* manuscripts.

	Edinburgh, Royal College of Physicians	*Oxford, Bodleian Library MS Ashmole 42*
Present participle	wonand	offirande, gangand
Gerund	biginning, welding	rysinge, fallinge
ANGEL	angel	angel
WH	qua, quat, quen	wha, what, when
<a>	**Consistent <a>** anfald, bathe, haligast, nan, sa	**Consistent <a>** hald, knawe, taken (for TOKEN), tald, wha
Graphology	[Thompson has silently replaced thorn with <th> so we cannot know]	[Thompson has silently replaced thorn with <th> so we cannot know]
Pronouns	Ic/I, thou/thee, he, scho, we, thai	I, thai, he, scho, we, you/yow
Use of I *v*. Y	**Tends to use <i>** blis, bring, mikel, spring, thing	**Uses <y> more than <i> but fairly indiscriminate** childe/child, him/hym, ilka, kith, mylde, servyse, Ynglihsse

As the table demonstrates, both manuscripts conform to 'fully Northern' rules for gerund and participle formation, but Edinburgh uses <qu> where Ashmole gives <wh>. It is interesting that Edinburgh, like **A**, also gives WHO in a <q> form, which *LALME* attests only in East Anglia. Both consistently use <a> for OE /aː/, and we find a greater tendency to spell in <i> in Edinburgh, while

Ashmole tends slightly towards <y>. They both spell ANGEL identically: *angel.* Both use ME *scho*, but Edinburgh, interestingly, shows some usage of 'ic' for I.

6.2. The lyrics of Richard Rolle

The second text to be considered here is the collection of Rolle lyrics found in Cambridge University Library, MS Dd. V. 64. This is a fourteenth-century manuscript, putting it diachronically level with **A, B, C** and **D,** and its lyrics have been edited transparently by Hanna (2007) in the EETS volume *Richard Rolle: Uncollected Prose and Verse,* which will be used here for data collection.

Richard Rolle was a fourteenth-century English hermit and mystic, who has been claimed as the author of a great volume of works. The *Officium et Miracula* tells us that Rolle was born at Thornton in Yorkshire and studied in Oxford under the auspices of the archbishop of Durham, although he left without a degree (Watson, 2007, p. 32). Hanna (1997, p. xiv) believes that his work was composed primarily in the 1340s or thereabouts.

The text comprises a set of seven lyrics on religious themes. The only comparable collection of materials is found in Longleat, Marquess of Bath MS 29 (Lt) (Hannah, 2007, p. lxi), which provides five of the poems found in Dd V. 64. The second and fifth of the seven lyrics in Dd V. 64 are unique to this manuscript. All the poems comprise monorhymed quatrains with lines usually of six stresses. These features, Hanna believes, make these unique poems 'every bit as apt to be Rolle's as those poems the two manuscripts share.'

For Dd V. 64, *LALME* (1986, vol. 1)took its analysis briefly from ff 1 – 4 and then mainly from Horstmann's edition. It claims 'varying language' and does not give a linguistic profile, nor is the manuscript entered on dot maps. As such, we are unable to use *LALME* to further our understanding of this manuscript's language or origins.

Hanna's description of Dd V. 64 is thorough enough that we may use it to help illuminate other findings in the same way that codicological studies of **A, B, C** and **D** have proven useful. Hanna dates the MS to s. xiv ex. It is a vellum manuscript, 184 x 125 mm, and comprises what were originally three separate manuscripts, each foliated individually. The lyrics fall into the third of these, and are written in textura, 26 lines to the page. The scrolls show catchwords, but no signatures.

Hanna (2007, p. xxix) notes *LALME*'s description of the language as 'varying' and notes that 'the variation is certainly among Yorkshire languages', suggesting a possible placement 'just north of Leeds.'

In accordance with our treatment of the previous text, the edited text has been scanned to determine where it fits amongst the other studied manuscripts:

	Cambridge, Dd. V. 64 f.101
Present participle	passande, lastand, cryand, byrnand
Gerund	chaungyng, wonyng, louyng, langyng
ANGEL	awngel, aungel
WH	whilk, when
<a>	alswa, ane, anely, bath, haly, mare, nane, sare, sari, swa, tald
Graphology	No ð. Thorn in similar set positions to those noted in other manuscripts: þe, þat, þow, þai, þam, þis. No thorn in words such as thynk or thyng. 'Oþer' is noted.
Pronouns	þou, þai, he, scho, we, þow
Use of I *v*. Y	begynnes, ill/yll, litell, mikell/mykel/mykele/mykell, pinne/pyne, sithen, synne, til, twynne, wille

The manuscript conforms to 'fully Northern' rules for gerund and participle formation and uses <wh> for WHEN and related items. We see consistent <a> for OE /aː/ and there appears to be no pattern in the use of <i>/<y>. We find two spellings of ANGEL: *aungel* and *awngel*. The pronoun *scho* is used, and we see thorn in the same 'set positions' as noted in **B** and **C**. We also see a notably frequent occurrence of <sch> – in, for example, the form *schort*.

6.3. The epistles of Richard Rolle

For further comparison, I also include a scan of a 'fully Northern' manuscript of Rolle's 'Epistles' or *Forma Viviendi*/The Fourme of

Parfit Liuyng. The Epistles form an anchoritic text, comprising a series of 'letters of instruction' to enclosed women, encouraging them to seek out Christ's presence.[4] The text exists (complete) in three Northern manuscripts: Cambridge. Dd. V. 64 (14th century), Oxford, Bodleian Library, Rawlinson C 285 fol. 40 and London, British Library, Harley 1022, fol. 49 (Ibid., p. xiv). Horstmann's 1862 edition, which I use here, is based upon Cambridge and Rawlinson only.

Rawl. C. 285, according to the editors of *LALME* (Benskin et. al, 1986, vol. 3), consists of two hands: 'Hands A and B, ff. 1 – 39, 69 – 73 (Hand A) and 40 – 68 (B)'. *LALME's* assessment is that, linguistically, the two hands are almost identical. The manuscript is not entered onto dot maps, but it is printed as LP 22. A survey of the linguistic profile indicates that the *LALME* team – who worked partly from Horstmann's edition (Ibid., vol. 1, p. 151) –were unable to find a very great degree of consistency in the orthography. The language of this manuscript, like that of Dd. V. 64, is quite variable, and has been classified by *LALME* (Benskin et. al, 1986, vol 3., p. 661) as NME. Given that *LALME* describes these manuscripts very similarly, it would seem useful to consider how far the two concur or differ.

Hanna (2007, p. 1) describes the Rawlinson manuscript as dating to s. xiv ex. It is a vellum manuscript, 220 x160 mm, in four main hands. The booklet in which the Epistles are contained has two hands and no signatures or catchwords. It is written in anglicana. Hanna does not offer any comment on the language beyond that it is 'pure Northern, probably Yorkshire'.

	Oxford, Rawl. C 285 f. 40
Present participle	lastand, passand
Gerund	schangeyng, wonynge
ANGEL	angel
WH	whilk, when
<a>	alswa, ane, anely, Haly, tald, mare, bath, sari, sal, swa,
Graphology	No ð. Thorn in similar set positions to those noted in other manuscripts: þe, þat, þow, þai, þam, þis. No

---

[4] Ibid., p. xiv.

	Oxford, Rawl. C 285 f. 40
	thorn in words such as thynk or thyng.
Pronouns	he, þou, þai, we, scho
Use of I *v*. Y	bygynnys, ill/ille/yll, litel/litil, sithen, thynk, whilk, wille

The manuscript conforms to 'fully Northern' rules for gerund and participle formation and uses <wh> for WHEN. We find, again, consistent <a> for OE /ɑ:/ and there appears no pattern in the use of <i>/<y>. ANGEL appears as *angel*. The pronoun *scho* is used, and we see thorn in the same 'set positions' as noted in **B** and **C**. As in the above Cambridge manuscript, we also see frequent instances of <sch>.

6.4. Durham Literary Manuscripts

We have discussed the lack of anchor texts for the Northern region, especially north of Yorkshire. The localised texts that are extant, almost all of them non-literary, proved insufficient for the *LALME* team to attempt to plot any NME manuscripts based on linguistic data alone. However, there are two literary texts localised, by internal evidence, to Durham.

The first, London, British Library, Arundel 507, is a religious miscellany in several 14th century hands, 'collected and augmented in English by Richard de Segbrok, monk of Durham, *ca.* 1400' (Benskin et. al, 2013). Friedmann (1995, p.245) concurs that the monk noted as its owner is almost certainly the manuscript's compiler. This is LP 10 in *LALME*. Horstmann notes that it is a small paper manuscript and contains, amongst a variety of Latin and French lyrics, some short ME texts, including two Rolle Lyrics. Its language has not been described except in the *LALME* profile.

The second, London, British Library, Egerton 3309, is a Metrical Life of St Cuthbert, from the library of Lord William Howard, of Castle Howard, County Durham. It is localised to Durham based upon this evidence. Fowler (1889, p. i), the only editor of this text, notes that no other version of this *Life* is known to exist. This is LP 13 in *LALME*. Fowler dates it to around 1450. The manuscript is vellum and written in a single uniform hand.

Fowler describes the language generally as 'Northern' but notes that it contains many Scandinavian forms, such as: *lund, thret, slyke.*

These manuscripts have been selected only because of their unique position as localised literary texts from within the NME region north of Yorkshire; as such, they are examined here, but do not offer as much information as some of the other texts.

	London, Arundel 507
Present participle	wonand
Gerund	comyng
ANGEL	—
WH	ye-whilke, when
<a>	alde, amang, ane, bathe
Graphology	<3> present in 3ow, 3e, etc; also 3ong. No thorn, <y> used in the 'set positions' for thorn in other MSS. No eth.
Pronouns	sche, sho, yai
Use of I *v.* Y	ilk, littil, mikel, think, til, wil

	London, Egerton 3309
Present participle	wonand
Gerund	comyng, singing
ANGEL	---
WH	Þe-whilke, when
<a>	alde, amange, ane, bathe (some 'both')
Graphology	<3> present in 3ow, 3e, etc, also 3ong, 3ere. Thorn present in set positions, for pronouns. No eth.
Pronouns	sho, he, þai, 3ow
Use of I *v.* Y	ilk, sister, sithen (some 'sythen'), syn

There is a considerable degree of consistency between the language of these two manuscripts, supporting the idea of a reasonably consistent Durham dialect – perhaps a specifically clerical or monastic dialect, given the nature of the texts and what is known of their origin. Comparing the two Linguistic Profiles beyond what the above table shows, we can see that both texts use <k> forms for such items as CHURCH, for which both give *kirk,* as does Edinburgh; both also form the past participle in *-id (deid, callid).*

The manuscripts conform to 'fully Northern' rules for gerund and participle formation and use <wh> for WHEN. We find, again, consistent <a> for OE /aː/ except for the occasional deviation in Egerton. It is interesting that Arundel gives *sche* rather than Northern *scho*. Both manuscripts utilise yogh; Arundel uses <y> in place of thorn. <i> is consistently used by Arundel; Egerton prefers <i> to <y>, but employs both.

6.5. Compiled data and its indications about varieties of NME

Given what we know of **A, B, C** and **D** with regard to these features and potential sociolinguistic backgrounds and origins, what kind of pattern, if any, can we identify by comparing these data? It might be useful, first, to present the following table for **A, B, C** and **D,** as an easily legible conflation of previous datasets about those manuscripts.

Conclusion

	A	B
Present Participle	-and, -ande	-and
Gerund	bigynnyng	bigynnyng
ANGEL	angel	aungel
WH	qwo, qwilk	Wha, whilk/whylk
<a>	Qwo, so, both, knawe, mare	Wha, swa, bath, both, knawe, mare
Graphology	þink, þe, base, þa, þam, þai, þair, bare, þan, þogh, erþe – not all words take thorn, but many more than in other ms.	þe, base, þa, þam, þai, þair, bare, þan, þogh, no thorn outside of these words (thynk, etc)
Pronouns	I, He, it, þai, þe, scho, sche	I, He, it, þai, þe, scho
Use of I v. Y	þink, wille, mykel, ilk	Þynk, will, mykell, ilk

158 *Dialect Variation in Northern Middle English*

	C	D
Present Participle	-and	-ande
Gerund	bygynnynge	begynnynge
ANGEL	angel	awngel
WH	Wha, whilk, wilk	Who, whylke
⟨a⟩	Wha, swa, bath, knawe, mare	Who, so, bothe, knawe, mare
Graphology	þe, þase, þa, þam, þai, þair, þare, þan, þogh, no thorn outside of these words (thynk, etc)	þe, þase, þa, þam, þai, þair, þare, þan, þogh, no thorn outside of these words (thynke, etc)
Pronouns	I, He, it, þai, þe, scho	I, He, it, þai, þe, scho
Use of I *v*. Y	þynk, wille, mykel, ilk	þynke, wylle, mykell, ylke

The table above presents us with an intriguing question, closely connected with the traditional perception of NME, and that is the variety of forms of the WHO item. If NME is characterised by continuation of OE /ɑː/ as <a>, then why do we find that two of our four manuscripts spell this item in <o>? This feature is especially notable because, unlike the <q>/<wh> differential, which is more likely to be an orthographic variation only, it could also be phonologically indicative. Like Williamson's findings in his study of present participle endings,[5] this data suggests that there are different dialects within the NME area, evolving independently and at different rates. Further investigation of this region as a home to many different dialects might enable the scholar to determine what sorts of linguistic changes were in progress synchronously within the region, and whether there was a pattern to these changes. Further investigation that incorporates sociolinguistics could subsequently enable us to guess at why the pattern – if one should emerge – is what it is. Having examined this feature in a further four manuscripts across two different texts, however, it is interesting that the pattern we are now finding is that the <o> ending so far only presents in manuscripts of the *Pricke of Conscience,* specifically **A, B** and **D**.

From a sociolinguistic standpoint, we might note that the move into a form in <o>, *who,* in **D** is in accord with the manuscript's use elsewhere of more cosmopolitan forms, suggesting some interaction with and influence from southerly dialects and training. In the fourteenth century, the language of the church was still firmly Latin, representative of its rank within the trilingual society of the time – priests and religious men who attested to the miracles of Thomas of Hereford in 1307, for example, gave testimony exclusively in Latin, while the laity witnessed 70% in English and 30% in French (Richter, 1979, pp. 206 – 17). Training in writing was always connected to the learning of Latin (Morgan and Thomson, 2008, p. 30), even where the medium of teaching Latin was usually Anglo-Norman French, with English unusual. At this time, we see an increase in didactic and religious works written in English, written by scribes who would have been more familiar with writing Latin or French (although Orme (2006, pp. 266 – 67) has suggested that

---

[5] For Williamson (2002), see Chapter One and Chapter Three.

novices in religious orders may have received their earliest instruction in the vernacular). However, Scribe **D**'s extravagant linguistic flourishes suggest an association not only with the Anglo-Norman commonly heard in England, but with the Central French literature entering the country at this time. They are not in accordance with the kind of training that would have been expected of a monastic house. Interestingly, there is evidence that Thomas Sampson, a teacher of grammar in Oxford in the later fourteenth century, taught a form of 'business training' in Oxford, instructing students in the use of French (Ibid., p. 35). Many consider Sampson to have been the writer of the *Orthographica gallica,* a treatise on French vocabulary and word usage (Kibbee, 1991, pp. 47 – 48). This evidence indicates that a university education may, at this time, have had a concentration on Central French and French usage not found elsewhere.

Our codicological investigation of **D,** alongside our assessment of this scribe's scholarly treatment and authoritative handling of the text, plus orthographical peculiarities like the doubled initial <f>, have already pointed us towards a theory that he may have an Oxford connection. If this is the case – and we have demonstrated in Chapter Five why historical context supports, rather than refutes, this supposition, although there is only circumstantial evidence for it – then there might certainly be a connection between this and the use of the more southerly <o> form. The evidence of one manuscript alone cannot be used to support a theory of university education as correlating with developments toward <o> in the NME region, but if we were able to find other manuscripts with similar possible connections and interrogate their language, the hypothesis could be properly sounded. Could it be that <o> emerged earlier in areas that had close ties with a university, as many places in the NME region did?[6]

If this were the case, it might shed some light, too, on the apparently peculiar adoption of final <o> alongside the <q> in the **A** manuscript's form 'qwo'. Across the other manuscripts, what has been noted is a tendency for <q> to appear as <wh> in wh- question words while the <a> ending is retained. The **A** form 'qwo', where the <o> appears alongside <qw>, is therefore anomalous. The

---

[6] See Chapter Five.

codicological evidence does not necessarily suggest a level of university connection for **A,** but it does appear that **A** was some form of highly trained scribe, not a cleric, and probably not the owner of the book. Moreover, the possible East Anglian connection suggested by this <q> form of the item WHO could indicate a connection to book production around the University of Cambridge at this time, the University being the largest non-monastic stimulus of production in this area. **A** – alongside **D** – is the manuscript whose language appears most different from all of the others considered. It could be that the only variation between <a> and <o> is orthographical and not phonological, with scribal training as to how a sound is represented bearing responsibility for the <o> forms we find in some *Pricke of Conscience* manuscripts. If so, this suggestion of a connection between the training of **A** and **D** is an interesting addendum to the hypothesis that Scribe **D** may have had some university connection, as it leads us to query whether the same might be said of **A**. Certainly, if we posit that <o> may have emerged earlier in areas with university ties, it might be likely that **A** was educated in such an area, or through one of Oxford's Northern schools. Notably, however, we do not find <o> in either of the Durham manuscripts described above. This may be because the Durham manuscripts are both traditionally monastic, and had no contact with university outposts in Durham. It may be that the <o>, in combination with the potential West Midlands features in **D** and East Midlands ones in **A,** suggests a more direct university connection, where the scribes are not clerics, but have worked or been trained in one of the university centres themselves, or by somebody who had been trained there.

Both of the manuscripts of *NHC* we have considered here have been localised, tentatively, to Yorkshire, but not to the university town of York. The language of both is fairly conservative and retains strongly Northern features, making consistent use of Northern <a>. Edinburgh also utilises <q> for <wh>. Geographical data alone does not enable us to draw any strong conclusions from this. We might suggest that language development in the NME region perhaps diverged more slowly away from its most characteristic Northern- isms in the vicinity of York, and that **D**, in particular, was perhaps written outside of this area, but there is no real evidence for this. Sociolinguistic considerations, however, point us back again to the origins of these texts and scribes. Scholars agree that *NHC* was a clerical, perhaps friarly, composition: while these manuscripts are not originals, we might infer from the fact that they are so early that a good deal of the original language features may have been retained, and also that they may have been copied within the same environment in which they were first written. Diachronically, these texts are not far removed from **D,** but **D's** language is far more cosmopolitan and, in some ways, advanced in the direction of more southerly language features. This might support the idea that monastic language retained a conservatism that had been lost earlier in non-clerical texts, particularly where the rate of development was altered by outside influence. The two localised Durham texts in many ways do show conservative language and orthography; the nature of the texts and the fact that the first was collated by a monk supports this idea of conservatism of grapheme and form in monastic language.

Examination of the two Rolle manuscripts presented here leads the scholar towards another question. Unlike the *NHC* manuscripts, neither of these has been localised any more accurately than to within the NME area. We know that Rolle himself was from Thornton in Yorkshire, but this is not necessarily reflected in these manuscripts, as they are not, of course, holographic. Attempts to localise manuscripts for the sake of localisation are not especially helpful to this dialect study, but it is interesting to compare how these manuscripts interrelate. While *LALME* lists their language both as 'variable', one can note some interesting points of consistency.

A, B, C and **D**, intriguingly enough, all seem to demonstrate a higher degree of internal consistency than these manuscripts of Rolle, which in their turn are more consistent than the *NHC* manuscripts considered. The table indicates, however, that there is a consistency between Cambr. Dd. V. 64 f.101 and Rawl. C 285 f. 40 when it comes to the question of initial <wh> and the usage of thorn in set positions only. This pattern of usage – where thorn is used in such words as *þai, þaim, þair, þan, þam*, but not *thynk* or *thyng* – is reflected in **B, C** and **D**. Given that Cambr. and Rawl. are not always consistent with their spellings of other words, it is interesting that this consistency exists. It might suggest, that these manuscripts are utilising a language similar to that of **B** and **C**, with similar history of scribal training, but which is developing along a different path, in that <a> for OE /ɑ:/ is still consistently used, although <wh> is used rather than <q> throughout.

In my comparative tables, I included the item ANGEL simply because it had proven so intriguing a word with regard to digraphs and their phonological implications in the original investigation. In **D**, the use of <w> in words such as SOUL (*sawle*) is fairly consistent, but also appears to be a feature associated only with **D**. **B** presents the form *aungels* for ANGELS, and we have discussed, in Chapter Three, the likelihood that this, like *awngels*, was intended to make explicit the fact that this word should be pronounced in the French fashion, rather than in the same way as the English word *angel*, meaning 'fish-hook'. Moreover, we discussed the fact that ANGEL and SOUL are in most cases spelled with the same digraph. The implication is, therefore, that if a manuscript gives *sawle* and *awngel* as **D** does, these two words are intended to be pronounced with the same vowel-sound.

This *awngel* form is very rarely recorded, which in the case of **D** is not hugely surprising – **D** is an often eccentric scribe, with his own sense of correct form and style. What is interesting, however, is that we also find *awngel* in Cambr. Dd. V. 64 f.101. The manuscript also gives *sawle*. We cannot necessarily claim that a form such as *awngel* represents a language's movement towards southerly forms, but it is interesting to find such an unusual form in this manuscript. Seen in accordance with the consistency of this manuscript in its placement of thorn, and with its consistent usage of <wh>, it appears that the language of Cambr Dd. V. 64 f.101 is developing in a different way and under different influences from the *NHC* manuscripts. If the *NHC* manuscripts represent one path for language development in this area, and the **D** manuscript represents a second, diverging from it, then this combination of features might place Cambr. between them, moving along a path that shares behaviours with the progression of both *NHC* and **D**. The Durham manuscripts, meanwhile, are highly consistent in feature, and seem to represent a monastic dialect from this region, forming a language group of their own. Although they, like the *NHC* manuscripts, show a degree of linguistic conservatism, they are clearly distinct in dialect.

Of course, the amount of data we are working with from these additional manuscripts is in no way of equal value to that used for **A, B, C** and **D**. No new transcriptions have been made, nor do we have, in some cases, a full understanding of the orthography of the original text, because the editor has chosen to silently emend. In a study such as this, which has striven to take into account the fact that a written language can exist and have value of its own, unrelated to any spoken dialect, this lack of proper orthographic data is problematic. However, even from this rough dataset, it has been possible to draw some conclusions. We have demonstrated, through our comparisons, that the beginnings of patterns can be seen, even from such a limited amount of data. If we were to place the manuscripts investigated on a map or net, with **D**, as the most cosmopolitan and, perhaps, the most variant from a 'traditional' NME model, at one side of it, we could attempt to place at least some of these other manuscripts around it, based upon their language features, even at this stage. The Edinburgh manuscript of *NHC*, for example, would fall at the opposite end of the net from **D**, with its consistent usage of <a> for <o>, and the occasional 'ic' for 'I', alongside its <q> for <wh>, making it very distinctive. Its <q> is not a traditionally NME feature, but *LALME's* dot maps attest this all over the north and east of England from East Anglia and upwards (Benskin et. al, 2013). Both manuscripts of *Epistles* would fall further across the map towards **D**, with the Cambridge manuscript, as discussed, the closest to the **B, C** group. **A** possesses some interesting variations, rendering it a sort of sub group of its own, but its language still fits somewhere between Edinburgh and **D**. The Durham manuscripts, likewise, possess some interesting variations, such as Arundel's <y> for <th>; like **A**, they utilise fairly conservative graphemes, especially in their use of yogh, and like **A**, they fall somewhere between Edinburgh and **D**, but rather in their own sub-group. They have a number of similarities to the Edinburgh dialect, particularly in their lexical usage, and similarities to **A** based upon orthography, but lack the distinctive <q> orthography of both Edinburgh and **A**. Rather, they appear to exist at a point equidistant from **A**, Edinburgh, and the **B-C** group. If these two manuscripts are representative of a (possibly monastic) Durham language, it does not appear that any of our other manuscripts are of the same origin.

On the forms of WHO in <q> found in both Edinburgh and **A**, the scholar is left considering an interesting question. Forms of WHO in <q> are attested by *LALME* only in East Anglia. The **A** manuscript does have a connection to this region through the language of Hand 4; Edinburgh, however, does not. It is interesting that two of the manuscripts considered by this study should show this feature. Given the consistency with which the manuscripts use these forms, and the internal consistency between the <q> forms of WHO and those of WHICH and WHEN, it seems they need not necessarily connote contamination or *Mischsprachen*. Potentially, this <qw> usage does suggest a connection to Fenland, or Cambridge-based, training or book production; potentially it is simply an analogous form that occurs in Northern manuscripts, but has not yet been attested in any beyond these two due to lack of study. However this <q> feature made its way into these manuscripts, the fact that it is found in two of nine manuscripts studied here is indicative that it is a viable language feature observable within the NME region, as part of consistent scribal usage.

The consistency with which the core scribes examined use their preferred forms, even when those forms deviate from those typically described as characterising NME, is one of the most interesting observations to have emerged from this study. Usage of <o> rather than Northern <a>, or *qwo* for WHO, for example, are, according to the general understanding of NME, 'non-Northern' forms, and a dialect that employs them might then be classified as being itself partly non-Northern – a form of *Mischsprache*. But application of this term, particularly in less-explored areas, is unhelpful. A true *Mischsprache* would comprise two dialects inorganically mixed by one scribe. However, where the variety is the consistent usage of a single scribe, whether or not it contains features that may suggest contact with other areas or specific influences, it remains a viable language variety from within the NME region, and it is dismissive of the witness to treat it as a *Mischsprache*. It is especially important to be cautious when we are dealing with an area so little studied and illuminated. Many of the language forms in use in the Northern region at this time are undocumented: the less data is available about an area, the more likely it is for scholarship to view forms as anomalous, when in fact, as new data is collected, we can see that a much wider degree of variation exists than had previously been held. Rather than assuming that a form used consistently by a scribe renders the language dialectally impure, it is more useful to consider how such a language variety may have emerged and who might have employed it, based upon the evidence.

London English, and the Types into which it has been divided by Samuels (1989, pp. 71-74), provides a useful illustration of this idea. This area has been very thoroughly and effectively studied: a huge amount of data is available about London English, to the extent that several separate London language varieties have been identified -- one of which, Type III, is demarcated by its characteristic Midlands features, showing the influence of immigrants from this area upon the English written in London. Yet this is rightly classified as a viable dialect type, representing the consistent output of a set of scribes, rather than as a *Mischsprache*. Naturally, in order for language change to occur, dialects are influenced by contact with others. In the same way, where we see features in NME dialects that suggest contact with West Midlands, East Midlands, or other southerly dialects, it is not useful to suggest that these are not, therefore, viable NME language features. It is more useful to scholarship to consider instead what these features indicate about the development of these language varieties and the training of the scribes who wrote them. The more data we acquire from this region, the more likely we are to find these features in more manuscripts, where they represent, for example, NME influenced by university contact, or by the book trade. Where a language variety is evidenced in one or more manuscripts as the consistent and organic product of a scribe, the fact that it contains some features not concurrent with Morris's basic description of NME does not render it a *Mischsprache*, but rather a viable variety of NME. Transcriptions of unedited manuscripts, as have been undertaken in this thesis, are particularly important for the purposes of adding more data to what currently exists, such that understanding of the variation attested in the NME area can be increased, and evidence of the range of scribal activity in this area can be clearly seen.

The manuscripts and their dialects, or types, might be sorted into groups that could be presented as follows:

Conclusion

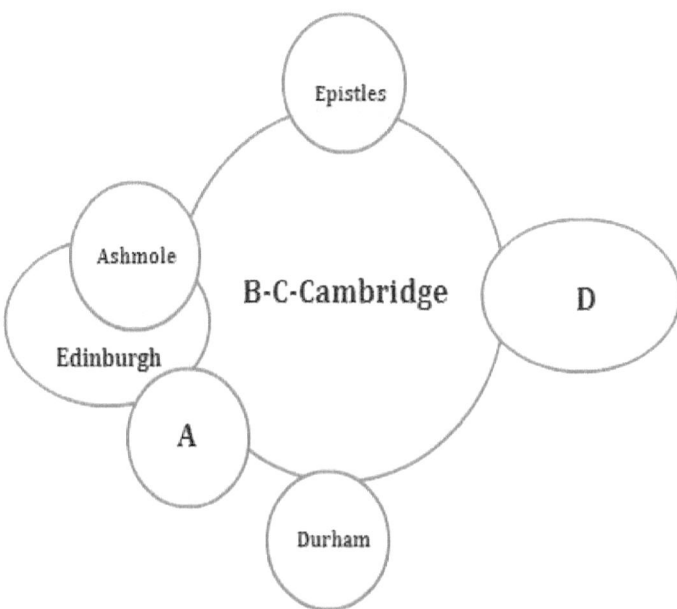

Edinburgh, the group **B-C**-Cambridge, and **D** represent the most distinct language varieties, taking up clear positions with regard to each other, while the language of **A**, with its unusual *o* in the WHO item alongside initial <qw>, and the Epistles with their unusually inconsistent dialect, are harder to categorise. The language of Ashmole is a slight variant on Edinburgh, falling somewhere between it and **B-C**-Cambridge. Of course, further study could reveal there to be other manuscripts very similar linguistically to **A**, making it more obvious why this language type has evolved and, perhaps, where. The Epistles are clearly related linguistically to **B, C** and Cambridge, and could be tentatively assigned to this group, but are less internally consistent. The Durham texts display a degree of graphemic conservatism akin to that of **A**, share a number of features with the **B-C** group, but do not contain the <q> of either Edinburgh or **A**, putting them therefore in their own linguistic group. It is possible, then, to present a set of potential dialects evident in these manuscripts, all of which are 'fully Northern', but have marked and specific variation within this umbrella category.

6.6. Identified varieties and their characteristic features

1. 'Edinburgh', or Variety 1. Retained <a> for OE /aː/; present participle in *–and*. Pronouns: *scho, thai, thaim, ic* alongside I. Initial <qu> for <wh> items. Gerund in *–ing*. Tendency towards <i> rather than <y>. *Angel* for ANGEL. *Qua* for WHO.
    a. Ashmole, as Variety 1 but, significantly, with <wh> items in <wh>. *Wha* for WHO.
2. 'A', or Variety 2. Sometimes <a>, sometimes <o>, approximate 50:50 division. Present participle in *–and(e)*. Pronouns: *scho/sche, pai, paim, I*. Initial <qw> for <wh> items. Gerund in *–yng*, tendency towards <i> rather than <y>. *Angel* for ANGEL. *Qwo* for WHO.
3. B-C-Cambridge, Variety 3. Almost always retained <a> for OE /aː/; present participle in *–and*. Pronouns: *scho, pai, paim, I*. <wh> for <wh> items. Gerund in *–yng(e)*. Indiscriminate <i> v <y>, no clear pattern. Various *aungel/angel/awngel* for ANGEL. *Wha* for WHO. The 'Epistles' fall tentatively into this group but are less internally consistent than B-C-Cambridge. Taking into account Hanna's localisation of Cambridge to 'probably north of Leeds', and *LALME*'s North Riding of Yorkshire localisation for B, it seems probable that this represents a dialect of scribes trained in North Yorkshire.
4. 'Durham', or Variety 4. Consistently retained <a>; present participle in *-and*. Gerund in *-yng*, occasional *-ing*. Pronouns: *sho, sche, pai, yai, ʒow*. Interesting consistent ye/þe before *whilk*. Preference for <i>. *Wha* for WHO.
5. 'D', or Variety 5. 30:20 retained <a> and <o> for OE /aː/. Present participle in *–and*. Pronouns: *scho, pai, paim, I*. <wh> for <wh> items. Gerund always in *–ynge*. Always <y> rather than <i>. *Awngel* for ANGEL. *Who* for WHO.

6.7. Re-assessing *Sir Tristrem* in the context of these varieties

We have discussed in Chapter Two how scholarship upon the language of *Sir Tristrem* has progressed over time. While Walter

Scott originally heralded it as a great Scots poem in his 1804 edition – a supposition based largely upon its presence in the Auchinleck manuscript, mostly comprised of Scots texts – Angus McIntosh argued in 1989 (McIntosh, 1989b, p. 94) that many forms previously thought to be Scots were actually more characteristic of NME. McIntosh noted that it is often difficult to discriminate between Northern and Scots texts, an idea this study supports: interestingly, however, other scholarship on this poem has argued that we cannot even assume a Northern origin at all. Vogel (1941, p. 542) noted that there were many 'anomalous' forms in this poem that deviated from the 'characteristic' Northern norms. He cites, for example, the fact that OE *hw* is always *wh*, never Nth. *qu(h)*, and that *scho* is not found. Given what this study has demonstrated already about the questionable ubiquity of these presumed 'norms', it would seem helpful to interrogate briefly the language of *Sir Tristrem*, too, to determine how removed it is from **A, B, C, D** and the manuscripts described above, and whether it can be placed into a pattern. The more study is conducted in the Northern area, the more accurately we can approach linguistic debates such as this one within their proper context.

This poem differs from all the others we have considered in that it is not a religious lyric, but a romance, found only in the Auchinleck Manuscript (National Library of Scotland Advocates' MS. 19.2.1). This makes it less easy to directly compare, given that there may have been differences in register between these two forms of writing, but the manuscript is generally considered to have been compiled between about 1330 – 1340, placing it, importantly, on a diachronic level with the others we are examining. This means that any conclusions we may draw about linguistic similarities and differences are more likely to be accurate.

'Non-Northern' forms have been isolated within the manuscript, but we have found 'non-Northern' forms in the other texts we have studied, and have suggested rationales based upon such socio-linguistic factors as university influence shifting the rate of development in one area before another, introducing words from outside of the region. In light of what this study has demonstrated so far, it seems that elements such as <wh> for OE <hw> do not constitute 'non-Northern' forms at all.

A scan of *Sir Tristrem* yielded the following data:

	Sir Tristrem (National Library of Scotland Advocates' MS. 19.2.1)
Present participle	coming, making, parting
Gerund	gadering, leteing, tidinge
ANGEL	---
WH	what, when, white, who
<a>	bath, knawe, mare, na mare, plawe, who
Graphology	[silently emended by editor]
Pronouns	thai, he, sche, ich, ye, we
Use of I v. Y	bright, bring, ich (for EACH), sink, tide, thing, yren

The results are intriguing in light of the data previously collected. It is quite evident that there are Northern forms present in this manuscript, such as the distinctive <a> for OE /ɑː/. However, Northern -[and] is not present in the present participle; we find *sche* instead of *scho* and *who* for WHO. Certainly, the manuscript's language does not seem to correlate with Scott's original description of it as 'clearly Scottish'. Nevertheless, it is interesting that the 'ic' form, echoing the 'ich' here, is also found in the Edinburgh MS of *NHC*, otherwise very traditionally Northern in feature. This is not a form unattested in the area. Likewise, we find consistent use of <a> for Southern <o> throughout this manuscript with the exception of 'who', the traditionally Northern form used more consistently than in several of the other manuscripts considered. We have established already that <wh> is actually more common than <q> for WH-items in the manuscripts we have studied, contrary to Vogel's remarks.

Importantly, the scribe of this text uses his forms consistently; they demonstrate genuine scribal usage, rather than a confused *Mischsprache*. In light of the variation we have noted, the language of *Sir Tristrem* could arguably be viewed as a viable NME dialect that has developed in slightly different ways, and at its own individual rate, to some of the others. If we were to map it alongside our existing manuscripts, it would fall beyond **D** as the most variant from a traditional NME model, based most of all on the fact that it has made the move into a present participle in -*ing*. However, viewed alongside our already fairly varied set of NME dialects, we can see that it is not anomalous in deviating from other NME varieties in several features. That it could, with these ostensibly 'non-Northern' features, still fit well enough into the net of 'fully Northern' ME dialects is evident; particularly the <wh> feature isolated by Vogel is not demonstrably a non-Northern feature. The -*ing* present participle form was not noted in any of the other manuscripts studied here, but as it later spread across the Northern area it must, naturally, have been first attested somewhere; inasmuch as all of the studied manuscripts show some features individual to them, this does not mean that further study would not attest these features elsewhere in the NME region. As we have discussed, language change is naturally influenced by language contact: evidence of such change and variation, where used consistently as the language of the scribe, need not indicate that the output dialect is not viable, or indeed, not Northern.

This manuscript is one that would need to be studied in detail, with attention to its sociolinguistic background and codicological implications, in order to be able to draw any firmer conclusions about the precise provenance of its dialect. However, as has been discussed, it is not precise localisation that will most help scholarship, but the understanding that the drawing of firm boundaries between language areas is not conducive to a proper appreciation of the language variation that could occur within regions at this time. Previous scholarship, focused intensely upon debates about localisation, has relied upon expectations of 'acceptable' Northern or Scots features to force texts onto one side of the border or the other, or outside of the region altogether. But artificial imposition of linguistic borders prevents scholarship from recognising the fluidity in language and the patterns that can be traced across the NME region and into Scotland. Considered in light of the heterogeneity in NME observed in this study, language varieties such as that of *Sir Tristrem* need not appear significantly more anomalous than many others.

6.8. Conclusions

From the data presented and analysed in this study, it is clear that suppositions about university influence stimulating language change in the North have been, to an extent, supported. It would be useful to undertake further and fuller consideration of manuscripts known to be from, and not from, areas of university influence, and see how deeply the correlation runs between this sociolinguistic context and the language variations observed by this study. The greatest problem remaining for the scholar of NME is not, as this study has shown, a lack of material, but simply a lack of scholarship. Were we able to investigate these, or other, manuscripts to the same depth to which we have studied **A, B, C** and **D,** it seems clear that much more valuable data concerning the development of language and language variation in this region could be gleaned. Even constrained only to *LALME* and edited texts and what codicological studies already exist, the study has made apparent that interesting patterns in language variation across the region stretch far beyond the *Pricke of Conscience.* It has established that the dialects within the NME region are not homogeneous, and that, moreover, some of them display language features, such as use of <o> for OE /ɑː/, that run contrary to what has previously been believed to characterise an NME manuscript.

The applications of this discovery are clear. Against this new context, it seems that some of the manuscripts that have puzzled scholars may have appeared anomalous simply because the context was not there into which they could be fitted. The example of *Sir Tristrem* seems to confirm the idea that the more Northern manuscripts are properly studied, the easier it becomes to understand and contextualise those manuscripts which have previously seemed isolated and linguistically confused. Previously, *Sir Tristrem* appeared anomalous, but the data accrued over the course of this study demonstrates that, in fact, its language can be fitted easily into the broad range of dialect variations that fall within the umbrella of NME.

This is a conclusion that could not have been drawn without transcriptions and close analysis of those Northern manuscripts previously unavailable in edited format. Having undertaken those transcriptions, we find that the evidence they provide fits interestingly into that already provided by the limited number of

Northern texts that have already been edited. Localisation is not necessarily achievable, but nor is it necessarily the only desirable aim of the dialectologist. It can aid us in adding sociolinguistic context to our analyses, but much of this context can also be deduced from manuscript study, and even textual study. Through codicological study of the manuscripts, and thorough analysis of the text, we have been able to suggest potential sociolinguistic circumstances in which the scribes under examination may have worked, and to indicate how these circumstances may have affected their language usage and handling of the text. Precise localisation has not been necessary here in order to demonstrate that there are interesting variations across the languages of NME, nor that these variations, and the differing rates and routes of language modification, have been clearly affected by specific and investigable sociolinguistic factors. Codicological and textual evidence, in combination, have enabled us to make reasonable judgements about the possible origins and contexts of the manuscripts studied, and consequently we can see that training and education, as well as monastic standing or lack of it, all have a significant influence on language variation within the NME region.

CHAPTER 7

Conclusion

The goal of this project was to interrogate the extent to which NME is a homogeneous dialect area. Through the compilation and comparison of new data from little-examined manuscripts, it has questioned whether the data shows greater variation than is typically expected of NME, and what can be uncovered about these manuscripts and their possible origins based upon textual and codicological evidence. Analysis of this data led to some interesting discoveries. Demonstrably, the data has shown a broader range of linguistic variables than traditional descriptions of NME would accommodate. Some items previously considered anomalous have been found to be in regular use in the NME region. Consideration of the data in context of other texts from the region has enabled the identification of a number of different language varieties, two of which can be firmly localised. Moreover, close study of the manuscripts, taking into account the codicological and textual evidence, has enabled us to hypothesise about the training, occupations and sociolinguistic circumstances of a number of previously little-examined scribes. Application of these ideas to the identified language varieties shows that training, register and sociolinguistic context may inform some of them, even where localisation is not yet possible.

This study has demonstrated that, when little-studied Northern texts are properly investigated, they can yield a wealth of information from which new conclusions can be drawn, new patterns of language presented, and new avenues opened for future study. We have considered already why usage of the term *Mischsprachen* can be unhelpful in less-explored areas where expectation of a very narrow range of features in NME has led to assessment of certain forms as 'non-Northern'. The new data acquired and considered by this study has expanded the idea of which features we find used consistently by Northern scribes, presenting a more complex model of the region within which linguistically-debated texts can be more usefully studied. Evidently, it is possible to nuance NME in the same way that other dialect areas have been nuanced.

7.1. Improvements to traditional dialect models

In discussing the dialects of the NME region, Morris (1863, p. v) makes the valuable point that to describe Northern English based purely upon 'that portion of it spoken in the North of England' is inadequate, suggesting that one needed to consider texts from lowland Scotland as well. However, his explanation for this – that, apart from some very minor differences, 'in Grammar and Vocabulary the idioms North and South of the Tweed belong to one and the same dialect' – is problematic and, as this study demonstrates, now misleading in light of new evidence. Morris's work was, in 1863, of enormous and ground-breaking value, and has been the basis of effectively all subsequent scholarship in the area. The issue is that his ideas about NME's homogeneity have been maintained well into a scholarly era where they are no longer appropriate or helpful.

Morris's suppositions must now be taken further. For example, in accordance with the time of writing, Morris (1863, p. v) disregarded orthographical differences as constituting any form of dialect variation; there is no distinction made between written and spoken dialects in his discussion, and no acknowledgement that orthographical or typographical variation can be worthy of study. These are elements that were simply not taken into account by scholarship at that time. But Morris's investigation into the language of the *Pricke of Conscience* has not been succeeded by another that has taken into account these scribal factors, and his account of the Northern dialect, his description of it as if it were homogeneous and his disregard of orthographical variation as important, has continued to be accepted as a valid general view of the NME region. However, while Morris was writing in an era before the input of the scribe was truly valued in its own right, we are not. This allows us to begin to differentiate dialects using orthographical differences and questions of sociolinguistic variation in a way that was not considered by Morris. As discussed in Chapter Six, study of pre-edited Northern texts alongside **A, B, C** and **D** led me to suggest that these texts could be divided, taking orthographical differences into account, into at least five, possibly more, language varieties.

What Morris (1863, p. xiii) described as the major characteristics of 'the Northumbrian dialect' have been reprinted without expansion in much subsequent scholarship, and indeed much of what Morris observed has been borne out in this study. However, Morris was working from only two manuscripts. The data accrued in this study, based upon a range of manuscripts, demonstrates that the variety of language features found within this region outstrips what Morris's model proposes, and furthermore that some NME texts lack what Morris deemed vital identifying features of NME dialects. Significantly, for example, we find that the relative pronouns in manuscripts such as **A** begin <qw>, rather than <wh> as in Morris's model, and, moreover, what he describes as 'the most striking peculiarity' demarcating Northern dialect texts – the preservation of <a> for OE/ɑ:/, which served as the identifier of 'fully Northern' texts still for Lewis and McIntosh in 1982 (p. 20) – is not consistently present across all manuscripts.

If all Northern texts are written in 'one and the same dialect', then all of the Northern texts studied ought to adhere to the fundamental identifying characteristics listed by Morris, but in testing this theory, this study found that they do not. The idea of NME as a basic 'norm' is no longer a useful one with which to work. The data examined in this study are sufficient to enable a reimagining of this region as one containing a number of language varieties, developing at different rates and under different influences. It is evident, then, that the more manuscripts and accompanying data we are able to incorporate into this picture, the more accurately we are able to present it as a region of numerous language varieties, each with their own different norms.

7.2. The NME region as home to many different language varieties

This study has taken the sociolinguistic circumstances of its scribes consistently into account, using these factors as a means of understanding and illuminating reasons behind language variation and change. Consequently, when I set my own accrued data from **A, B, C** and **D** against what context already existed, these factors were invaluable in exploring the pattern of language variation that emerged, and deducing the possible rationale behind it.

As laid out in Chapter Six, I set the findings from **A, B, C** and **D** alongside those from some of the limited number of already edited NME texts. Having studied **A, B, C** and **D** in depth, it was easy enough to identify the points of most obvious variation, and data was then taken from further texts to illuminate these points only, in order to make the most useful comparison we could without being able to explore these new texts in the same depth afforded to the main four. The intention was to determine whether correlations could be found between sociolinguistic setting and the rate of language development, and whether patterns could be seen when setting the data from **A, B, C** and **D** within a wider net as illuminated by further edited texts. As the previous chapter discusses, patterns certainly did emerge, and some earlier theories – for example, about correlation between universities and language development towards more southerly preferred forms – were substantiated. **A, B, C** and **D** could be set within a useful bigger picture of dialectal and sociolinguistic variation across this region. Variation in the major areas, such as in the retention or otherwise of <a> for OE /ɑ:/ and in the forms of WHAT and WHO, could be tracked across the manuscripts, the pattern of change obvious in a way that it was not with only the first four.

Ultimately, I identified five distinct language varieties. One of these, Variety 4, is firmly localisable to Durham. A second, Variety 3, is probably a North Yorkshire dialect, although the localisation is less certain. However, as this exercise demonstrated, it is still very possible to usefully differentiate a number of dialects by their features, even before firm localisation is possible. Because codicological and textual evidence have shed light on the sociolinguistic circumstances of the scribes, we are still able to posit reasons behind the pattern of language variation that emerges. Certain language features can be connected to monastic usage, to university influence and to commercial production, and these might, indeed, eventually aid in localisation when further data is accrued. The logical continuation of this study would be the close investigation of further NME manuscripts, of the *Pricke of Conscience* and other texts, to determine how their language relates to the varieties identified here, what further data they can contribute, and what information they can add to our understanding of the language variety they most closely resemble.

The five dialect forms, and one sub-form below, were identified:

Conclusion

1. 'Edinburgh', or Variety 1. Possibly a West Yorkshire dialect, very conservative Northern lexis (*kirk* for CHURCH, *kythe* for SHOW). Retained <a> for OE /ɑ:/; present participle in *–and*. Pronouns: *scho, thai, thaim, ic* alongside I. Initial <qu> for <wh> items. Gerund in *–ing*. Tendency towards <i> rather than <y>
   a. Ashmole, as Variety 1 but, significantly, with initial <wh> for WHO, WHAT, WHEN.
2. 'A', or Variety 2. Probably not monastic, perhaps some East Anglian connection in scribal training or place of copying. Sometimes <a> for OE /ɑ:/, sometimes <o>, approximate 50:50 division. Present participle in *–and(e)*. Pronouns: *scho/sche, pai, paim, I*. Initial <qw> for <wh> items. Gerund in *–yng*, tendency towards <i> rather than <y>. The most graphemically conservative.
3. B-C-Cambridge, Variety 3. Probably language of commercial scribes trained in North Yorkshire. Almost always retained <a> for OE /ɑ:/; present participle in *–and*. Pronouns: *scho, pai, paim, I*. <wh> for <wh> items. Gerund in *–yng(e)*. Indiscriminate <i> v <y>, no clear pattern.
4. 'Durham', or Variety 4. Monastic Durham dialect. Conservative lexis, consistently retained <a> for OE /ɑ:/; present participle in *-and*. Gerund in *-yng,* occasional *-ing*. Pronouns: *sho, sche, pai, yai, ȝow*. Interesting consistent ye/þe before *whilk*. Preference for <i>.
5. 'D', or Variety 5. Non-monastic dialect, indicating some connection to West Midlands and perhaps university training. 30:20 retained <a> and <o> for OE /ɑ:/. Present participle in *–and*. Pronouns: *scho, pai, paim, I*. <wh> for <wh> items. Gerund always in *–ynge*. Always <y> rather than <i>.

In Chapter Six, we discussed how studies of the text *Sir Tristrem* have usually been concerned with attempts to identify it as either Scots, Northern English, or some sort of *Mischsprachen*, with 'anomalous' forms confusing the issue. Examination of this text in light of the above investigation demonstrated that, the more Northern manuscripts are properly studied, the easier it becomes to understand and contextualise those manuscripts which have previously seemed isolated and linguistically confused. The data accrued over the course of this study demonstrates that, in fact, the language of *Sir Tristrem* is not at all unusual in deviating from more than one of the features that have traditionally characterised NME. The implications of this are that, in the future, other ostensibly anomalous texts might be illuminated through the use of the more complex model of NME demonstrated here. Scholars could compare the language and orthography of debated manuscripts to the features noted in the language varieties identified here. The more data is accrued, the more easily we will be able to say with certainty whether a feature is actually anomalous, or whether it is, in fact, attested in other manuscripts from the region.

McIntosh and others have noted the lack of anchor texts in the NME region as one of the major reasons scholarship has not been able to make as many inroads in this area as elsewhere. As part of an attempt to set this study in context, I did investigate whether any such anchor texts – deeds, letters, or other localised texts in English, from an appropriate time period – could be readily found in the mostly likely collections. One of the ways in which scholarship could now advance, using my identified language types, would be to compare a localised text to these languages and determine to which group its language is closest. As such, I examined the holdings of Durham Cathedral, and of those those colleges in Oxford associated with the bishopric of Durham and the north during this period in time: University, Balliol and Trinity (formerly Durham College).

Balliol College, which retains its manuscripts and statutes on site, does have some manuscripts from the relevant period, but the statutes – which have been printed by Salter as Oxford Balliol Deeds (1913) – are, as we might expect, in Latin. There are a small number of manuscripts in English but none from the appropriate time and none apparently Northern. Trinity and University College have both deposited their manuscript collections in the Bodleian, and as with Balliol, there are no appropriate documents in English from the relevant period that appear to be Northern. The archives and collections of Durham Cathedral for this period in time remain, again, overwhelmingly in Latin and French; what little material there is in English mostly begins to creep in from the fifteenth century. Because of the shift in attitudes towards English across the pivotal hundred year period between these manuscripts, still few, and those of the *Pricke of Conscience* I have studied, studies of these would not be especially helpful. These discoveries are in keeping with previous statements by the *LALME* team that there were few anchor texts for this region: in the obvious places, they are not easy to find. However, what my study has undertaken is an approach to the question of Northern dialect study from a different angle where the more traditional ones are not possible. Taking my linguistic findings as a starting point, a larger future study could mine the less obvious sources of records and other Northern material for texts that could map onto the sets of dialect features I have identified, working, as it were, in the opposite direction from the usual method, which has proven so difficult to apply in the NME region.

7.3. Conclusions about scribes and manuscripts based on codicological evidence

One of the original goals of this study was to determine what close manuscript study, approached from a number of scholarly angles, could contribute to our understanding of NME. The outcome of my manuscript study has served to encourage further questions about linguistic variation and its relation to scribal training and motivations. Close reading of each manuscript, particularly when compared line by line against the other three, served to illuminate the attitude of each scribe with regard to his text and his audience, allowing us to consider each one as a living person with a purpose and history, rather than simply as the anonymous host of a language variety. As such, even where texts are unlocalised, sociolinguistic deductions enabled us to consider in what sort of setting a scribe may have been working, and thus which language features may be particular to monastic scribes, for example, or those who have been university-educated. The addition of codicological to textual evidence enabled us to make more accurate interpretations. While Scribe **A** is the more orthographically traditional of the four, the codicological evidence strongly dissuades us from any assumption that this traditionalism reflects a scribe producing manuscripts in a monastic house – although of course, there is nothing to say he was not trained in one. Questions of training raise their heads still more pointedly in the case of Scribe **D,** whose French-influenced spellings and orthography, combined with his authoritative handling of the text and occasional Midlands features, perhaps suggest a university connection.

This idea of the scribe as mobile – as a man who might have been trained in one institution and then carried his skills elsewhere – is an important one to keep in mind, particularly in the case of Scribes **A** and **D**. Both of these scribes appear to have been in some kind of contact with people using language varieties from outside of the NME area. For **A**, the major connection is that his writings occur alongside additional sections in a variety of different languages. We have discussed in Chapter Five what this could indicate: potentially, **A** could have originated from and written this manuscript within the NME area, with the manuscript then left to travel elsewhere to acquire its additional quires. Equally, however, **A** could have written his NME section from outside of the dialect area, making the idea of 'localising' all the more interesting. Certainly, the manuscript – which seems to have ended its journey in the Fens – cannot help us. We are really only able to localise the language to the place where the scribe was trained; but there is nothing to say that this trained language did not vary over time, with features acquired and lost by the scribe, depending upon external factors.

The **D** manuscript appears to have been strongly influenced by some kind of scholarly impetus. Its doubled-f, as discussed in Chapters Three and Five, is an uncommon feature, found in other West Midlands manuscripts, while much of its French orthography also reflects more southerly interactions, although the core language is clearly Northern. We might therefore suggest that the language of **D** is the organic language of an Oxford-educated Northerner, without implying that this is therefore a *Mischsprache*. Perhaps the **D** manuscript was produced within a commune of Northerners living in a university town, or perhaps in some Northern outpost. Perhaps the scribe was educated in Oxford itself, or perhaps by Oxford men teaching in the North. In any event, the fact remains that what we see is a valid output dialect, the language of this scribe, but not one necessarily localisable to a single specific place. Rather, we might argue that such a language is connected more to the education, motivations and personal history of the scribe than to a particular town or house.

This does not, and should not, make the language unworthy of being considered as a useful and illustrative dialect form. On the contrary, envisaging it in this way enables us to ask a lot of interesting questions about features we see in other Northern manuscripts, too, and the potential reasons behind their spread. We have noted, for example, the potential for a connection between final <o> in WHO in the Northern region, and a university education. Historical context indicates how widespread was the influence of the universities, particularly Oxford, across the North. Some features we have already connected to university education, and the spread of these across the Northern region becomes both more interesting and more useful when viewed against this background. When, as seen in Chapter Six, we are able to posit connections between university men working and teaching in the North, and instances of language change within the greater pattern, it can serve as an excellent means of illuminating that pattern and the reasons behind it. Moreover, if we can acknowledge this proposed Oxford-influenced or university-influenced Northern English as a 'real' dialect or language variety based upon our knowledge of its sociolinguistic context, it could ultimately help future scholars to identify the provenance of manuscripts that use a similar dialect. Information about the scribe, and the manuscript itself, are vitally important in accurately studying the language variety they use. The study of Scribe **D** as part of this project has supported this idea.

It would, as discussed, be enormously useful to Northern dialectology if we were able to transcribe and electronically tag all Northern manuscripts of the *Pricke of Conscience* in order to run the sorts of comparisons we have run here across all of the lines in all of these, rather than utilising transcribed tranches. This would enable us to create a far broader and denser picture of language variation across the NME area at this time. However, a study such as that would require not only an army of researchers, but also a stimulus, and an understanding of what the ultimate purpose would be. The current study is intended to serve as such a stimulus, demonstrating the ways in which an exploration of unstudied Northern manuscripts, in their sociolinguistic contexts, can challenge and advance outdated ideas about NME. Scholars such as Angus McIntosh and Margaret Laing have suggested for many years that a large-scale study of the NME region might be useful. I hope that this study, in demonstrating how investigation of only four manuscripts can reconfigure our understanding of the dialect structure of this region, has shown why such a study on a grand scale could prove a monumental advance.

The dialects of the NME region are not homogeneous. Rather, it appears that they behave in similar ways to dialect varieties in other regions, to which more attention has been paid. This project has demonstrated that there is a distinct pattern of language variation detectable in this region at this time. In dividing NME into five major sub-varieties, we have provided a coarse initial dialect net for future studies, even small-scale, in-depth studies such as this one, to tighten with new data. The *Pricke of Conscience* is a major key to the Northern dialect area, but it is far from the only text that has much information still to yield. The investigation discussed in Chapter Six demonstrates clearly the value of adding even one or two new texts to a comparative study, in that each new set of data illuminates the others, even where the matrix connects manuscripts only to each other, rather than to points on a map.

The scholarly idea of NME has been allowed to become outdated because of lack of attention to Northern manuscripts and lack of analysis of the social factors behind the scribes who wrote them. The major scribes considered in this study have previously been entirely anonymous: as a result of textual and codicological examination, we have been able to contribute to scholarship our hypotheses as to their probable origins and occupations. The current study has demonstrated how vital is the use of sociolinguistic and codicological evidence in order to identify and explain language varieties within NME, and the connections between them. It presents a figure of the NME region that shows it to be an area of productive language growth and development, where a number of distinct language varieties flourish beneath the larger umbrella of NME. This understanding opens a number of avenues for future research in this area. Primarily, the mass transcription and logging of all 'fully Northern' manuscripts of the *Pricke of Conscience* would show the full extent of language variation across this text, and enable us to assign the manuscripts to the relevant language variety group, as identified in this study. Subsequently, full sociolinguistic and codicological surveys of each manuscript would illuminate what is known about each language variety, and increase the accuracy of initial suppositions. Ultimately, it will be very rewarding if a thorough search of Northern holdings could uncover overlooked anchor texts which will then firmly localise one or more of the language varieties identified here. However, as this study has demonstrated, when witnesses are investigated from new angles, linguistic data can expand scholarly ideas and make valuable contributions, even where firm localisation is not yet possible.

APPENDIX 1: Manuscript Transcriptions

1.1. A – Rawlinson C.891

Book 5

þe v parte þat es of þe day of dome
And of tokens þat before sal come
Ilkman suld þink and undirstand
On þe day of dome þat es comand
In þis parte may men x þinges rede
þat toudies þe grete dai of drede
And before þat day sal be
And some at þe day als men sal se
þe firste es wondirful tokenes sere
That before þat day sal be schewed here
þe second es of þe fire þat sal brynne
þe world 7 alle þat es þare inne
þe iii es of risyng genale
Pf al men boþe grete 7 smale
þe iv. of cristes comyng doun
To þe dome in his propre persoun
þe v. es of þe certayne stede
þat crist sal deme boþe qwik 7 deade
þe vi. es of þe fourme of man
In qwilk crist sal schewe hym þan
þe vii es of accusers many
þat þe synful sal accuse openly
þe viii es of þe rekennyng
þat þai sal 3elde of þair lyvyng
þe ix of men þat efter þai wrou3t
Some sal be demed 7 some nou3t
Pe x es of þe dome fynalle
Wen Crist sal make endyng of alle
Of þir sal fal even als þai
Some before some at þe day

Before þat day sal tokenynges come
Of qwilk may here fynde some
Als of anticrist 7 his pouste
And oþer þat before sal be
35 þe qwilk tokenynges men sal fynde hard
Als men may here afterward
And qwo so wille avise hym wele
He may ilk day here se 7 fele
Tokenes þat he may understand
40 þat þe day of dome es nere comand
For many þinges þat sal fal 7 trowe
Al remes þe worldes end er sene nowe
þurgh qwilk grete clerkes knawes
þat þe worlde to þe ende fast drawes
45 For þi we schulde us redy here
Als þe day of dome ware comand nere
Ffor Cristes disciples wold have knowyng
Some tokenyng of his last comyng
þai spak to crist als 3e may here
50 In þe gospel on þis maniere:
[rubric]

Book 6

Here bygynes þe sexte part þat spekes of þe paynes of helle.

Many man here spekes of helle
Bot of þe paynes þare of fewe can telle
5 Bot qwo so here must knowe wele
What payn þe synful þare sall fele
In grete drede he schulde be brou3t
And qwen he of þase paines þou3t
Ffor þe mynde of þaim schulde him fere
10 So bitter and so horible þai her
Bot for þi þat many knawes nou3t r13t
Whate kyn þaines in helle ere di3t
Wiþ outen ende for sinful man

þare I wille schewe 3owe als I can
A party of þase paynes sere
Als 3e sal sove afterward here
Bot fust I wille schewe 3ouse ware es helle
Als I have herde grete clerkes telle
And seþen I wille schewe 3owe mare
And speke of grete paynes þat ar þare
Som clerk says als þe boke wrtues
þat helle is þe tolk of þe erþe es
Ffor al þe erþe be skille may likned be
In til a rounde appille of a tre
þat even in myddes has a tolk
And so it may be to a negg 3olke
Ffor ri3t als a dalk es in mydward
þe 3olk of egge qwen it es harde
Ri3t so es hell as clerkes telles
In mydwarde & nouware dies
And als þe 3olk in midward þe egge lyse
And þe qwite a boute on þe same wise
Ri3t es þe erþe wiþ outen doute
In myddes þe hevens þat gone aboute
þus man a man se be a negge harde d13t
How helle heven & ertþe standes ri3t
Fful hidus & mirk helle es kidde
Ffor it es wiþ in þe ertþe hidde
þider þe sinful sal bedryven
Als sone als þe last douie es gyven
Wiþ alle þe fendes þare to dwelle
þat nowe ar un þe mire & in helle
þate sal þai alle ben stopped togider
Wo sal þam be þat sal wwende þider
Ffor þare es so mykel sorowe & bale
And so many paynes wiþouten tale
þat alle þe clerkes þat ev hade wite
þat ai was or þat lives 3itte
Couþe nou3t telle ne schewe þurgh lare
Howe mykel sorow & pyne es þare
And 3if it þurgh kynde may be so

þat a hundre þousand men or mo
Had a hudre þousand tunges of stele
And ilk a tunge mi3t speke wiseli & wele
55 And alle þase tunges of ilka man
Had bigun first qwen þe worlde bigan
To speke of helle & so to speke aye
qeiles þe world schuld last to domesday
Yit mi3t þai uou3t þase pannes tel ri3t
60 þat synful man in helle es di3t
Ffor mwy no wyt can ymagyn
Qwat paynes þare ar ordayned for syn
Bot may fynd qwo so wille loke
Some general paynes writen in þis boke
65 Among alle oþer paynes in helle
Als men has herde wise clerkes telle
Bot qwat man es so wise & witty þat couþe telle þase paynes pperly
Bot it were he þat had bene þare
And sene þase paines les & mare
70 Bot mwo so comes þare for certayn
He may on no wise turne agayn
Bot dwelle þare & nev agayn come
Ffor þe boke sais þus of wisdome
[non est agintus qui veusus est ab inferis]

1.2. B – MS. Rawlinson Poetry 175

Book 1

Here bigynnes þe first part þat es of mans wrechedness.

First when god made althing of noght
Of þe fowlest mater man he wroght
Þat was of erthe for twa skils to hard
Þe tane es for þi þat god wald
Of foule mater mak man in despyte
Of Lucifer þat fell als tyte
Till hell als he had synned thurgh pryde
And of all þat with him fell þat tyde
For þai suld have þan þe mare schenschepe
And þe mare sorow when þai tuke kepe
Þat man of swa foule mater suld dwell
In þat place fraw whilk þai fell
Þe tother skill es þis to se
For man suld here þe meker be
Ay when he ses and thinkes in thoght
Of how foule mater he es wroght
For god thurgh his gudnes and his myght
Wald þat sen þat place in heven bright
Was made voyde thurgh þe syn of pryde
Till it was fylled ogayne on ilk a syde
Thurgh þe vertu of mekenes
Þat even contrary till pryde es
Þan may no man þider come
Bot he þat meke es and bowsome
Þat pines þe gospell þat sais us
How god said till his disaples þus
Nisi efficiamini sicut parvulus, non intrabitis in regnum celorum.
Bot yhe he said be als a child
Þat es to say both meke and myld
Yhe sall noght entre bi na way
Hevenryke þat sall last ay

```
           þan bihoves a man ay here seke
35         þat þat may tittest mak him meke
           Bot na thing here may meke him mar
           þan to think in hert als i said are
           How he was made of a foule matere
           And es noght els bot erth here
40         For þi sais a clerk als I now say
           What es man bot erth and clay
           And powder þat with þe wynd brekes
           And þarfor Job þus to god spekes
           [rubric]
```

Book   2

Here bigyns þe secund part þat es of þe world.

```
           All þe worlde se wyde 7 brade
           Our Lord specially for man made
5          And al other thung als clerkes can pue
           He made anely till mans bihove
           Sen he all þe world 7 all thing wroght
           Till mans bihove þan man aght noght
           Lufe nouther werldlyisch thing nebodily
10         Mare þan our lord god all myghty
           Ne als mykell als god þof þat war los
           And wha so dose unkynd he es
           For god war worthy mare to be loved
           þan any creature 7 swa bihoved.
15         Sen he es maker of all hyng
           And of all creature þe bigynnyng
           þis say I be men þat gyfes þam mykell
           Till þis werld þat es fals 7 fykell
           And hises all thing þat till it falles
20         swilk men werldlyisch men men calles
           þat þair hif mast on þe werld sette
           And þat hife þe lyfe of god lettes
           þarfor gud it es þat a man him kepe
```

Fra wardlylische 7 vayne wirschepe
For thurgh luf of þis world 7 vanyte
A man at þe last forbarred may be
Of þe blysfull warld whare all ioy es
Whare þe lyfe of man sall be endles
þat dose to god here þat him falles
þat warld þis clerkes world of world calles
Bi all þe world þat god wald make
For man of whilk I bifore spake
þat swa generally here es tane
haþ be understanden ma warldes þan ane
For a gret clerk says þat hight Bertolmewe
þat til a werldes er pryncepaly to schewe
þat þe ele [hole in parchment] 7 all þe hevens
Contenes als he þain in boke nevens
And all þe creatures þar god wroght
Swa þat witouten þa warld es noght
þe tane es gastly munsible 7 clene
þe tother es bodily 7 may be sene
þe gastly world þat na man may se
Es heven whare god lyttes in tinte
And ye neghen orderes of aungels
And haly spirites in þat warld dwelles
And þider sall we com 7 part lyfe ay
If we þiderward hald þe ryght way.

Book 3

Here bigyns þe thred part þat es of þe dede.

Ded es þe mast dred thing þat es
In all þis world als þe buke witnes
For here es na qwyk creature lyfand
þat it ne es for þe ded dredand
And flese þe ded ay whils it may
Bot at þe last it most be þe dedes pray
Ded of all þat it comes to abates

10	And chaunges all in myghtes and states
	Na man may wele ogaynst it stand
	Whare þat it comes in any land
	þat es to say bodily ded
	Ogayns þe whilk may nane help ne red
15	For all þat lyfe has bi hones it fele
	þat aght ilk man to knaw wele
	Bot bi þe name of ded may be tane
	And understanden ma dedes þan ane
	For als þis clerkes fyndes wryten and redes
20	Thre maners of dedes er þat men dredes
	Ane es bodily ded þat thurgh kynd es
	Ane other gastly þe thred endles
	Bodily ded þat es kyndely
	Es twynyng bitwene þe saul and þe body
25	And þat dedes full bitter afterward
	Gastly ded es a twynyng thurgh syn
	Bitwene god and mans saule within
	For als þe saule es lyf of þe body
	Swa þe lyfe of þe saule es god all myghty
30	And als þe body withouten dout
	Es ded when þe saul es passed out
	þe saule of man es ded ryght swa
	When god es departed þarfra
	For whare syn es es þe devell of hell
35	And þare whare þai er god will noght dwell
	For dedly syn and þe devell and he
	In a sted may noght togyder le
	þarfor when þe saule es wounded with syn
	God passes out and þe fend gase in
40	þan es þe saule onence god ded
	Ay whils syn and þe dwevell dwels in a sted
	And als þe body may be slayne
	Thurgh wapen þat men may ordayne
	Swa es þe saule slane thurgh syn
45	Wharfor god and it bihoves twyn.

Book 4

Here bigyns þe ferth part þat es of purgatory.

Many spekes and in buke redes
Of purgatory bot fone it dredes
For many wate noht what it es
Þarfor þai dred it wele þe les
Bot if þai knew wele what it ware
Or trowed þai wald dred it þe mare
And forþi þat som has na knawyng
Of purgatory ne understandyng
Þarfor I will now speke a party
In þis buke of purgatory
And first shew yhow what it es
And whare it es als þe buke wytnes
And whatkyn payns er þare in
And whylke saules gase þider and for what syn
And al swa what thing es mast certayne
Þat þam moght help and slake þair payne
Of þir ser poyntes I will spek and rede
And swa I sall þis ferthe part spede.
Purgatory es na thing elles
Bot a clensyng sted þare saule dwelles
Þat has synned and had contricion
And er in þe way of salvacion
And er noght parfytely clensed here
Of all venyele synnes sere
Bot þare bihoves þam payn fele
Till þai be clensed parfytely and wele
Of alkyn syn þat þai ever wroght
In word in ded in will in thoght
For swa pured and fyned never gold was
Als þai sall be ar þai þethen was
Wharfor þe payn þat þe saule þare hentes
Es mare bitter þan all þe tourmentes
Þat all þe marters in erth thold
Sen god was for us boght and sold

For þe lest payn of þe paynes þare sere
Es mare þan es þe mast payn here
Als says a gret clerk þus shortly
40 In a buke of þe payns of purgatory
[rubric]

Book 5

Here bigyns þe fift part þat es of þe
day of dome and of takens þat sall com bifore.

In þis part men may of ten thinges rede
þat towches þe gret day of drede
Of whilk som bifor þat day sall be
And at þe day als men sall se.
þe first es þe wonderfull takens sere
þat bi for þat day sall be shewed here
þe secund es of þat fyre þat sall bryn
þe world 7 all þat es þarein.
þe thred es of þe rysyng generall
Of all men bah grete 7 small
þe forth es of cristes comyng donne
Till þe dome in his propre persoune
þe fift es of þe certaine stede
Whare crist sall deme bath whik 7 dede
þe sext es of þe fourme of man
In whilk crist sall shew him þan
þe sevend of þe accusers many
þat þe synfull saules sal accuse þar openly
þe aghtend of þe account & rekenyng
þat þai sall þheld of all þair lyfyng
þe neghend of all men eft þai have wroght
Of whylke som sall be demed 7 som noght
þe tend es of þe gret dome fynall
þat crist sall gyf 7 mak end of all
Of þir sall som fall als yhe herd me say
Bifore þat day 7 som at þe day
Bifore þe day sere takens sall come
Of whilk men may here fynd wryten som
Als of ancrist comyng 7 hys pouste
And of other ma þat bi for þat day sall be
þw hilk takens men sall thynk ful hard
Als yhe may here 7 se afterward
And wha swa will avyse him wele

```
        He may ilk day here se 7 fele
        Takens whare thurgh he may understand
        þat þe day of dome es fast comand
40      For wonders þat suld fall als 7 trow
        Ogayn þe worldes end er sene now
        Thurgh whilk wonders gret derkes knawes
        þat þe world fast to þe endward drawes
        Wharfor we suld mak us redy here
45      Als þe day of dome was comand here
        Cristes disciples þat yherned to have knawyng
        Of som takens ogaynes þe last comyng
        Spak to crist als may yhe here
        In ye godspell on þis maniere:
50      [rubric]
```

Book 6

Here bigyns ye sext part þat es
of ye peyns of hell.

```
        Many men heve spekes of hell
5       Bot of ye payns þare few kan tell
        Bot wha swa heve mught wit & knaw wels
        What payns þe synfull þare sall fele
        þai suld in gret fridlayke be broght
        riþ when þai on þa payns thoght
10      For þe mynt of þam might men fere
        Swa bytte & swa horrible þai ere
        Bot for þe þat many knawes noght ryght
        What kyn paynes in hell er dyght
        Withouten end for synfull man
15      þarfor I will shew þow als I kan
        bi party of þa payns sere
        rus þe may sone effward here
        Bot furst I will shew whare es hell
        2iis I have herd som gret clerkes tell
20      And sithen will I shew þhow mare
```

And spek of þe payns þat er þare
Som clerkes says als ye buke bers witnes
þat hell even in myddes þeerth es
For all erthe bi skyll may lykend be
Till a round appell of a tre
þat even in myddes has a tolk
And swa it may be till ane egge yholk
For als a talk es even in mydward
þe yholk of þe egge when it es hard
Right swa es hell pytt als clerkes telles
In myddes þe erth & nowrwhare elles
And fils þe yholk in mydes ye egge lyse
And þe white o bout on þe same wise
Right swa es þe erth wt outen tout
In mydes ye hevens þat gase o bout
þus may men se bi ane egge hard dight
How heven & erth & hell standes ryght
Full hydns & myrk hell es kyd
For wln rt es with in þye erth hyd
þider þe synfull sall be dryven
alls tyte als þe last tome es gyfen
Wt all þe tevels ay þare to dwell
þat now er in þe aþre & in hell
þare sall þai all be stowerd togyder
Wa sall þam be þat sall wend þider
For þare es swa mykll sorow & bale
And swa many payns wt outen tale
þat all þe clerkes þat e'er had witt
þat en was or þat lyfes yhit
Touth noght tell ne shew thurgh lave
How mykell sorow & payne es þare
And if it thurgh kynd myght be swa
þat ane hundreth thowsand men or ma
Had ane hundreth thousand tonges of stele
And ilk tong myght speke wisely & wele
And ilk a tong of ilk a man
Had bigonnen when þe world bigan
So spek of hell & swa suld speke ay

Whils ye world suld last till domesday
60 Yhit moght þai noght ye sorow tell
þat to synfull es ortaind in hell
For why na witt of man may ymagyn
What paynes þare er ordaynd for fyn
Bot men may bynd wha swa will luke
65 Som mane of payns wryten in buke
Omang all other payns þat er in hell
Als men has herd wise clerkes tell
Bot what man es swa wise & witty
þat cowth tell þa vayns pprley
70 Bot it war he þat had bene þare
And sene þa paynes bath les & mare
Bot he þat þare romes for certayne
May noght lyghtly turne ogayne
He most dwell þare & nei oway torne
75 For þe buke says þus of wisdome.
[rubric]

1.3. B2 – MS. Harley 4196

Book 2

Here bigyns þe secund part
þat es of þe world.

Al þe world so wydee and brade
Our lord specialy for man made
And all oth' thyng als clerkes kan prove
He made anely tyllmans bi hove
Sen he [crossed out iii] Pe world and all thyng wroght
Till mans bihove þan man aght noght
Luf nouth worldysshe thyng ne bodily
Mare þan our lord god all myghty
Ne als mykell als god þogh yt war les
And wha so dose unkyng he es
Ffor god war worthy mare to be lufed
þan any creature is swa bihoved
Sen he es maker of all thyng
And of all creatures þe bigynyng
þis say II be men þat gyvesþam mykell
Tylll þis world þat els fals and fykell
And lufes all thing þattyll it falles
Swilk men worldysshe men men calles
þat þair luf mast on þe world lettes
And þat luf þe luf of god lettes
þen fore gud it es þat a man him kepe
Ffra worldysshe luf and wany worschepe
Ffor thurgh luf of þis world and vanite
Al man at þe last forhard may be
Of þe blyssfull world þare all ioy es
Whare þe lyfe of man sall be endeles
þat dose to god here þat him falles
þat world þis clerkes world of world calles
Why all þe world þat god wald make
Ffor man of whilk I be fore spake
þat swa genally here es tane
May be understanden ma worldes þan ane

Ffora gret clerk says þat hight Berthelmewe
þat twa worldes er princypaly to schewe
þat þe elementes and all þe hevens
Contenes als he þam in boke nevens
40 And all þe creatures þat god wroght
Swa þat witouten þa worldes es noght
Þe tane es gastlyunsible and clene
Þe tother es bodily and may be sene
Þe gastly world þat no man may se
45 Is heven whare god syttes in trinite
And þe neghen orters or aungels
And haly spirrites in þat world dwels
And þider sall we com and þare lyf ay
If we þiderward hald þe ryght way
50 þat world was made for mans wonyng
Omang aungels in ioy and lykyng
All mare þare in for to dwel
Als men may here þir clerkes tell
Now here on will is no langer stand
55 Ffor afterward comes þis mat tyll hand.
[rubric]

Book 6

There is no red 'Here begins...' rubric, only an ornamental 'M' to mark the beginning.

Many men here spekes of hell
Bot of þe payns þare sone kan tell
What payns þe synful þare sall fele
5 þaild in gret ferdlayk be broght
Ay when þei on þa payns thoght
Ffor þe mynde of þam moght men fere
Swa pyst and swa horrible þai er
Bot for þi þat many knawes noght ryght
10 What kyn payns in hell er dyght
Witouten ende for synfull man
Þarfor I will schew yhowals I kan
Al party of þa payns sere

Als yhe may sone aftirward here
Bot fyrst I will schew whare es hell
Als I have herd som gret clerkes tell
And sythen will I shew yhow mare
And speke of þe payns þat er þare
SOm clerkes says als þe bokes bers witnes
þat hell even in myddes þe erth es
Ffor all erth bi skyll may lykend be
yll a round appell of a tre
þat even in myddes has a roll
And swa it may be tyll ane egg yholk
Ffor alsa dalk es even in mydward
þeyholk of þe egge when it es hard
RIght swa es hell pytt als clerkes telle
I myddes þe erth and nouwhare elles
And als þeyholk in myddes þe egge lyse
And þe white of lout is on þe same wyse
Ryght swa es þe erth wtouten dout
I myddes þe hevens þat gaseobout
þusmay men se be ane egge hard dyght
How heven and erth and hell standes ryght
Fful hyd es it myrk hell es kyd
Ffor well it es wtin þe erth hyd
þider þe synfull Sall be dryven
Als tyte als þe last dome es gyven
Wt all þe devels ay þare to dwell
þat now er in þe ayre and in hell
þare sall þai all be storred togyder
Wa sall þam be þat sall wend þider
Ffor þares swa mykell foron and sale
And swa many papirs witouten tale
þat all þe clerkes þat ev had wytt
þat ev was or þat lyfes ryght
Couth noght tell ne shew thurgh lare
How mykell sorow and payne es þare
And if it thurgh kynde myght be swa
þat a undreth thousand men or ma
Had a hundreth thousand tonges of stele
And ilk tong moght speke wisely and wele
And ilk a tong of ilka man

Had bigon when þe world bigan
55 To speke of hell and swa suld speke ay
Whils þe world suld last tyll domesday
Yhit moght þai noght þe sorow tell
þat to synfull es ordaynd in hell
Ffor why na wytt of man may ymagyn
60 What payns þare er ordaynd for syn
Bot men may fynd wha swa will loke
Som mare of payns wryten in boke
Omang all other payns þat er in hell
Als men has herd wise clerkes tell
65 Bot what man es swa wise and wytty
þat couth tell þa payns pprety
Bot et war he þat had bene þare
Whid seve þa payns both les and mare
Bot he þat þare cours for crayne
70 May noght lyghtly turne ogayne
He most dwell þare and nev oway come
Ffor þe buke says þus of wysdome.
[rubric]

1.4. C – MS. Cotton Galba E.ix

Book 1

Here bygynnes þe first part
þat es of mans wrechednes.

First whan God made al thyng of noght
Of the foulest matere man he wroght
þat was of erthe for twa skyls to halde
þe tane es forthy þat God walde
Of foul matere mak man in despite
Of Lucifer þat fel als tyte
Til helle als he had synned thurgh pride
And of alle þat with him fel þat tyde
For þai suld have þan þe mare shenshepe
And þe mare sorow when þai tuk kepe
þat men of swa foul matere suld duelle
In þat place fra whilk þai felle
þe tother skille es þis to se
For man suld here þe meker be
Ay when he sese and thynkes in thoght
Of how foul mater he is wroght
For God thurgh his gudnes and his myght
Wald þat sen þat place in heven bright
Was made voyde thurgh þe syn of pride
It war filled ogayne on ilka syde
Thurgh þe vertu of mekenes
þat even contrary til pryde es
þan may na man þider come
Bot he þat meke es and boghsome
þat proves þe gospelle þat says us
How God sayd til his disciples thus:
Nisi efficiamini sicut parvulus, non intrabitis in regnum celorum.
Bot yhe he sayde be als a childe
þat es to say bathe meke and mylde
Yhe sal noght entre be na way
Hevenryke þat sal last aye.
þan byhoves a man ay here seke

　　　　þat may tittest make him meke
　　　　Bot nathyng here may meke him mare
　　　　þan to thynk in hert als I sayde are
　　　　How he was made of a foul matere
40　　　And es noght elles bot herthe here
　　　　For þi says a clerk als I now say
　　　　What es man bot herth and clay
　　　　And poudre þat with þe wynd brekes
　　　　And þarfor Iob þus to God spekes
45　　　[rubric]

Book 2

Here bygynnes þe secunde part þat es of þe world.

　　　　Alle þe world so wyde and brade
　　　　Our Lord speciali for man made
5　　　 And al other thynge, als clerkes can profe
　　　　He made anly to mans byhove
　　　　Sen he al þe world and alle thynge wroght
　　　　Til mans byhove, þan man aght noght
　　　　Lufe nowther worldlisshe thyng ne bodily
10　　　Mare þan our Lord God almyghty
　　　　Ne als mykel as God þogh þat war les
　　　　And wha-so dos unkynd he es
　　　　For God war worthy mare to be lufed
　　　　þan any creature and swa byhufed
15　　　Syn he es maker of althynge
　　　　And of alle creatures þe bygynnynge.
　　　　þis say by men þat gyves þam mykel
　　　　Til þis world þat es fals and fikel
　　　　And lufes alle thynge þat til it falles
20　　　Swilk men worldlisshe men men calles
　　　　þat þair luf mast on þe world settes
　　　　And þat luf þe luf of God lettes.
　　　　þarfor gude it es þat a man him kepe
　　　　Fra worldlisshe luf and vany worshepe.
25　　　For thurgh luf of þis world and vanite
　　　　A man at þ last forbard may be

Of þe blisful world þar al ioy es
Whar þe lyfe of man sal be endles
þat dos to God here þat hym falles þat world þer clerkes 'world of
world' calles.
Whi alle þe world þat God walde make
For man of whilk I byfor spake
þat swa generaly here is tane
May be undirstanden ma worldes þan ane
For a grete clerk says þat hight Berthelmewe
þat twa worldes er principaly to shewe
þat þe elementes and al þe hevens
Contenes, als he þam in boke nevens,
And alle þe creatures þat God wroght
Swa þat withouten þa worldes es noght.
Þe tan es gastly, invisile and clene,
Þe tother es bodyly and may be sene.
Þe gastly world, þat na man may se
Es heven whar God syttes in trinite.
And þe neghen ordres of angels
And haly spirytes in þat world duelles
And þider sal we com and þar lyf ay
If we þederward hald þe right way.
[rubric]

Book 3

Here bigynnes þe thred part
þat es of þe ded.

Ded es þe mast dred thing þat es
In all þis world als þe boke witnes
Ffor here es na qwyk creature lyfand
þat it ne es for þe ded dredand
And flese þe ded ay whils it may
Bot at þe last he most be þe dedes pray.
Ded of all þat it comes to abates
And chaunges all myghtes and states
No man may wele ogayn it stand
Whare þat it comes in any land

þat es to say bodily ded
15 Ogayns þe whilk no man may help ne red
Ffor all þat lyf has bihoves it fele
þat aght ilk man to knaw wele
Bot bi þe name of ded may be tane
And understanden ma dedes þan ane
20 Ffor als þir clerkes fyndes writen and redes
Thre maners of dedes er þat men dredes
Ane es bodily ded þat thurgh kynd es
Ane other gastely þe thred endeles
Bodily ded þat is kyndely
25 Es twynyng betwene þe saule and þe body
And þat ded es full bytter and hard
Of whilk I sall schew yhow afterward.
Gastely ded es twynyng thurgh synne
Bitwene God and man saule within
30 Ffor als þe saule es lyf of þe body
Swa þe lyfe of þe saule es God allmyghty
And als þe body with outen dout
Es ded when þe saule es passed out
þe saule of man es ded ryght swa
35 When God es departed þarefra
For whare syn es es þe devell of hell
And þare whare þai er will God noght dwell
For dedely syn and þe devell and he
In a stede may noght togyder be
40 þarfor when þe saule es wounded with syn
God passes out and þe fende gase in
þan es þe saule onence God ded
Ay whils syn and þe devell dwelles in þat stede
And als þe body may be slayne
45 Thurgh wapen þat men may ordayne
Swa es þe saule slane thurgh syn
Wharfor God and it bihoves twyn.

Book 4

Here bygynnes þe ferth part
þat es of purgatory.

Many spekes and in buke redes
Of purgatory but fon it dredes
For many wate noght what it es
þarfor þai drede it wele þe les.
Bot if þai knew wele what it ware
Or trowed þai walde drede it þe mare
And forthy þat sum has na knawyng
Of purgatory ne undirstandyng
þarfor I wille now speke aparty
In þis boke of purgatory
And first shew yhow what it es
And whare it es als þe buke wittenes,
And whatkyn payns er þar-in
And whilk saules gas þeder, and for what syn
And alswa what thyng es mast certayn
þat þam mught help and slake þair payn
Of þir sex poyntes I wil spek and rede
And swa I sal þis ferth part spede.
Purgatory es nathyng elles
Bot a clensyng sted þar saules duelles
þat has synned and had contricyon
And er in þe way of salvacion
And er noght parfytly clensed here
Of al veniel syns sere
Bot þar byhoves þam payne fele
Til þai be clensed parfytely and wele
Of alkyn syn þat þai ever wroght
In worde in dede, in wille or thoght
For swa pured and fyned never gold was
Als þai sal be ar þai þethen pas.
Wharfor þe payn þat þe saul þar hentes
Er mare bitter þan alle þe tourmentes
þat alle þe marters in erthe tholed
Sen God was for us boght and sold
For þe lest payn of þe payns þar sere

Es mare þan es þe mast payn here
Als says a grete clerk þus shortly
In a buke of þe paynes of purgatory:
[rubric]

Book

Here bygyns þe fifte part þat es of
þe day of dome and of takens þat sal cum byfor.

    In þis part men may of ten þinges rede,
5 þat touches þe grete day of drede,
    Of whilk sum byfor þat day sal be,
    And at þe day, als men sal se.
    þe first es of the wonderful takens sere
    þat byfor þat day sal be shewed here.
10 þe secunde es of þe fire þat sal bryn
    þe world and al þat es þar-in.
    þE thred es of þe rysyng generale
    OF alle men, bathe grete and smale.
    þe ferthe es of crystes commyng don
15 Til þe dome in proper parson.
    þe fifthe es þe certayn stede
    Whar Crist sal deme bathe qwik and dede.
    þe sexte es of þe fourme of man
    In whilk Crist sal shew him þan.
20 þe sevend of þe accusers many
    þat þe synful saul sal accuse þar openly.
    þe aghtynd, of þe acunt and þe rekennyng,
    þat þai sal yheld of alle þair lyfyng.
    þe neghend of al men aftir þai haf wroght
25 Of wilk som sal be demed and som noght
    þe tend es of þe grete dome final
    þat Crist sal gyf and make ende of al.
    Of þir sal som falle, als yhe herd me say
    Byfor þat day and sum at þe day.
30 Byfor þe day sere takens sal com
    Of whilk men may here fynd wreten some
    Als of ancris commyng and his pouste

And of other ma þat byfor þat day sal be
þe whilk takens men sal thynk ful harde
Als yhe may se and here afterwarde.
And what-swa wille avise hym wele
He may ilk day here se and fele
Takens war thurgh he may understande
þat þe day of dome es fast comande.
For wonders þat shuld falle als I trow,
Agayn þe worldes hend er sene now,
Thurgh whilk wondres grete clerkes knawes
þat þe worlde fast to þe endeward drawes.
Wharfor we shuld make us redy here
Als þe day of dome war command nere.
Crist disciples, þat yherned haf knawyng,
Of sum takens agayns his last commyng
Spak to Crist, als yhe may here,
In þe godspelle on þis manere:

Book 6

Here bygynnes þe first part
þat es of mans wrechednes

First whan God made al thyng of noght
Of the foulest matere man he wroght
þat was of erthe for twa skyls to halde
þe tane es forthy þat God walde
Of foul matere mak man in despite
Of Lucifer þat fel als tyte
Til helle als he had synned thurgh pride
And of alle þat with him fel þat tyde
For þai suld have þan þe mare shenshepe
And þe mare sorow when þai tuk kepe
þat men of swa foul matere suld duelle
in þat place fra whilk þai felle
þe tother skille es þis to se
For man suld here þe meker be
Ay when he sese and thynkes in thoght
Of how foul mater he is wroght

20   For God thurgh his gudnes and his myght
     Wald þat sen þat place in heven bright
     Was made voyde thurgh þe syn of pride
     It war filled ogayne on ilka syde
     Thurgh þe vertu of mekenes
25   þat even contrary til pryde es
     þan may na ma man þider come
     Bot he þat meke es, and boghsome,
     þat proves þe gospelle þat says us,
     How God sayd til his disciples þus
30   Nisi efficiamini sicut parvlus, non intrabitis
     in reghum celorum
     Bot yhe, he sayde, be als a childe
     þat es to say bathe meke and mylde
     Yhe sal noght entre be na way
35   Hevenryke þat sal last ay.
     þan byhoves a man ay here seke
     þat may tittest make him meke
     Bot nathyng here may meke him mare
     þan to thynk in hert als I sayde are
40   How he was made of a foul matere
     And es noght elles bot herthe here.
     For-þi says a clerk als I now say
     What es man bot herth and clay
     And poudre þat with þe wynd brekes?
45   And þarfor Iob þus to God spekes:
     memento, queso, quod sicut lutum feceris
     me et in pulverem reduces me.
     He says, thynk, Laverd, þat als þow made me
     Foul erthe and clay here to be
50   Right swa þou sal turne me agayne
     Til erthe and poudre, þis es certayn.
     þan says our Laverd God alymyghty
     Agayne til man þus shortly :
     Memento, homo, quod cinis es,
55   et in cinerem reverteris.
     Thynk man, he says, askes er-tow now
     And in to askes agayn turn sal-tow.
     þan es a man noght elles to say
     Bot askes and pouder, erthe and clay

Of þis suld ilk man here haf mynde
And knawe þe wrechednes of mans kynde
Þat may be sene, als I shewe can
In al þe partys of þe lyfe of man
Alle mans lyfe casten may be
Principaly in þis partes thre,
Þat er þir to our understandyng
Bygynnyng, midward, and endyng.

1.5. D – MS Wellesley 8

Book 1

Se unserin humane condicione

    Fyrst when godd made all thyng of noght
    Of þe fowlest mater man he wroght
5   þat was of þe erthe for twa skylles to hald
    þe tane es for þi þat godd walde
    Of fowle mater he made man for despyte
    Of licfer þat fell als tyte
    Tyll helle als he had synned though pryde
10 And of alle þat felle with hym þat tyde
    For þai solde have þan þe more schenschepe
    And þe more sorow when þai toke kepe
    þat man of so fowle mater solde dwelle
    In þat place fro whylke þai felle
15 þe tothyr skylle es þis to se
    Ffor man solde here þe maker be
    Ay when he seese and thynkes in thoght
    Of how fowle matere he is wroght
    Ffor godd throgh hys godnes and hys myght
20 Walde þat son þat place in hefen bryght
    Was made voyde thorgh þe synne of pryyde
    He was fylled agayne on ylke a syde
    Thorgh þe vertow of maeknes
    þat even contrary to pryde es
25 þan may no man þider come
    Bot he þat maeke es and bowsome
    þat prwfes þe godspell þat sayse us
    How godd sayde tyll hys dyscyples thus
    Bot yhe be he sayde als a chylde
30 þat es to say bothe maeke and mylde
    Yhe sall noght entre be no way
    Hefenryke þat sall last ay
    þan behofes a man ay here saeke

þat tyttest may mak hym maeke
Bot nothyng may meeke hym here mare
þan to thynke in hert als I sayde are
How he was made of a fowld matere
And es noght elles bot erthe here
For þi says a clerke als I now say
What es a man bot erthe and clay
And powder þat wit þe wynde brakes
And þarfor Iob þus to godd spekes.

Book 2

Part secunda: De conditione mundi

Alle þe worlde so wyde and brade
Owre lorde specialy for man made
And all othyr thunges als clerkes can prove
He made only to mans behove
Sen he þe worlde and alle thyng wroght
Tytt mans behofe þan man aght noght
Lufe nowther worldely thyng ne bodely
Mare þan hys lord godd almyghty
He als mykell als godd þogh þat war lesse
And who so dose unkynde he es
For godd war worthy mare to be luffed þan any creature and so be hofed
Sen he es maker of all thung
And of all creatures þe begynnyng
þis say I be men þat gyffed þamme mykell
So þis worlde þat es fals and fykell
And luffes all thyng þat to it falles
Swylke men worldlysche men men calles
þat þair luf most on þe worldes settes
And þat luf þe luf of godd lettes
þarfore godd es þat man hym keepe
Fro worldly luf and vayne worscheepe
For thorgh luf of þis worlde and vanyte

A man at last forbarred may be
Of þe blysfull worlde þar all joy es
Whare þe lyfe of man sall be endles
þat dose to godd here þat hym falles
30 þat worlde þee clerkes world of worlds calles
Be alle þe world þat godd walde make
For man of whylke I before spak
þat sa generally here es tone
May be undyrstanden ma worlde þan one
35 For a grete clerke says þat hyght bertylmowe
þat twa worldes are pryncipally to schewe
þat þe elementes and all þe hefens
Contenes als he þanne in boke nefens
And alle þe creatures þat godd wroght
40 Swa þat witouten þase worldes es noght
þe tane es gasteley invisibyll and cleene
þe tother es bodily and may be seene
þe gostly world þat no man may see
Es hefen whare godd syttes in trynyte
45 And þe neghene orders of awngels
And holy spyrytes in þat world dwelles
And þider sall we come and þare lyffe ay
yf we þiderward hald þe ryght way.

Book 3

Dede es þe moste dredde thyng þat es
In alle mo worlde als þe boke wytnes
Ffor here es no whykk creature lyfand
þat it ne es for þe dede dredande
5 And fleese þe dede ay whyle it may
Bot at þe last it behofes be þe dedys pray
Dede of all þat it comes to abates
And chawnges alle myghtes and states
No man may wele agayne it stande
10 Whare þat it domes in any lande
þat es to say bodily dede

Agayne whylke may helppe no rede
Ffor alle þat lyfe has behofes it fele
þan aught ylk man to knawe it weele
Bot by þe name of dede may be tone
And undyrstanden mo dedes þan one
For als þere clerkes fyndes wryten and redes
One es badely dede þat thrugh kynde es
Another es gostly þe thredd endeles
Bodely dede þat es kyndly
Es twynyng by twene þe sawle and þe body
And þat ded es full byttyr and hard
Of whylke I sall schewe yhowe eftyrward
Gostly dede es a twynning thorgh syn
Be twene godd and man sawle within
This manere of dedes are þat man dredys
Ffor als þe sawle es lyf of þe body
SSo þe lyf of þe sawle es godd alle myghty
And als þe body witouten dowte
Es dede when þe sawle es passed owte
þe sawle of man es dede ryght so
When godd es departed þarfro
For whare syn es es þe devel of helle
And þare whare he es godd wyll noght dwelle
For dedly syn and þe devel and he
In astede may noght togyder be
þarfore when þe sawle es wounded withyn
Godd passes owte and þe feende gose in
þan es þe sawle anence godd dede
A ye whyls syn and þe feende dwelles in þat stede
And als þe body may be slayne
Thurgh wapen þat men may ordayne
Swa es þe sawle slayne thorgh synne
Wharfore godd it and t behofes twynne.

Book 4

de purgatorio þo quarta

      Many spekes and in boke redys
      Of purgatory bot fone it dreedys
5   For many wate noght what it es
      þare ffore þai drede it wele þe les
      Bot yf þai knewe weele what it ware
      Or trowed þai walde dreede it þe mare
      And for þi þat sum has no knawyng
10 Of purgatory ne undyrstandyng
      þarefore I wylle nowe speke a party
      In þis boke of purgatory.
      And fyrst schewe yhow what it es
      And whare it es als þe boke wyttnes
15 And whatkyn paynes are þare in
      And whylke sawles gas þider and for what syn
      And alswa what thyng es moste certayne
      þat þamme moght helpe and slake þaire payne
      Of þese sex poyntes I wyll speke and reede
20 And so I sall þis fferth part speede.
      Purgatory es nothyng elles
      Bot clensyng stede þare sawles dwelles
      þat has synned and hadd contryciowne
      And ar in þe way of salvacyowne
25 And war noght parfytely clenssed heere
      Of bodely and venyale synnes dere
      Bot þare byhofes þanne paynes feele
      So þai be clenssed parfytely and weele
      Of alkyn syn þat þai ever wroghte
30 In worde in dede in wylle in thoght
      For so powred and fyned never golde was
      Als þai sall be ar þethen pas
      Wharfore þe payne þat þe sawle þare henttes
      Are more byttyr þan alle þe towymenttes

þat alle þe martyrs in erthe tholde
Sythen godd was for us boght and sold
Ffor þe leste payne of þe paynes þare seere
Es more þan es þe moste payne heere
Als says a grete clerke þus sleghly
In a boke of þe paynes of purgatory
He says þe leste payne þat es þare
In purgatory es weele mare.

Book 5

In þis part men may often thynges reede
þat towches þe grete day of dreede
Of whylke som before þat day sall be
And at þat day als men sal se
þe fyrst es of þe wondyrfull takenes seere
þat before þat day salle be schewed here
þe secunde es of þe fyre þat salle brynne
þe worlde and alle þat es þare inne
þe thrydd es of þe rysyng generalle
Of alle men bothe grete and smalle
þe fyerthe es of crystes comyng downe
To þe doome in hys propyr persowne
þe fyft es of þe certayne stede
Where cryste sal deeme bothe whykk and dede
þe sexte es of þe fowrme of man
In whylkk cryste salle schewe hym þan
þe sevend of þe accuseres many
þat þe synfull sal accuse þare openly
þe aghtend of þe acownte and reckenynge
þat þai sal yheelde of alle þaire lyffynge
þe neghend of alle men after þas hase wroght
Of whylke som salle be dampned and som noght
þe tend es of þe grete dome fynalole
þat cryste salle gyffe and mak ende of alle
Of þeere sal dom falle als yhe herd me say
Before þe day and sum at þe day

Before þat day sere takenes sall come
Of whylke men may heere fynde wryten some
Also of antecryste comyng and of hys powste
30 And of other mo þat before þat day salle be
þe whylke takenes men sall thynk full hard
Als yhe may se and here aftyrwarde
And who so wylle avyse hym wele
He may ylk day (ylk day) here se and feele
35 Takes whare thogh he may undyrstand
þat þe day of dome es fast comand
For wonderes þat solde falle als I trowe
Agaynes þe worlde ende are seene nowe
Thorgh whylke wonderes grete clerkes knawes
40 þat þe worlde faste to þe endeward drawes
Wharfore we solde mak us redy here
Als þe day of dome ware comand neere
Cryste dyscyples þat yherned hafe knawyng
Of som tokenes agayne hys last comyng
45 Spakk to cryste als yhe may here
In þe gospelle on þis manere

APPENDIX 2: Questionnaire

ITEM	Manuscript				
	A	B	B2	C	D
AFTERWARD	afterward	effward	aftirward	afterwarde	effward
AGAIN	agayne	ogayne	agayne	agayne	ogayne
AGAINST	agaynes	ogaynes	ogaynes	agaynes	ogaynes
ALL	alle	all	alle	alle	all
AMONG	among	omang	omang	amaunge	omang
ANY	any	any	any	any	any
ARE	ere	er	er	er	are
AS	als	als	als	als	als
AWAY	away	oway	oway	away	oway
BE	be	be	be	be	be
BEFORE	before	bifore	byfor	before	bifore
BEGAN TO	bigan	bigan	bygan	byganne	bigan
BEHOVES	bihove	bihove	byhove	behofe	bihove
BETWEEN	betwene	bitwene	betwene	by twene	bitwene
BOTH	both	bath, both (50:50)	bath	bothe	bath, both
BUT	bot	bot	bot	bot	bot
BY	bi	bi	by	by	bi
CALL	calle	calle	calle	calle	calle
CAN	can	kan	can	can	kan
COULD	couþe	cowth	couth	couthe	couth, cowth
DAY	day	day	day	day	day
DEATH	ded	ded	ded	dede	ded
DOWN	doun	donne	don	downe	donne

DREAD (n)	drede	fridlayke	ferdlayke	dreede	ferdlayk
EACH	ilk	ilk/ilka	ilk	ilk/ilka	ylke
EARTH	erþe	erth	erthe	erthe	erth
FAR	fer	fer	fer	ferre	fer
FATHER	fader	fader	fader	fader	fader
FIGHT	fight	fight	fyght	fyghte	fight
FIRE	fire	fyre	fire	fyre	fyre
FIRST	first	first	first	fyrst	first
FIVE	five	five	fyve	fyve	five
FLESH	flesche	flesh	fleshe	flesshe	flesh
FOLLOW	folow	folow	folow	folowe	folow
FOUR	four	fowr	four	fowre	fowr
FRIEND	frend	frend	frende	frende	frend
GIVE	gyve	gyf	gyve	gyffe	gyf
GO	wende	wend	wende	wende	wend
GOOD	gud	gud	gude	gude	gud
HAVE	have	have	have	have	have
HEAD	hede	hede	hede	heede	hede
HEAVEN	heven	heven	heven	hefen	heven
HELL	helle	hell	helle	helle	hell
HER	hir	hir	hir	hir	hir
HIM	hym	him	hym	hym	him
HITHER	hi(eth)er	hider	hider	hider	hider
HOLD	hald	hald	hald	hald	hald
HOLY	haly	haly	haly	holy	haly
HOW	how	how	how	how	how
HUNDRED	hundre	hundreth	hundreth	hundreth	hundreth
IF	ȝif	if	if	yf	if

Appendix II

IS	es	es	es	es	es
IT	it	it	it	it	it
KNOW	knawe	knawe	knawe	knawe	knawe
LAND	land	land	land	lande	land
LAW	law	law	law	lawe	law
LESS	les	les	les	les	les
LIFE	lyfe	lyfe	lyfe	lyfe	lyfe
LIVE (vb)	live	lyfe	lyve	lyve	lyfe
LORD	lord	lord	lord	lorde	lord
LOVE	luf	luf	luf	luf	luf
LOW	lawe	lawe	lawe	lawe	lawe
MAKES	makes	makes	makes	makes	makes
MAN	man	man	man	man	man
MANY	many	many	many	many	many
MAY	may	may	may	may	may
MIGHT	myght	might	myght	myght	might
MON	man	man	man	man	man
MORE	mare	mare	mare	mare	mare
MUCH	mykel	mykell	mykell	mykel	mykell
NAME	name	name	name	name	name
NEVER	nev	nev	never	never	never
NOT	noght	noght	noght	noght	noght
NOW	now	now	now	nowe	now
OLD	ald	ald	ald	alde	ald
ONE	ane	ane	ane	one	ane
OR	or	or	or	or	or
OTHER	oþer	other	other	other	other
OUR	our	our	our	owre	our

OUT	out	out	out	owte	out
POOR	pover	pover	pover	povere	pover
PRAY	pray	pray	pray	pray	pray
SAY	say	say	say	say	say
SELF	self	self	self	selffe	self
SHALL	salle	sall	sal	salle	sall
SHE	scho (2 sche)	scho	scho	scho	scho
SHOULD	schulde	suld	suld	solde	suld
SIN	sin	syn	syn	syn, synne (50:50)	syn
SINCE	seþen	sithen	sythen	sytthen	sithen
SOME	some	som	som	som	som
SORROW	sorowe	sorow	sorow	sorow	sorow
SOUL	saul	saule	saul	sawle	saule
SUCH	swilk	swilk	swilk	swilk	swylke
SUN	son	son	son	sonne	son
THAN	þan	þan	þan	þanne	þan
THE	þe	ye	ye	þe	þe
THEIR	þair	þair	þair	þair	þair
THEM	þam	þam	þam	þam	þam
THEN	þan	þan	þan	þanne	þan
THERE	þare	þare	þar	þare	þare
THESE	þase	þa	þa	þa	þa
THEY	þai	þai	þai	þai	þai
THINK	þink	thynk	thynk	thynke	thynk
THOSE	þase	þase	þase	þase, 3 þese	þase, þese
THOUGH	þogh	þof	þogh	þogh	þogh
THREE	thre	thre	thre	three	thre

THROUGH	þurgh	thurgh	thurgh	thorgh	thurg
TO + inf	to	to	to	to	to
TO + subject	to (some till)	to (occasional tyll)	to (occasional tyll)	to (occasional tylle)	to (occasional tyll)
TOGETHER	togider	togyder	togider	togyder	togyder
TWO	twa	twa	twa	two	twa
WAS	was	was	was	was	was
WELL	wele	wele	wele	weele	wele
WERE	war	war	war	war	ware
WH -	qw	wh	wh	wh	wh
WHEN	qwen	when	when	when	when
WHERE	ware	whare	whare	whare	whare
WHICH	qwilk	whilk, whylk	whilk	whilk, wilk	whylke
WHO	qwo	wha	wha	wha	who
WILL	wille	will	wille	wylle	will
WITHOUT	wiþouten	witouten	withouten	witouten	withouten
WORLD	worlde	world, worlde	world	worlde	world
WOULD	wold	wald	wald	walde	wald
YET	ȝitte	yhit	yhitt	yette	yhit
YOU	ȝowe	yow	yhow	yhow	yow

BIBLIOGRAPHY

PRIMARY SOURCES

London, British Library, Cotton Galba E. IX.

London, British Library, Harley 4196

Oxford, Bodleian Library, Rawlinson C.319

Oxford, Bodleian Library, Rawlinson Poetry 175

Wellesley, Massachusetts, Wellesley College Library, 8.

SECONDARY LITERATURE

Abrams, M.H. (1961) *A Glossary of Literary Terms*. New York: Wadsworth.
Aitchison, J. (2001) *Language Change: Progress or Decay?* 3rd edn. Cambridge: Cambridge University Press.
Andrew, M. and Waldron, R.A. (1982) *The Poems of the Pearl Manuscript*. Berkeley: University of California Press.
Antilla, R. (1989) *Historical and Comparative Linguistics*. 2nd edn. Amsterdam: John Benjamins.
Aston, T.H. and Faith, R. (1984) 'The Endowments of the University and Colleges to *circa* 1348', in Catto, J.I. (ed.) *The History of the University of Oxford: Volume I, The Early Oxford Schools*. Oxford: Oxford University Press, pp. 265 – 311.
Barber, C.L. (2000) *The English Language: A Historical Introduction*. Cambridge: Cambridge University Press.
Beadle, R. (1994) 'Middle English Texts and Their Transmission, 1350–1500: Some Geographical Criteria', in Laing, M. and Williamson, K. (eds.) *Speaking in Our Tongues: Proceedings of a Colloquium on Medieval Dialectology and Related Disciplines*. Woodbridge: Boydell & Brewer.
Beadle, R. (ed.) (2009) *The York Plays: The Text*. Oxford: Oxford University Press.

Beadle, R., Doyle, A.I. and Piper, A.J. (eds.) (1995) *New Science out of Old Books: Studies in Manuscripts and Early Printed Books in Honour of A.I. Doyle.* Aldershot: Scolar Press.

Benskin, M. (1977) 'Local Archives and Middle English Dialects', *Journal of the Society of Archivists*, 5, pp. 500-514.

Benskin, M. (1992) 'The 'Fit' Technique Explained', in Riddy, F. (ed.) *Regionalism in Late Medieval Manuscripts and Texts: Essays Celebrating the Publication of a Linguistic Atlas of Late Mediaeval English.* Cambridge: D.S. Brewer.

Benskin, M. (2004) 'Chancery Standard', in Kay, C.J., Hough, C.A. and Wotherspoon, I. (eds.) *New Perspectives on English Historical Linguistics: Selected papers from 12 ICEHL, Glasgow, 21 26 August 2002. Volume II: Lexis and Transmission.* Amsterdam: John Benjamins, pp. 1–40.

Benskin, M. et al (eds.) (2013) *An Electronic Version of A Linguistic Atlas of Late Mediaeval English* (http://www.lel.ed.ac.uk/ihd/eLALME/eLALME.html)

Benskin, M. and Laing, M. (1981) 'Translations and Mischsprachen in Middle English Manuscripts', in Benskin, M. and Laing, M. (eds.) *So Meny Peple Longages and Tonges: Philological Essays in Scots and Mediaeval English Presented to Angus McIntosh.* Edinburgh: Middle English Dialect Project.

Benskin, M., McIntosh, A. and Samuels, M.L. (eds.) (1986) *A Linguistic Atlas of Late Medieval English.* Aberdeen: Aberdeen University Press.

Benson, C.D. (1980) *Chaucer's Drama of Style: Poetic Variety and Contrast in the Canterbury Tales.* Chapel Hill: University of North Carolina Press.

Blake, N.F. (1977) *The English Language in Medieval Literature.* London: Dent and Sons.

Blake, N.F. (1992) 'Introduction', in Burchfield, R.W. *et al.* (eds.) *The Cambridge History of the English Language.* Cambridge: Cambridge University Press.

Boffey, J. and Thompson, J.J. (1989) 'Anthologies and Miscellanies: Production and Choice of Texts', in Griffiths, J. and Pearsall, D. (eds.) *Book Production and Publishing in Britain, 1374–1475.* Cambridge: Cambridge University Press.

BIBLIOGRAPHY

Born, E. and Born, W. (1986) 'The Medieval Monastery as a Setting for the Production of Manuscripts', *The Journal of the Walters Art Gallery,* 44, pp.16-47.

Bradley, H. (1919) 'Remarks on the Corpus Glossary', *The Classical Quarterly,* 13, pp. 89–108.

Braswell, M.F. (ed.) (1995) *Ywain and Gawain.* Kalamazoo: Medieval Institute Publications.

Brown, K. and Ogilvie, S. (2009) *Concise Encyclopedia of the Languages of the World.* Oxford: Elsevier.

Brown, M. (2007) *A Guide to Western Historical Scripts: From Antiquity to 1600.* London: The British Library.

Brown, P. (2009) *A Companion to Medieval English Literature and Culture c.1350–c.1500.* Oxford: Wiley-Blackwell.

Burrow, J.A. and Turville-Petre, T. (1996) *A Book of Middle English.* Oxford: Blackwell.

Burton, T.L. (1991) 'On the Current State of Middle English Dialectology', *Leeds Studies In English,* n.s. 2. pp 167-208.

Carver, J. (1938) 'The Northern Homily Cycle, and Missionaries to the Saracens', *Modern Language Notes,* 53(4), pp. 258–261.

Cawley, A.C. (1958) *The Wakefield Pageants in the Towneley Cycle. Vol. 1.* Manchester: Manchester University Press.

Chambers, J.K. (1983) 'The Miller's Tale', in Ross, T.W. (ed.) *The Miller's Tale.* Oklahoma: University of Oklahoma Press.

Chambers, J.K. and Trudgill, P. (1998) *Dialectology.* Cambridge: Cambridge University Press.

Chaytor, H.J. (1945) *From Script to Print: An Introduction to Medieval Vernacular Literature.* Cambridge: Cambridge University Press.

Christianson, C.P. (1989) 'Evidence for the Study of London's Late Medieval Manuscript-Book Trade', in Griffiths, J. and Pearsall, D. (eds.) *Book Production and Publishing in Britain, 1375–1475.* Cambridge: Cambridge University Press.

Conlee, J. (ed.) (2004) *William Dunbar: The Complete Works.* Kalamazoo: Medieval Institute Publications.

Copeland, R. (1991) *Rhetoric, Hermeneutics, and Translation in the Middle Ages: Academic Traditions and Vernacular Texts.* Cambridge: Cambridge University Press.

Cowen, J. and Kane, G. (eds.) (1995) *Geoffrey Chaucer: The Legend of Good Women.* East Lansing: Michigan State University Press.

Cunningham, I., Ker, N.R. and Watson, A.G. (eds.) (1977) *Medieval Manuscripts in British Libraries. Vol. II.* Oxford: Clarendon Press.

Dahood, R. (1997) 'The Current State of Ancrene Wisse Group Studies', *Medieval English Studies Newsletter,* 36, pp. 6-14.

Dance, R. (2002) 'The AB Language: The Recluse, the Gossip and the Language Historian', in Wada, Y. (ed.) *A Companion to Ancrene Wisse.* Woodbridge: Boydell & Brewer.

Darau, M. and McIntosh, A. (1971) 'A Dialect Word in Some West Midlands Manuscripts of the *Prick of Conscience*', in Aitkin, A.J. and McIntosh, A. (eds.) *Edinburgh Studies in English and Scots: A Collection of Essays Dedicated to O.K. Schram (1900-1968).* Edinburgh: Palsonn Hermann.

DaRold, O. (2014) 'Codicology, Localization and Oxford, Bodleian Library, Ms. Laud. Misc. 108' in Meale, C. (ed.) *Makers and Users of Medieval Books: Essays in Honour of A.S.G. Edwards.* Woodbridge: Boydell & Brewer.

Davis, N. (1967) 'Style and Stereotype in Early English Letters', *Leeds Studies In English.* n.s. 1. pp. 7–15.

De Hamel, C. (1992) *Medieval Craftsmen: Scribes and Illuminators.* London: The British Museum Press.

De Roover, F.E. (1939) 'The Scriptorium', in Thompson, J.W. (ed.) *The Medieval Library.* Chicago: University of Chicago Press.

Deansley, M. (ed.) (1920) *The Lollard Bible and Other Medieval Biblical Versions.* Cambridge: Cambridge University Press.

Denholm-Young, N. (1954) *Handwriting in England and Wales.* Cardiff: University of Wales Press.

Destrez, J. (1935) *La Pecia Dans Les Manuscrits Universitaires Du Xiiie Et Du Xive Siècle.* Paris: Jacques Vautrain.

Doyle, A.I. (1983) 'English Books in and out of Court from Edward III to Henry VII', in Scattergood, V.J. and Sherborne, J.W. (eds.) *English Court Culture in the Later Middle Ages.* London: Duckworth.

Doyle, A.I. (2008) 'Introduction to Neil Ker's Elements of Medieval English Codicology', in Edwards, A.S.G. (ed.) *English Manuscript Studies 1100-1700 Vol. 14: Regional Manuscripts 1200-1700.* London: The British Library.

BIBLIOGRAPHY

Dunbabin, J. (1984) 'Careers and Vocations' in Catto, J.I. (ed.) *The History of the University of Oxford: Volume I, The Early Oxford Schools.* Oxford: Oxford University Press, pp. 565 – 607

Edwards, A.S.G. (2008) *Regional Manuscripts, 1200-1700.* London: The British Library.

Edwards, A.S.G. and Pearsall, D. (1989) 'The Manuscripts Of The Major English Poetic Texts', in Griffiths, J. Pearsall, D. (eds.) *Book Production and Publishing in Britain, 1375 – 1475.* Cambridge: Cambridge University Press.

Ellis, R. (ed.) (1989) *The Medieval Translator: The Theory and Practice of Translation in the Middle Ages.* Cambridge: D.S. Brewer.

Fernández-Cuesta, J. (2013) *Seville Corpus of Northern English.* Available at: http://ingles3.us.es/ (Accessed 01 May 2013).

Fernández-Cuesta, J. and Rodriguez-Ledesma, M.N. (2008) 'Northern Middle English: Towards Telling the Full Story', in Dossena, M., Drury, R. and Gotti, M. (eds.) *English Historical Linguistics 2006.* Amsterdam: John Benjamins, pp.91-109.

Fisiak, J. (1995) *Medieval Dialectology*, Vol. 79. London: Walter de Gruyter.

Fowler, J.T. (ed.) (1889) *Metrical Life of St Cuthbert.* Durham: Surtees Society.

Friedman, J.B. (1995) *Northern English Books, Owners, and Makers in the Late Middle Ages.* New York: Syracuse University Press.

Ganim, J. (1983) *Style and Consciousness in Middle English Narrative.* Princeton: Princeton University Press.

Gardela, W. (2011) 'Spelling Variants of the Present Participle in a Selection of Northern English and Scots Texts of the Late 14th and the 15th Centuries', in Gregerson, F., Parrott, J.K. and Quist, P. (eds.) *Language Variation – European Perspectives III: Selected Papers from the 5th International Conference on Language Variation in Europe (ICLaVE 5), Copenhagen, June 2009.* Vol. 7. Amsterdam: John Benjamins.

Gillespie, V. (2008) 'Religious Writing' in Ellis, R. (ed.) *The Oxford History of Literary Translation in English, Vol. 1: 700-1550.* Oxford: Oxford University Press.

Gillieron, J. (1915) *Étude de géographie linguistique: Pathologie et thérapeutique verbales... Résumé de conférences faites à l'École pratique des hautes études.* Canton de Berne (Suisse): Beerstecher.

Graddol, D., Leth, D. and Swann, J. (1996) *English Language: History, Diversity and Change*. London: Routledge.

Gradon, P. (1971) *Form and Style in Early English Literature*. London: Methuen.

Gregory, E.D. (2010) *The Late Victorian Folksong Revival: The Persistence of English Melody, 1878 – 1903*. London: Scarecrow Press.

Guest, E. (1968) *A History of English Rhythms*. New York: Haskell House.

Hanna, R. (1993a) *Pursuing History: Middle English Manuscripts and Their Texts*. Stanford: Stanford University Press.

Hanna, R. (1993a) *William Langland*. Vol. 3, *Authors of the Middle Ages: English Writers of the Late Middle Ages*. Cambridge: Variorum.

Hanna, R. (1996) 'Miscellaneity and Vernacularity: Conditions of Literary Production in Late Medieval England', in Nichols, S.G. and Wenzel, S. (eds.) *The Whole Book: Cultural Perspectives on the Medieval Miscellany*. Kalamazoo: University of Michigan Press, pp. 37-51.

Hanna, R. (1997) *The Index of Middle English Prose, Handlist XII: Manuscripts in Smaller Bodleian Collections* Cambridge: D.S. Brewer.

Hanna, R. (2003) 'Yorkshire Writers', in *Proceedings of the British Academy, Volume 121, 2002 Lectures*. Oxford: Oxford University Press.

Hanna, R. (2005) *London Literature, 1300–1380*. Cambridge: Cambridge University Press.

Hanna, R. (ed.) (2007) *Richard Rolle: Uncollected Prose and Verse, with Related Northern Texts*. Oxford: Oxford University Press.

Hanna, R., and Wood, S. (eds.) (2013) *Richard Morris's Prick of Conscience*. Oxford: Early English Text Society.

Heffernan, T.J. (1985) 'The Authorship of the "Northern Homily Cycle": The Liturgical Affiliation of the Sunday Gospel Pericopes as a Test', *Traditio*, 41, pp. 289–309.

Hoad, T. (1994) 'Word Geography: Previous Approaches and Achievements', in Laing, M. (ed.) *Speaking in Our Tongues: Proceedings of a Colloquium on Medieval Dialectology and Related Disciplines*. Cambridge: Cambridge University Press.

BIBLIOGRAPHY

Hockett, C.F. (1955) *A Manual of Phonology*. Baltimore: Waverly Press, p. 246.

Horobin, S. (1998) 'A New Approach to Chaucer's Spelling', *English Studies,* 79, pp. 415-424.

Horobin, S. (2001) 'J.R.R. Tolkien as a Philologist: A Reconsideration of the Northernisms in Chaucer's Reeve's Tale', *English Studies*, 82, pp. 97-105.

Horobin, S. (2009) *Studying the History of Early English*. London: Palgrave Macmillan.

Horobin, S. (2011) 'Mapping the Words', in Gillespie, A. (ed.) *The Production of Books in England 1350–1500*. Cambridge: Cambridge University Press.

Horobin, S. and Smith, J.J. (2002) *An Introduction to Middle English*. Edinburgh: Edinburgh University Press.

Horstmann, C. (ed.) (1892) *The Minor Poems of the Vernon M.S., Part 1. Vol. 98*. London: Early English Text Society.

Horstmann, C. (1895) *Yorkshire Writers: Richard Rolle of Hampole, an English Father of the Church, and His Followers. Vol. I.* London: S. Sonnenschein & Co.

Hudson, A. (1983) 'Observations on a Northerner's Vocabulary', in Gray, D. and Stanley, E.G. (eds.) *Five Hundred Years of Words and Sounds: A Festschrift for Eric Dobson*. Cambridge: D.S Brewer.

Jensen, V. (2012) 'The Consonantal Element (Th) in Some Late Middle English Yorkshire Texts', *Studies in Variation, Contacts and Change in English,* 10. Available at: https://varieng.helsinki.fi/series/volumes/10/jensen/ [Accessed May 2 2022].Johnson, I. (1997) 'Vernacular Valorizing: Functions and Fashionings of Literary Theory in Middle English Translation of Authority', in Beer, J. (ed.) *Translation Theory and Practice in the Middle Ages*. (Studies in Medieval Culture, 38). Kalamazoo: Medieval Institute Publications, pp. 239-254.

Johnston, P.A. (2011) 'Appendix: Notes on the Dialect of the York Plays', in Davidson, C. (ed.) *The York Corpus Christi Plays*. Kalamazoo: Medieval Institute Publications, pp. 535-558.

Jones, M.J. (2002) 'The Origin of Definite Article Reduction in Northern English Dialects: Evidence from Dialect Allomorphy', *English Language and Linguistics,* 6(2), pp. 325-345.

Jordan, R. (1974) *Handbook of Middle English Grammar: Phonology*. Translated from the German by E.J. Crook. The Hague and Paris: Mouton.

Kaiser, R. (1937) *Zur Geographie Des Mittelenglischen Wortschatzes*. Leipzig: Mayer & Müller.

Ker, N.R, Parkes, M.B. and Watson, A.G. (eds.) (1978) *Medieval Scribes, Manuscripts & Libraries: Essays Presented to N.R. Ker*. London: Scolar Press.

Ker, N.R. and Watson, A.G. (1987) *Medieval Libraries of Great Britain: A List of Surviving Books*. London: Offices of the Royal Historical Society.

Kibbee, D.A. (1991) *For to Speke Frenche Trewely: The French Language in England, 1000-1600: Its Status, Description, and Instruction*. Amsterdam: John Benjamins.

Kitson, P. (1992) 'Old English Dialects and the Stages of Transition to Middle English', *Folia Linguistica Historica*, 24 (Historica-vol-11-1-2), pp 27-88.

Kristensson, G. (1967) *A Survey of Middle English Dialects, 1290-1350: The Six Northern Counties and Lincolnshire*. Lund: C.W.K. Gleerup.

Kroch, A. and Taylor, A. (1997) 'Verb Movement in Old and Middle English: Dialect Variation and Language Contact', in Van Kemenade, A. and Vincent, N. (eds.) *Parameters of Morphosyntactic Change*. Cambridge: Cambridge University Press, pp. 297-325.

Kwakkel, E. (2003) 'A New Type of Book for a New Type of Reader: The Emergence of Paper in Vernacular Book Production', *The Library*, 4(3), pp. 219-248.

Laing, M. (1991) 'Anchor Texts and Literary Manuscripts in Early Middle English', in Riddy, F. (ed.) *Regionalism in Late Medieval Manuscripts and Texts*. Cambridge: Cambridge University Press.

Laing, M. (2004) 'Multidimensionality: Time, Space and Stratigraphy', in Dossena, M. and Lass, R. (eds.) *Methods and Data in English Historical Dialectology*. Bern: Peter Lang, pp. 49-93.

Laing, M. (2007) 'A Linguistic Atlas of Early Medieval English, 1150–1325 (LAEME, Version 1). Available at: http://www.lel.ed.ac.uk/ihd/laeme/laeme.html [Accessed May 2 2022])

BIBLIOGRAPHY

Laing, M. (2008) 'The Middle English Scribe: *Sprach Er Wie Er Schrieb?*', in Dossena, M., Drury, R. and Gotti, M. (eds.) *English Historical Linguistics 2006.* Amsterdam: John Benjamins, pp. 1-44.

Laing, M. and Lass, R. (2006) 'Early Middle English Dialectology: Problems and Prospects', in Van Kemenade, A. and Los, B. (eds.) *The Handbook of the History of English.* Oxford: Blackwell Publishing.

Lewis, R.E. (1976) 'Medieval Popularity, Modern Neglect: The Case of the *Pricke of Conscience*', *14th Century English Mystics Newsletter*, 2(April), pp. 3-8.

Lewis, R.E. (2001) *Middle English Dictionary.* Ann Arbor: University of Michigan Press.

Lewis, R.E. and McIntosh, A. (1982) *A Descriptive Guide to the Manuscripts of the Pricke of Conscience, Medium Ævum Monographs Vol. 12.* Oxford: Society for the Study of Medieval Language and Literature.

Lightfoot, D.W. (1991) *How to Set Parameters: Arguments from Language Change.* Cambridge, MA: MIT Press.

Locock, K. (ed.) (1899) *The Pilgrimage of the Life of Man.* London: Early English Text Society.

Logan, F.D. (2012) *A History of the Church in the Middle Ages.* London: Routledge.

Loomis, L.H. (1942) 'The Auchinleck Manuscript and a Possible London Bookshop of 1330-1340'. *Publications of the Modern Language Association of America,* 57(3), pp.595-627.

Lupack, A. (ed.) (1994) 'Sir Tristrem', in *Lancelot of the Laik and Sir Tristrem.* Kalamazoo: Medieval Institute Publications, pp. 143-278.

Lyall, R.J. (1989) 'Materials: The Paper Revolution', in Griffiths, J. and Pearsall, D. (eds.) *Book Production and Publishing in Britain, 1375–1475.* Cambridge: Cambridge University Press.

Machan, T.W. (2005) *English in the Middle Ages.* Oxford: Oxford University Press.

Matto, M. and Momma, H. (2009) *A Companion to the History of the English Language.* Oxford: Wiley-Blackwell, 2009.

McColly, W.B. (1987) 'Style and Structure in the Middle English Poem "Cleanness"', *Computers and the Humanities* (1987), pp. 169–76.

McIntosh, A. (1956) 'The Analysis of Written Middle English', *Transactions of the Philological Society,* 55 (1956), 26-55.

McIntosh, A. (1989a) 'Word Geography in the Lexicography of Medieval English', in Laing, M. (ed.) *Middle English Dialectology: Essays on Some Principles and Problems.* Aberdeen: Aberdeen University Press, pp. 92 - 227.

McIntosh, A. (1989b) 'Is *Sir Tristrem* an English or a Scottish Poem?', in Mackenzie, J.L. and Todd, R. (eds.) *In Other Words: Transcultural Studies in Philology, Translation, and Lexicology Presented to Hans Heinrich Meier on the Occasion of His Sixty-Fifth Birthday.* Foris: Dordrecht and Providence, pp. 12 -39.

McIntosh, A. (1989c) 'Scribal Profiles from Middle English Texts', in Laing, M. (ed.) *Middle English Dialectology: Essays on Some Principles and Problems.* Aberdeen: Aberdeen University Press, pp. 66 - 90.

McIntosh, A. (1989d) 'A New Approach to Middle English Dialectology', in Laing, M. (ed.) *Middle English Dialectology: Essays on Some Principles and Problems.* Aberdeen: Aberdeen University Press, pp. 20 - 35.

McMahon, A. and McMahon, R. (2006) *Language Classification by Numbers.* Oxford: Oxford University Press.

Medcalf, S. (1981) *The Later Middle Ages.* New York: Holmes and Meier.

Meech, S.B., Moore, S. and Whitehall, H. (1935) 'Middle English Dialect Characteristics and Dialect Boundaries', *Essays and Studies In English And Comparative Literature. U. Of Michigan Publications, Language and Literature XIII.* Ann Arbor: University of Michigan Press, pp. 1–60.

Melzer, D. (2008) *French Influence on the English Language in the Middle English Period.* Hamburg: GRIN Verlag oHG.

Michael, M.A. (2008) 'Urban Production of Manuscript Books and the Role of the University Towns', in Morgan, N.J. and Thomson, R. (eds.) *The Cambridge History of the Book in Britain. Volume 2, 1100-1400.* Cambridge: Cambridge University Press, pp. 168-194.

Milroy, J. (1992) *Linguistic Variation and Change: On the Historical Sociolinguistics of English.* Oxford: Blackwell.

Minkova, D. (1991) *The History of Final Vowels in English: The Sound of Muting.* Berlin: Mouton de Gruter.

BIBLIOGRAPHY

Mitchell, B. and Robinson, F.C. (2002) *A Guide to Old English.* 6th edn. Malden, MA: Blackwell.

Mooney, L.R. (2011) 'Vernacular Literary Manuscripts and Their Scribes', in Gillespie, A. and Wakelin, D. (eds.) *The Production of Books in England, 1350–1500.* Cambridge: Cambridge University Press, pp. 192-211.

Morgan, N. and Thomson, R.M. (2008) 'Language and Literacy', in Morgan, N. and Thomson, R.M. (eds.) *The Cambridge History of the Book in Britain. Volume 2, 1100-1400.* Cambridge: Cambridge University Press, pp. 22-38.

Morris, R. (ed.) (1863) *The Pricke of Conscience (Stimulus Conscientiae): A Northumbrian Poem.* Berlin:: Published for the Philological Society by A. Asher.

Nevanlinna, S. (1972) *The Northern Homily Cycle: The Expanded Version in MSS Harley 4196 and Cotton Tiberius E 7.* Helsinki: Société Néophilologique.

Nicholson, P. (1984), 'Gower's Revisions in the *Confessio Amantis*'. *The Chaucer Review,* 19(2), pp. 123-143.

Oliver, R. (1970) *Poems without Names: The English Lyric, 1200–1500.* Berkeley: University of California Press.

Orme, N. (2006) *Medieval Schools: From Roman Britain to Renaissance England.* New Haven: Yale University Press.

Osberg, R.H. (ed.) (1996) *The Poems of Laurence Minot, 1333–1352.* Kalamazoo: Medieval Institute Publications.

Pahta, P. (2012) 'Code-switching in English of the Middle Ages', in Nevalainen, T. and Closs Traugott, E. (eds.) *The Oxford Handbook of the History of English.* Oxford: Oxford University Press.

Parkes, M.B. (1978) 'The Production of Copies of the Canterbury Tales and the *Confessio Amantis* in the Early Fifteenth Century', in Parkes, M.B. and Watson, A. (eds.) *Medieval Scribes, Manuscripts and Libraries: Essays Presented to N.R. Ker.* London: Scolar Press.

Parkes, M.B. (1991) *Scribes, Scripts, and Readers: Studies in the Communication, Presentation, and Dissemination of Medieval Texts.* London: Hambledon Press.

Parkes, M.B. (1992) 'The Provision of Books', in Catto, J.I. and Evans, R. (eds.) *The History of the University of Oxford, II: Late Medieval Oxford.* Oxford: Oxford University Press.

Parkes, M.B. (1993) *Pause and Effect*. San Diego: University of California Press.

Pearsall, D. (ed.) (1979) *The Auchinleck Manuscript*. London: Scolar Press.

Pearsall, D. (1989) 'Introduction', in Griffiths, J. and Pearsall, D. (eds.) *Book Production and Publishing in Britain, 1375 – 1475*. Cambridge: Cambridge University Press, pp. 1-10.

Pietsch, L. (2005) *Variable Grammars: Verbal Agreement in Northern Dialects of English*. Berlin: De Gruyter.

Plummer, J.F. (2000) 'Style', in Brown, P. (ed.) *A Companion to Chaucer. Blackwell Companions to Literature and Culture 6*. Oxford: Blackwell, pp. 414-427.

Pollard, G. (1970) 'The Names of Some Fifteenth Century Binders', *The Library*, 5(3), pp. 193-218.

Purser, T. (2004) *Medieval England 1042-1228*. London: Heinemann.

Richter, M. (1979) *Sprache Und Gesellschaft Im Mittelalter: Untersuchungen Zur Mündlichen Kommunikation in England Von Der Mitte Des Elften Bis Zum Beginn Des Vierzehnten Jahrhunderts*. Stuttgart: Hiersemann.

Rissanen, M. (2005) 'The development of till and until in English', in Fisiak, J. and Kang, H.K. (eds.) *Recent Trends in Medieval English Language and Literature in Honour of Young-Bae Park*. Seoul: Thaehaksa, pp. 75-92.

Rothewell, W. (1994) 'The Trilingual England of Geoffrey Chaucer'. *Studies in The Age of Chaucer*, 16(1), pp. 45–67.

Rygiel, D. (1981), 'Ancrene Wisse and Colloquial Style: A Caveat'. *Neophilologus*, 65 (1), pp. 137–143.

Salter, H.E. (1913) *The Oxford Deeds of Balliol College*. Oxford: Clarendon Press.

Samuels, M.L. (1963) 'Some Applications of Middle English Dialectology', *English Studies*, 44(1-6), pp. 81-94.

Samuels, M.L. (1989) 'Some Applications of Middle English Dialectology', in Laing, M. (ed.) *Middle English Dialectology: Essays on Some Principles and Problems*. Aberdeen: Aberdeen University Press.

Samuels, M.L. (1992) 'Scribes and Manuscript Traditions', in Riddy, F. (ed.) *Regionalism in Late Medieval Manuscripts and Texts: Essays Celebrating the Publication of a Linguistic Atlas of Late Mediaeval English*. Cambridge: D.S. Brewer, pp. 1-7.

BIBLIOGRAPHY

Sands, D.B. (1986) *Middle English Verse Romances*. Exeter: University of Exeter Press.

Savage, A (2003) 'The Communal Authorship of "Ancrene Wisse"', in Wada, Y. (ed.) *A Companion to Ancrene Wisse*. Woodbridge: Boydell & Brewer, pp. 45-55.

Scase, W. (ed.) (2007) *Essays in Manuscript Geography: Vernacular Manuscripts of the English West Midlands from the Conquest to the Sixteenth Century*. Turnhout: Brepols Publishers.

Scott, W. (ed.) (1804) *Sir Tristrem; a Metrical Romance of the Thirteenth Century; by Thomas of Erceldoune, Called the Rhymer*. Edinburgh: Archibald, Constable and Co.

Scragg, D.G. (1974) *A History of English Spelling*. Manchester: Manchester University Press.

Shepherd, G. (ed.) (1959) *Ancrene Wisse Parts Six and Seven*. London and Edinburgh: Nelson.

Shonk, T.A. (1985) 'A Study of the Auchinleck Manuscript: Bookmen and Bookmaking in The Early Fourteenth Century', *Speculum*, 60(1), pp. 71-91.

Simpson, J. (2002) *The Oxford English Literary History: Reform and Cultural Revolution, 1350-1547. Vol. 2*. Oxford: Oxford University Press.

Sisam, K. (ed.) (1921) *Fourteenth Century Verse and Prose*. Oxford: Clarendon Press.

Skeat, W.W. (1912) *English Dialects from the Eighth Century to the Present Day*. Oxford: Oxford University Press.

Small, J. (ed.) (1862) *English Metrical Homilies from Manuscripts of the Fourteenth Century*. London: Paterson.

Smith, J.J. (ed.) (1988) *The English of Chaucer and His Contemporaries: Essays by M. L. Samuels and J. J. Smith*. Aberdeen: Aberdeen University Press.

Smith, J.J. (1992) 'The Use of English: Language Contact, Dialect Variation and Written Standardisation in the Middle English Period', in Machan, T.W. and Scott, C.T. (eds.) *English in Its Social Contexts: Essays in Historical Sociolinguistics*. Oxford: Oxford University Press.

Smith, J.J. (1993) 'Dialectal Variation in Middle English and the Actuation of the Great Vowel Shift', *Neuphilologische Mitteilungen*, 94(3-4), pp. 259-77.

Smith, J.J. (1994) 'The Great Vowel Shift in the North of England, and Some Spellings in Manuscripts of Chaucer's Reeve's Tale', *Neuphilologische Mitteilungen*, 95(4), pp. 433-37.
Smith, J.J. (2005) *Essentials of Early English: Old, Middle and Early Modern English*. London: Routledge.
Smith, J.J. (2012) *Older Scots: A Linguistic Reader*. Woodbridge: Scottish Text Society.
Spearing, A.C. (1964) *Criticism and Medieval Poetry*. London: Edward Arnold.
Sprouse, J.R. (2003) 'The Scribal Dialect of the Bodleian Library, Manuscript Ashmole 42', *Neuphilologische Mitteilungen*, 104(1), pp. 95-113.
Steinman, M. (2010) 'Lesen Und Schreiben in Den Klöstern Des Frühen Mittelalters ', in Robinson, P.R. (ed.) *Teaching Writing, Learning to Write: Proceedings of the XVIth Colloquium of the Comité International de Paléographie Latine*. London: King's College London Centre for Late Antique & Medieval Studies, pp. 25-35.
Stenroos, M. and Thengs, K. (2020) *Records of Real People: Linguistic variation in Middle English Local Documents* Amsterdam: John Benjamins.
Strang, B. (1970) *A History of English*. London: Methuen.
Sweet, H. (1888) *A History of English Sounds from the Earliest Period, with Full Word Lists*. Oxford: Clarendon Press.
Taavitsainen, I. (1994) 'Subjectivity as a Text-Type Marker in Historical Stylistics', *Language and Literature*, 3(3), pp. 197-212.
Tatlock, J.P. (1935) 'The Canterbury Tales in 1400', *PMLA*, 50(1), pp. 100-139.
Thompson, A.B. (ed.) (2008) *The Northern Homily Cycle*. Kalamazoo: Medieval Institute Publications.
Thompson, J.J. (1998) *The Cursor Mundi: Poem, Texts and Contexts*. Oxford: Society for the Study of Medieval Languages and Literature.
Thornton, R. (1995) 'Sir Perceval of Galles', in Flowers Brassell, M. (ed.) *Sir Perceval of Galles and Ywain and Gawain*. Kalamazoo: Medieval Institute Publications.
Tolkien, J.R.R. (1929) 'Ancrene Wisse and Hali Meiðhad', *Essays and Studies by Members of the English Association, Volume 14*. Oxford: Clarendon Press, pp. 104-126.

BIBLIOGRAPHY

Tolkien, J.R.R. (1933) 'Chaucer as a Philologist: The Reeve's Tale', *Transactions of the Philological Society,* 33(1), pp.1-70.

Townend, M. (2002), *Language and History in Viking Age England: Linguistic Relations between Speakers of Old Norse and Old English.* Turnhout: Brepols Publishers.

Traherne, E. (2012) *Living through Conquest: The Politics of Early English, 1020 to 1220.* Oxford: Oxford University Press.

Traherne, Elaine and Swan, M. (eds.) (2000), *Rewriting Old English in the Twelfth Century.* Cambridge: Cambridge University Press.

Traherne, E. and Walker, G. (eds.) (2010) *The Oxford Handbook of Medieval Literature in English.* Oxford: Oxford University Press.

Trips, C. (2002) *From Ov to Vo in Early Middle English.* Amsterdam: John Benjamins.

Trudel, G. (2005) 'The Middle English Book of Penance and the Readers of the Cursor Mundi', *Medium Ævum,* 74(1), pp. 10-33.

Turville-Petre, T. (1983) 'Some Medieval English Manuscripts in the North-East Midlands', in Pearsall, D. (ed.) *Manuscripts and Readers in Fifteenth-Century England: The Literary Implications of Manuscript Study.* Cambridge: D.S. Brewer, pp. 125-141.

Turville-Petre, T. and Turville, P. (1996) *England the Nation: Language, Literature, and National Identity, 1290-1340.* Oxford: Clarendon Press.

University of Virginia, 'The Piers Plowman Electronic Archive' http://www3.iath.virginia.edu/seenet/piers/archivegoalsbarchet.htm [Accessed March 2 2022].

Van Herk, G. (2012) *What Is Sociolinguistics?* Oxford: Wiley-Blackwell.

Vogel, B. (1941) 'The Dialect of Sir Tristrem', *Journal of English and Germanic Philology,* 40(4), pp. 538-544.

Wakelin, M.F. (1977) *English Dialects: An Introduction.* London: Athlone Press.

Waters, S.A., 'A History of *Pricke of Conscience* Studies', *Studia Neophilologica,* 55(2), pp. 147-151.

Wathey, A. (1989) 'The Production of Books of Liturgical Polyphony', in Griffiths, J. and Pearsall, D. (eds.) *Book Production and Publishing in Britain, 1375–1475.* Cambridge: Cambridge University Press, pp. 143-162.

Watson, N. (1995) 'Censorship and Cultural Change in Late-Medieval England: Vernacular Theology, the Oxford Translation Debate, and Arundel's Constitutions of 1409', *Speculum*, 70(4), pp. 822–864.

Watson, N. (1991) *Richard Rolle and the Invention of Authority*. Cambridge: Cambridge University Press.

Wells, J.E. (1938) *A Manual of the Writings in Middle English, 1050-1400: Supplement*. Vol. VII. New Haven: Yale University Press.

Wełna, J. (1998) 'The Functional Relationship between Rules (Old English Voicing of Fricatives and Lengthening of Vowels before Homorganic Clusters)', in Fisiak, J. and Krygier, M. (eds.) *Advances in English Historical Linguistics*. Berlin: De Gruyter.

White, R.M. (ed.) (1878) *The Ormulum, Vol. 1*. Oxford: Clarendon Press.

Whitelock, D. (ed.) (1939) *Sermo Lupi Ad Anglos*. London: Methuen.

Williamson, K. (2002) 'The Dialectology Of "English" North of the Humber, C. 1380–1500', in Fanego, T., Méndez-Naya, B. and Seoane, E. (eds.) *Sounds, Words, Texts and Change*. Amsterdam: John Benjamins, pp. 253–286.

Woolf, R. (1968) *The English Religious Lyric in the Middle Ages*. Oxford: Clarendon Press.